*The Mystery of "A Public Man"*

# The Mystery of
# "A PUBLIC MAN"

A HISTORICAL DETECTIVE STORY

BY

## Frank Maloy Anderson

UNIVERSITY OF MINNESOTA PRESS · Minneapolis

LONDON · GEOFFREY CUMBERLEGE · OXFORD UNIVERSITY PRESS

PRINTED AT THE COLWELL PRESS, INC., MINNEAPOLIS

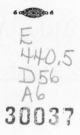

# Contents

*The Story*

# I

This little book is an attempt to clear up one of the long-standing mysteries of American history. In 1879 the *North American Review*, then one of the most widely read of American magazines, published in four installments "The Diary of a Public Man." It was or purported to be a diary kept during the Secession Winter of 1860–1861. Not all the diary was published. Extracts for twenty-one days lying between December 28, 1860, and March 15, 1861, were included. On twenty of the twenty-one days the Diarist was in Washington. On the other day, February 20, 1861, he was in New York City. The name of the diarist was withheld.

Interest in this real or purported diary lies chiefly in two things. If genuine, it is a Lincoln document of capital importance. It is also important and of absorbing interest for its portrayal of leading men and its narration of significant events at Washington during the critical days just before the outbreak of the Civil War.

Before asking the reader to go with me along the detective trail I think it will be well to supply him with a more detailed description of the Diary and especially to make him acquainted with a few of its more significant passages. Thus equipped he can follow the search with added interest and a keener appreciation of the finer points involved in the mystery whose solution we are seeking.

As a Lincoln document the Diary is important because historians and the biographers of Lincoln have depended upon it for several of the well-known sayings of Lincoln and for a number of the most striking anecdotes about him. For all of these, save in one instance, the Diary is the sole authority for the matter in question.

3

The Diarist had or claimed to have had three interviews with Lincoln. The earliest occurred in New York City on February 20, 1861, while Lincoln was there en route to Washington for his inauguration. The Diarist reports:

My conversation with Mr. Lincoln was brief and hurried, but not entirely unsatisfactory—indeed on the main point quite the reverse. He is entirely clear and sensible on the vital importance of holding the Democrats close to the Administration on the naked Union issue. "They are," he said to me, "just where we Whigs were in '48 about the Mexican war. We had to take the Locofoco preamble when Taylor wanted help, or else vote against helping Taylor; and the Democrats must vote to hold the Union now, without bothering whether we or the Southern men got things where they are, and we must make it easy for them to do this, because we can't live through the case without them," which is certainly the simple truth. He reminded me of our meeting at Washington, but I really couldn't recall the circumstances with any degree of clearness. He is not a great man certainly, and, but for something almost woman-like in the look of his eyes, I should say the most ill-favored son of Adam I ever saw; but he is crafty and sensible, and owned to me that he was more troubled by the outlook than he thought it discreet to show. He asked me a number of questions about New York, from which I gathered for myself that he is not so much in the hands of Mr. Seward as I had been led to think. He was amusing about Mayor Wood and his speech, and seems to have a singularly correct notion of that worthy. He asked me what I had heard about the project said to be brewing here for detaching New York City not only from the Union but from the State of New York as well, and making it a kind of free city like Hamburg. I told him I had only heard of such visionary plans, and that the only importance I attributed to them was, that they illustrated the necessity of getting our commercial affairs back into a healthy condition as early as possible. "That is true," he replied; "and nobody feels it more than I do. And as to the free city business—well, I reckon it will be some time before the front door sets up housekeeping on its own account," which struck me as a quaint and rather forcible way of putting the case.

I made an appointment for Washington, where he will be at Willard's within a few days, and agreed to write to ———.

4

The second interview took place on February 28, 1861, at the Willard Hotel in Washington, where Lincoln was staying until his inauguration. The Diarist thus records it:

Half an hour with Mr. Lincoln to-day, which confirms all my worst fears. I should say he is at his wits' ends, if he did not seem to me to be so thoroughly aware of the fact that some other people are in that condition. I told him frankly, on his own provocation to the subject, what I thought would be the advantages to his Administration, and to the country, of putting ———— into the Cabinet, and gave him to understand, as plainly as I thought becoming, that he must not look on me as acting in concert with any set of men to urge that nomination, or any other nomination, upon him. I think he saw that I was in earnest; and, at all events, he advised me to write to ———— in the terms in which I wished to write to him.

I was sorry to find him anxious about the safety of Washington, and he asked me some questions about Captain Stone, which surprised me a little, and annoyed me more. I told him what I knew of Stone personally, and what had been said to me about him, by the most competent men in the army, at the time when he first came here, by General Scott's wish, to reorganize the militia of the District. He seemed very glad to hear of this, and was very much taken with a story which I told him, and for the accuracy of which I could vouch, that when Captain Stone, upon an urgent recommendation of General Scott, was appointed to the command of the District militia, in January, Governor Floyd was excessively enraged, and tried to get his own nephew, "Charley Jones," who had been previously nominated for the post, and who is a desperate fellow, to insult Stone, pick a quarrel with him, and shoot him. Mr. Lincoln's melancholy countenance lighted up with a twinkle in his eye, "That was not a bad idea of Floyd's," he said, in a slow, meditative sort of way. "Of course I'm glad Stone wasn't shot, and that there wasn't any breach of the peace; but—if the custom could be generally introduced, it might lubricate matters in the way of making political appointments!" After a little, he recurred to the dangerous condition of Washington. I then spoke very earnestly, for it was clear to me that he must be still under the pressure of the same evil counsels which had led him into that dreadful business of the night-ride from Harrisburg; and I urged him to put absolute confidence in

5

the assurances of Captain Stone. I told him, what I believe to be perfectly true, that the worst stories about the intended incursions into Washington, and the like, all originate with men like George Saunders, of New York, and Arnold Harris, of Tennessee, once a particular follower of President Buchanan, but now a loud and noisy secessionist—men who came into my mind because I had passed them in the hall of the very hotel in which we were talking, and in which they have been telling wonderful stories of conspiracy and assassination, from the hotel porches, to anybody who will listen to them for weeks past. He listened to me very attentively, and, suddenly stretching out his hand, picked up and handed me a note to look at. I recognized Senator Sumner's handwriting as I took it, and was not, therefore, particularly surprised to find it alarmish and mysterious in tone, bidding Mr. Lincoln, for particular reasons, to be very careful how he went out alone at night. I saw that Mr. Lincoln watched me while I read the note, and I may have perhaps expressed in my countenance an opinion of the communication which I did not think it civil to put into words, merely reiterating, as I laid it on the table, my own conviction that there was nothing to fear in Washington, and no occasion for measures likely to influence the public mind unfavorably in other parts of the country. As I rose to go, Mr. Lincoln pulled himself together up out of the rocking-chair, into which he had packed himself, and, scanning me good-naturedly for a moment, said, very abruptly, "You never put backs with Sumner did you?" I suppose I looked as much surprised as I felt; but I laughed and said that I did not think I had ever done so. "Well, I suppose not," he said; and then hesitating a moment, went on: "When he was in here I asked him to measure with me, and do you know he made a little speech about it." I tried to look civilly curious, and Mr. Lincoln, with an indescribable glimmer all over his face, continued: "Yes," he said, "he told me he thought 'this was a time for uniting our fronts and not our backs before the enemies of the country,' or something like that. It was very fine. But I reckon the truth was"— and at this point I was compelled against my will to laugh aloud —"I reckon the truth was, he was—afraid to measure!" And with this he looked down with some complacency on his own really indescribable length of limb. "He is a good piece of a man, though—Sumner," he added, half quizzically, half apologetically, "and a good man. I have never had much to do with bishops down

6

where we live; but, do you know, Sumner is just my idea of a bishop." At that moment a door opened, and a lady came in, in not a very ceremonious way, I thought, dressed as if either just about to go into the street, or having just come in. Mr. Lincoln presented me to her as his wife, and I exchanged a few words with her. Perhaps I looked at her through the mist of what Senator Douglas had intimated to me; but certainly she made a disagreeable impression on me. She is not ill-looking, and, though her manners are not those of a well-bred woman of the world, there would be nothing particularly repulsive about them, were it not for the hard, almost coarse tone of her voice, and for something very like cunning in the expression of her face. With the recollection of Mr. Douglas's account of her relations with her husband, the thought involuntarily occurred to me of the contrast between his own beautiful and most graceful wife and this certainly dowdy and to me most unprepossessing little woman. I think if the wives had been voted for, even by the women, Mr. Douglas would be President-elect to-day.

The third interview took place at the White House three days after Lincoln's inauguration. On the day preceding the interview, the Diarist tells us, he had a call from a man who represented that he had just come from visits to Montgomery and Charleston. While at Charleston he had visited Fort Sumter and had there talked with Major Robert Anderson, "a connection by marriage of his wife." He had learned thereby that Anderson did not expect to see the authority of the United States re-established over the states which had already seceded from the Union and that his own action would be determined by the course which his own state, Kentucky, would pursue. When the Diarist insisted that this information ought to be taken to President Lincoln, the man from Montgomery and Charleston was reluctant but finally consented to go with the Diarist to the White House. A note to Lincoln from the Diarist brought an answer the next morning, making an appointment for the afternoon. The Diarist recorded the interview as follows:

Early this morning I received a message from the President making an appointment for this afternoon. I called for ———— at his hotel and we drove to the White House. I could not help observing the disorderly appearance of the place, and the slovenly way in which the service was done. We were kept waiting but a few moments, however, and found Mr. Lincoln quite alone. He received us very kindly, but I was struck and pained by the haggard, worn look of his face, which scarcely left it during the whole time of our visit. I told the President, in a few words, why we had asked for this interview, and ———— then fully explained to him, as he had to me yesterday, the situation at Fort Sumter. It seemed to me that the information did not take the President entirely by surprise, though he asked ———— two or three times over whether he was quite sure about Major Anderson's ideas as to his duty, in case of any action by Kentucky; and, when ———— had repeated to him exactly what he had told me as to the language used to himself by Major Anderson, Mr. Lincoln sat quite silent for a little while in a sort of brooding way, and then, looking up, suddenly said: "Well, you say Major Anderson is a good man, and I have no doubt he is; but if he is right it will be a bad job for me if Kentucky secedes. When he goes out of Fort Sumter, I shall have to go out of the White House." We could not resist a laugh at this quaint way of putting the case, but the gloomy, care-worn look settled back very soon on the President's face, and he said little more except to ask ———— some questions about Montgomery, not I thought of a very relevant or important kind, and we soon took our leave. He walked into the corridor with us; and, as he bade us goodby, and thanked ———— for what he had told him, he again brightened up for a moment and asked him in an abrupt kind of way, laying his hand as he spoke with a queer but not uncivil familiarity on his shoulder, "You haven't such a thing as a postmaster in your pocket, have you?" ———— stared at him in astonishment, and I thought a little in alarm, as if he suspected a sudden attack of insanity, when Mr. Lincoln went on: "You see it seems to me kind of unnatural that you shouldn't have at least a postmaster in your pocket. Everybody I've seen for days past has had foreign ministers, and collectors, and all kinds, and I thought you couldn't have got in here without having at least a postmaster get into your pocket!" We assured him he need have no concern on that point, and left the house, both of us, I think, feeling, as I certainly did, more anxious and disturbed than when we entered it. Not one word had Mr. Lincoln

8

said to throw any real light either on his own views of the situation or on the effect of ——'s communication upon those views. But it was plain that he is deeply disturbed and puzzled by the problem of this wretched fort, to which circumstances are giving an importance so entirely disproportionate to its real significance, either political or military.

In addition to these interviews, highly significant if genuine, the Diary contains three interesting anecdotes about Lincoln. For two of these the Diary is the sole source. None of them, save one, is supported by any other contemporaneous evidence.

The most famous of these tells how Stephen A. Douglas held Lincoln's hat while Lincoln was delivering his first inaugural address. In describing the scene at the inauguration the Diarist, after remarking that neither Buchanan nor Lincoln appeared to advantage and that Chief Justice Taney could hardly speak plainly, went on to say:

I must, however, except Senator Douglas, whose conduct can not be overpraised. I saw him for a moment in the morning, when he told me that he meant to put himself as prominently forward in the ceremonies as he properly could, and to leave no doubt on any one's mind of his determination to stand by the new Administration in the performance of its first great duty to maintain the Union. I watched him carefully. He made his way not without difficulty—for there was literally no sort of order in the arrangements—to the front of the throng directly beside Mr. Lincoln, when he prepared to read the address. A miserable little rickety table had been provided for the President, on which he could hardly find room for his hat, and Senator Douglas, reaching forward, took it with a smile and held it during the delivery of the address. It was a trifling act, but a symbolical one, and not to be forgotten, and it attracted much attention all around me.

Two days before the inauguration, the Diarist, if he can be trusted, put on record a remarkably interesting and significant episode:

There can be no doubt about it any longer. This man from Illinois is not in the hands of Mr. Seward. Heaven grant that he

9

may not be in other hands—not to be thought of with patience! These New York men have done just what they have been saying they would do, and with just the result which I have from the first expected; though I own there are points in the upshot which puzzle me. I can not feel even sure now that Mr. Seward will be nominated at all on Tuesday: and certainly he neither is nor after this can be the real head of the Administration, even if his name is on the list of the Cabinet. Such folly on the part of those who assume to be the especial friends of the one man in whose ability and moderation the conservative people at the North have most confidence; and such folly at this moment might almost indeed make one despair of the republic!

———— has just left me. He was one of the party who called on Mr. Lincoln to-day to bring matters to a head, and prevent the nomination of Chase at all hazards. A nice mess they have made of it! Mr. Lincoln received them civilly enough, and listened to all they had to say. Speaking one after another, they all urged the absolutely essential importance of the presence of Mr. Seward in the Cabinet, to secure for it either the support of the North or any hearing at the South; and they all set forth the downright danger to the cause of the Union of putting into the Cabinet a man like Mr. Chase, identified with and supported by men who did not desire to see the Union maintained on its existing and original basis at all, and who would rather take their chances with a Northern republic, extending itself to Canada, than see the Union of our fathers kept up on the principles of our fathers. After they had all said their say in this vein, Mr. Lincoln, who had sat watching them one after another, and just dropping in a word here and there, waited a moment, and then asked what they wanted him to do, or to forbear. They all replied that they wished him to forbear from nominating Mr. Chase as a member of his Cabinet, because it would not be possible for Mr. Seward to sit in the same Administration with Mr. Chase. He wouldn't wish it, and his friends and his State would not tolerate it—it must not be.

Then Mr. Lincoln sat looking very much distressed for a few moments, after which he began speaking in a low voice, like a man quite oppressed and worn down, saying, it was very hard to reconcile conflicting claims and interests; that he only desired to form an Administration that would command the confidence of the country and the party; that he had the deepest respect for Mr. Seward, his services, his genius, and all that sort of thing; that Mr. Chase has great claims also, which no one could contest—perhaps not so great as Mr. Seward; but what the party and country wanted was the hearty cooperation of all good men and of all sections, and so on, and so on, for some time. They all thought he was weakening, and they were sure of it, when after a pause he opened a table-drawer and took out a paper, saying: "I had written out my choice here of Secretaries in the Cabinet after a great deal of pains and trouble; and now you tell me I must break the slate and begin all over!"

He went on then to admit, which still more encouraged them, that he had sometimes feared that it would be as they said it was—that he might be forced to reconsider his matured and he thought judicious conclusions. In view of that possibility, he said he had constructed an alternative list of his Cabinet. He did not like it half as well as the one of his own deliberate preference, in which he would frankly say he had hoped to see Mr. Seward sitting as Secretary of State, and Mr. Chase sitting as Secretary of the Treasury—not half as well; but he could not expect to have things exactly as he liked them; and much more to the same effect; which set the listeners quite agog with suppressed expectations of carrying their great point.

"This being the case, gentlemen," he said, finally, after giving the company time to drink in all he had said—"this being the case, gentlemen, how would it do for us to agree upon a change like this?" Everybody, of course, was all attention. "How would it do to ask Mr. Chase to take the Treasury, and to offer the State Department to Mr. William F. Dayton, of New Jersey?"

——— told me you could have knocked him or any man in the room down with a feather. Not one of them could speak. Mr. Lincoln went on in a moment, expatiating on his thoughtfulness about Mr. Seward. Mr. Dayton, he said, was an old Whig, like himself and like Mr. Seward. He was from New Jersey, which "is next door to New York." He had been the Vice-Presidential candidate with General Fremont, and was a most conservative, able, and sensible man. Mr. Seward could go as Minister to England, where his genius would find great scope in keeping Europe straight as to the troubles here, and so on, and so forth, for twenty minutes.

When he got through, one of the company spoke, and said he thought they had better thank him for his kindness in listening to them, and retire for consultation, which they did. But I fear from the tone and the language of ——— that there is more cursing than consultation going on just now. I must own that I heard him with something like consternation. Whether this prefigures an exclusion of Mr. Seward from the Cabinet, who can tell? Nor does that possibility alone make it alarming. It does not prefigure—it proves that the new Administration will be pitched on a dangerous and not on a safe key. It makes what was dark enough before, midnight black. What is to come of it all?

When Lincoln was in New York City on February 20, 1861, Moses H. Grinnell, a leading business man, gave a breakfast in his honor and in the evening he attended the opera. The Diarist, though not present on either occasion, was able through an informant to give interesting reports as to what Lincoln said, how he looked, and how he acted. The guests at the breakfast included quite a number of millionaires. When somebody said to him that he would not be likely to meet so many millionaires at any other table in New York, Lincoln remarked "Oh, indeed, is that so? Well, that's quite right. I'm a millionaire myself. I got a minority of a million in the votes last November."

The Diarist's account of Lincoln at the opera reads:

"My cousin V—— came to me with a most amusing account of the President-elect at the opera in Mr. C——'s box, wearing a huge pair of *black* kid gloves, which attracted the attention of the whole house, hanging as they did over the red velvet box-front. V—— was in the box opposite, where some one, pointing out the strange, dark looking giant opposite as the new President, a lady first told a story of Major Magruder of the army, a Southern man, who took off his hat when a procession of Wide-awakes passed his Broadway hotel last year and said, "I salute the pallbearers of the Constitution"; and then rather cleverly added, "I think we ought to send some flowers over the way to the undertaker of the Union."

During one of the *entr'actes*, V—— went down into what they call the "directors' room" of the Academy, where shortly after appeared Mr. C—— with Mr. Lincoln, and a troop of gentlemen all eager to be presented to the new President. V—— said Mr. Lincoln looked terribly bored, and sat on the sofa at the end of the room with his hat pushed back on his head, the most deplorable figure that can be imagined, putting his hand out to be shaken in a queer, mechanical sort of way. I am afraid V—— has a streak of his sarcastic grandmamma's temper in him.

In addition to this unique information about Lincoln, the Diary contains a great deal that is of exceptional human and historical interest. Its picture of Washington during the Secession Winter is one of the most graphic we possess. The Diarist was, or represented himself to have been, a man of wide acquaintance among the prominent public men of the day. Many of them talked to him with amazing frankness. He was on particularly intimate terms with William H. Seward and Stephen A. Douglas. Both men are represented as frequently seeking his counsel and employing his assistance. Both at times revealed to him closely guarded secrets. His reports about these conversations and his estimates of their characters present pen portraits seldom more strikingly drawn.

Lord Lyons, the British minister to the United States, was among those who talked freely and frankly with the Diarist about the critical situation then existing. Seven states having already seceded, His Lordship said to the Diarist, three days before Lincoln's inauguration: "How are you going to dispose of the actual occupation unlawfully, or by force, of United States premises in these seceded States? . . . How can the new President acquiesce in that occupation? And if he does not acquiesce in it, how will he put an end to it?" These were questions, the Diarist confessed, he could not answer and which he said now haunted him as they had not done before.

Several persons deeply interested in the formation of Lincoln's Cabinet tried to enlist his influence to further their designs. One of these was Senator Charles Sumner of Massachusetts who sent for him and begged for his aid in a last minute endeavor to prevent the appointment of Simon Cameron to a place in the Cabinet. Incidentally Sumner told the Diarist in considerable detail a characteristic instance of Cameron's use of shady financial transactions in Pennsylvania politics.

The Diarist was also on intimate terms with a good many Southern leaders. James L. Orr, one of the South Carolina commissioners to Washington, tried to use him as an intermediary with William H. Seward. Senator Judah P. Benjamin of Louisiana gave him a detailed analysis of the existing situation and an accurate forecast of the plans subsequently followed in organizing the Confederate government. He was in touch with W. C. Rives and J. A. Seddon, of the Virginia delegation to the Washington Peace Convention, and with M. J. Crawford, one of the Confederate commissioners to Washington. His knowledge of Southern affairs and his understanding of the South, both in its strength and in its weakness, were exceptional.

Despite the interest in the Diary aroused at the time of its publication in the *North American Review* in 1879 and despite the constantly increasing interest in Abraham Lincoln and in almost everything connected with the Civil War, the Diary long remained little known to the general reading public, except for small portions of it quoted by historians and biographers of Lincoln. This singular circumstance was doubtless due to the fact that the Diary was accessible only in the pages of the *North American Review* for 1879 and sets of that publication were usually to be found only in the larger libraries. Quite recently this difficulty of access has been removed. Early in 1945 the Abraham Lincoln Bookshop of Chicago brought out a limited edition of the Diary, admirably edited by the distinguished Lincolnist, F. Lauriston Bullard. This was soon followed (1946) by a popular edition published by the Rutgers University Press. Interest in the Diary has been further enhanced through an entertaining and provocative essay which Bernard De Voto published as his Easy Chair contribution to the May, 1945, issue of *Harper's Magazine*. Since then additional discussion of the Diary has appeared in a number of recent review articles and books, most notably by Burton J. Hendrick in his *Lincoln's War Cabinet* and James G. Randall in his *Lincoln the President.*[1]

In the light of these circumstances an attempt to solve the mystery which has always surrounded the Diary seems to be in order.

# II

The opening chapter, I hope, will have prepared the reader to recognize the desirability of getting answers to a number of questions which the character of the Diary and the circumstances attending its first appearance in print at once bring to mind. Is it a genuine diary, actually written in 1860–1861? Who was the Diarist? If not exactly what it purports to be, what is its real character?

Answers to these questions, I presently discovered, could be found only by approaching them in the manner of the detective. That in this instance the problems to be solved are historical rather than criminal need not detract from interest in the solution of the mystery that envelopes the Diary. That these problems have considerable historical importance adds further interest to the story.

My own interest in the Diary and its problems began about 1913. In the intervening years I have at times given those problems considerable attention. At other times I have permitted my interest to lie dormant for long periods. Much of my effort at a solution of the mystery has been a by-product of a larger task upon which I have been and am still engaged. These circumstances have controlled the course that the investigation has taken and may explain in part at least the method in which the results are presented in this book.

At an early stage in my search I recognized that the Diary might be any one of three different things. (1) It might be substantially what it purports to be, i.e., an actual diary written from day to day in 1860–1861. (2) It might be wholly fictitious, the product of some clever literary impostor. (3) It might be in part a genuine diary to which additions and revisions had been made at a subsequent time.

At first, however, I proceeded upon the assumption that the Diary was genuine, being influenced in that supposition by the fact that an impressive array of historical scholars had long considered it as genuine and had drawn upon it extensively in historical and biographical books, especially those devoted to Abraham Lincoln.[2] So believing, I was interested primarily to discover who was the author.

My first hypothesis was that the Diarist was John Van Buren, "Prince John," the brilliant son of President Martin Van Buren, a man well known and greatly admired in his day but now almost forgotten. There is much in the Diary to indicate that the Diarist may have been a man of the "Prince John" type. But beyond that general possibility and evidence that "Prince John" had been among Lincoln's callers in New York on February 20, 1861, and so conceivably might have had the interview with Lincoln reported in the Diary for that day, I could not discover anything to sustain the theory. As the more likely possibilities came in sight, I presently abandoned the theory as untenable.

For several years most of my efforts simply resulted in the exclusion of various possible authors. Taking well-known men of the general type that the author seemed to be, I excluded a considerable number of them as possible authors. This was usually done by discovering for each man that on one or more of the days when the Diarist was in Washington the man in question was somewhere else.

In 1923, being in London I took advantage of the opportunity to follow a clue suggested by the Diary entry of March 1, 1861. On that day the Diary records that the Diarist called on Lord Lyons, then the British minister at Washington. The purpose of his call was "in relation to ——'s business with those vexatious people in Barbadoes and Antigua." This seemed to afford a possible means of discovering the Diarist. If the official papers of Lord Lyons contained any documents in regard to such a matter, it seemed quite possible that they might include the name of a man with whom Lord Lyons had discussed the business on March 1, 1861. That man would almost certainly be the Diarist. At the very least the man in question would become a likely possibility.

In 1923 the official papers of Lord Lyons were at the Public Record Office in London. In accordance with a rule of the Foreign Office they were open to inspection up to January 1, 1861, but not beyond that date. The matter in which I was interested lay just beyond the deadline. I was in a dilemma. I knew that occasionally special permission could be obtained to go beyond the fixed line. I thought I knew that application for such an indulgence would be granted, if at all, only after a long delay. I had, however, only a few days for my stay in London. By chance I mentioned my predicament to a member of the staff at the Public Record Office whom I met in a social way. To my surprise and gratification he told me that occasionally the Foreign Office would grant the needful permission very promptly if the applicant was properly introduced. He further suggested that I call at the Record Office and try my luck. I did so promptly the next morning. Within ten minutes I was busily engaged in examining Lord Lyons' papers. A telephone call from the Record Office to the Foreign Office had brought the necessary permission. Red tape can sometimes be cut quickly. But, alas, my clue led nowhere. There was nothing in the official papers of Lord Lyons "in relation to ——'s business with those vexatious people in Barbadoes and Antigua." Some years later, to make assurance doubly sure, I had the private papers of Lord Lyons at Arundel Castle examined in the hope that they might contain something that did not get into the official papers. But that effort also led to no result.

While those efforts were in progress I never had been in a position to give much continuous attention to the problem or to have ready access to a great deal of the materials in the way of newspapers of 1860–1861, letters of that period now gathered in manuscript collections, and other sources which possibly might furnish information that would lead to a solution of the mystery. Late in the summer of 1927, however, I determined that during the coming summer I would go to

Washington and search the extensive newspaper files and, so far as might be needful, the thousands of letters in the Manuscript Division of the Library of Congress.

Shortly after this decision had been reached I was invited to express an opinion about the validity of a hypothesis advanced by another investigator. His theory was an intriguing one. It looked plausible. It was based upon a considerable array of evidence. On careful examination, however, I found it untenable. The incident led me to renewed effort and furnished me with several suggestions which afterward I was able to use with good results.

My work in Washington during the summer of 1928 led me to think that probably I had discovered the Diarist. I did not regard the conclusion to which I had arrived as fully established, but I did think it highly probable. So thinking, I read an elaborate paper on the subject at the December meeting of the American Historical Association at Indianapolis. The paper was entitled "Who Wrote the Diary of a Public Man? Amos Kendall, Henry Wikoff, or X?"

In that paper I recognized the three possibilities about the Diary already mentioned. Without pronouncing definitely for any one of the three, I presented briefly the most cogent arguments for the view that the Diary is what it purports to be. Taking that view as probably the correct one, I argued that Amos Kendall was almost certainly the author of the Diary. At a later point in this story I shall set forth much of the evidence and arguments then adduced.

An interesting discussion followed the reading of the paper. Most of the participants were men who had at some time tried to discover the identity of the Diarist. None of them took issue with my conclusion.

At the time of the Indianapolis paper I expected to put it into print, possibly with some revision, within a year or two at the latest. My intention was to republish the Diary, accompanied by my paper in regard to it. I intended before doing so to look further into certain matters about which I had not been able to fully satisfy myself. I was particularly anxious to pursue one line of investigation which I had not yet explored. That was the question of the manner in which the Diary had been received at the time of its publication in 1879. I hoped and expected that discussion in regard to it at that time would include considerable speculation and argument as to its authenticity and its authorship. From such discussion I hoped to obtain valuable information and suggestive clues which might be followed up.

Circumstances delayed the pursuit of the inquiry. When finally undertaken it proved time-consuming but disappointing. The results, which will be set forth at a later point in the story, did not materially aid me except in a negative way. Meanwhile I had been led by new discoveries to consider more thoroughly than hitherto the possibility that the Diary was not altogether what it purported to be. As a result, I began to search for a possible diarist whose actual diary, probably rather meager, could have been revised and added to until it became "The Diary of a Public Man" as published in the *North American Review* in 1879. Considerable search led me presently to discover a man who apparently met many of the requirements. Since that discovery I have by search in many places and often under unusual circumstances endeavored to determine whether the man in question was the actual Diarist. I have also scrutinized the Diary more thoroughly than in the earlier stages of my investigation in order to determine, if possible, whether it could have been written in 1860–1861.

# III

From an early stage in my quest I perceived that in the end I might be forced to make considerable use of internal evidence drawn from the Diary. As results obtained from that form of evidence are often much disputed, I determined, if possible, to solve the problem of the Diary by more direct methods.

One of these was to ascertain whether anything could be learned about how the editor of the *North American Review* had obtained the copy of the Diary, or rather the extracts from it which he had published. Information upon that point might lead to the disclosure of the Diarist.

So far as I could discover only three efforts had been made to learn the identity of the Diarist by application to the editors or publishers of the *North American Review,* though others may have been made. In each instance the effort failed to produce the desired result.

George Ticknor Curtis while preparing his life of James Buchanan applied to Allen Thorndike Rice, the editor and owner of the *Review* at the time the Diary appeared, for information as to the identity of the Diarist. His request was refused.[3]

Hiram Barney, who figured in the Diary entry for February 20, 1861, wrote to a friend in October, 1886, that he had applied to D. Appleton and Co., the publishers of the *Review,* for the name of the Diarist, but they would not or could not inform him.[4]

At a much later date the late James Westfall Thompson, who was much interested in the Diary, wrote the office of the *North American Review* to learn whether the archives of the publication contained any information about the Diary. The reply, which he once showed me, was that the publication having changed hands several times, the management then in control had no correspondence going back as far as 1879.

Wishing to be perfectly sure that there could be no mistake about the information given to Professor Thompson, I went to the office of the *North American Review*, then located in New York City. I was courteously received but obtained only the same information that had been given to him. While there I asked and received permission to examine the office file of the *Review*, hoping that the authorship of anonymous contributions might have been set down in that file. There was, however, no indication in the file as to the authorship of the Diary.

I also sought information at the office of D. Appleton and Co., thinking that possibly payments to contributors to the *Review* might have been made through the publishers and that thereby the identity of the Diarist, or a clue which would lead to it, might be discovered. But I found that D. Appleton and Co. had acted only as printers and distributors. Their records contained no information as to editorial matters connected with the *Review*.

At various times I made persistent efforts to discover what had become of the papers of Allen Thorndike Rice, the editor of the *Review*, after his death in 1889, believing that his correspondence would be likely to contain something in regard to the Diary. These efforts yielded some interesting personal experiences but no tangible results. The Rice papers seem to have disappeared without leaving a trace.

Another possibility failed to yield any positive results. Knowing that the Widener Library at Harvard University had a file of the *North American Review* in which during the early years of publication men who were closely connected with it had written in the names of the writers, all of the articles being unsigned during the early years, I examined that file in the hope that the practice had been continued in later years as regards unsigned articles. But I found that the practice had been discontinued long before 1879.

22

All these efforts to discover direct evidence which would solve the mystery of the Diary having led to no result, there seemed to be only one other recourse before attempting to find the solution by a more thorough-going examination of the internal evidence afforded by the Diary than anything I had as yet attempted. I could examine the manner in which the Diary had been received at the time of its publication in 1879. At that time only eighteen years had elapsed since the period covered by the Diary. There must have been, accordingly, among its readers many men who could reasonably feel themselves entitled to believe that they were well qualified to pronounce upon it with considerable authority. Their speculation as to the identity of the Diarist and their discussion as to whether the Diary was what it purported to be ought, therefore, to afford valuable suggestions that could be followed up and accepted or rejected in the light of all the pertinent evidence available. Accordingly, I began an extensive examination of newspapers, magazines, and any other available material which would show how readers of the Diary in 1879 had reacted to it. The result will be set forth in the next chapter.

# IV

The investigation which I pursued in an endeavor to utilize the method of solving the mystery of the Diary by enlisting the aid of its original readers extended over a long period. Much of it had to be done as opportunity offered in conjunction with other work. During the course of it I tried to examine as many newspapers and magazines of 1879 as was possible. I did include all the leading magazines and more than fifty newspapers. Among the latter were nearly all the leading newspapers of New York, Philadelphia, Boston, Washington, Baltimore, Cincinnati, Chicago, and St. Louis. I also included a considerable number of newspapers in other cities, selected in most cases because there appeared to be some special reason for supposing that the editor of the paper in question would be likely to take a decided interest in the Diary. Such papers were numerous in 1879. Among the many included were the *Springfield Republican*, the *Providence Journal*, the *New Haven Register*, the *Richmond Whig*, the *Atlanta Constitution*, the *Charleston News and Courier*, the *Nashville American*, the *Cleveland Leader*, the *Indianapolis Journal*, the *Des Moines Register*, the *Illinois State Journal*, and the *San Francisco Examiner*.

I found that the publication of the Diary had evidently aroused much interest. It had given rise to a great deal of discussion, but not the sort that would be of much assistance to me.

So far as I could discover only one editor sent a reporter to interview a survivor who had been mentioned in the Diary in a way which indicated that if properly questioned he might have been able to identify the Diarist. The one survivor so interviewed was Thurlow Weed. Apparently he was

24

not asked to identify the Diarist. Nor was he asked anything bearing upon the authenticity of the Diary.[5] The report of the interview furnished nothing to aid me in my search.

Many editors made use of the Diary, or something that appeared in it, as a basis for editorials. Quite a number of contributors wrote letters to the editors about it. But in none of these discussions was there any serious attempt to canvass the question whether the Diary actually was what it purported to be and not much in the way of argument or conjecture about the identity of the Diarist. In all I found only six suggestions advanced as to the authorship of the Diary. Five of them can be dismissed very quickly. The sixth will require more extended attention.

One of the six was Thurlow Weed himself. The suggestion that he might be the Diarist came shortly after the appearance of the first installment. Presumably the maker of that suggestion would not have made it if he had waited and critically examined the third installment,[6] for in that Weed is mentioned in a way to preclude the possibility that he could have been the Diarist. On February 26, 1861, the Diarist tells about having received a note from Weed and also about seeing him on that day. As Weed would not have been writing a note to himself, he manifestly was not the Diarist.

Another suggestion was that the Diarist was Charles Edward Stuart. Several reasons might have been advanced in support of that opinion. Stuart had been United States senator from Michigan from 1853 to 1859. He was a close friend of Stephen A. Douglas and obviously had a strong admiration for him. Stuart in that particular seemed to fit into the picture perfectly. A dispatch from Chicago which appeared in the *New York World* on August 24, 1879, reported that the *Chicago Tribune* of the next day would contain a report that Stuart was the author of the Diary. An effort to find the article in the *Chicago Tribune* proved fruitless. Apparently for some undiscoverable reason the article did not appear. But the report that Stuart was the author of the Diary reached Kalamazoo, Stuart's home town. The *Kalamazoo*

*Gazette* questioned him about the matter and received from him a positive denial. Stuart was not the Diarist.

The third suggestion was D. H. Strothers.[7] In 1860–1861 Strothers was a well-known writer and illustrator of popular books and magazine articles. Much of his output appeared over the *nom de plume* of "Porte Crayon." I was able to satisfy myself that he was not the Diarist by finding that in an article which he published in *Harper's Magazine* for June, 1866, he had said, "During the winter of 1860–1861 I was residing at my father's house in Martinsburg [then Virginia, now West Virginia], occupied with my private affairs and arranging for a future of peace and seclusion." Quite evidently Strothers could not have been the Diarist, who at that time was in Washington, thinking about other things than his own personal affairs and "a future of peace and seclusion." As the entries in the Diary were made by a man who was almost continually in Washington from December 28, 1860, to March 15, 1861, it is evident that Strothers was not the Diarist.

The fourth suggestion was Joseph C. G. Kennedy, at one time superintendent of the Census.[8] In that capacity he was at Washington during the period covered by the Diary. In personality, however, he did not in any marked degree resemble the Diarist as incidentally depicted in the Diary. One circumstance, moreover, seemed to exclude him. Lincoln had first met the Diarist at Washington in 1848. But Kennedy was in 1848 living on a farm near Meadville, Pennsylvania.[9] A meeting between the two men at that time could scarcely have occurred.

The fifth suggestion was Horatio King, postmaster general during the closing days of the Buchanan administration.[10] He was in Washington during the period covered by the Diary. In personality he resembled the Diarist in several particulars. But in his case, too, one circumstance definitely excluded him. Chapter eight of his *Turning on the Light,* a reminiscent volume, is entitled "My first and last sight of President Lincoln." It begins: "There is no more vivid or apparently indelible impression on the tablet of my memory than my first and last sight of President Lincoln. . . . The first occasion was when he called on President Buchanan, in company with Senator Seward on the 23d of February, 1861 . . ." Such words could not have been written by a man who had interviewed Lincoln at New York on February 20, 1861, as the Diarist reported that he had done. Manifestly King was not the Diarist.

The sixth suggestion was made in a *Chicago Tribune* editorial on August 26, 1879, apropos of the second installment of the Diary. It suggested that Jacob Collamer was the Diarist. Collamer was in 1860–1861 United States senator from Vermont.

This suggestion came to me as a great and exceptionally interesting surprise for in my Indianapolis paper I had closely examined that possibility, recognizing in it one of considerable plausibility.

My examination had begun by utilizing a discussion in regard to the Diary by the late Allen Johnson, who had been professor of history at Yale University and editor of the *Dictionary of American Biography*. He was a man with an exceptionally penetrating and critical mind. In 1926 he had published a little book entitled *The Historian and Historical Evidence*. In a short passage at pp. 59–61 he discussed the authorship of the Diary. Without venturing to name the Diarist, he described upon the basis of internal evidence the kind of man the Diarist appears to have been. He was, according to the description drawn by Professor Johnson, (1) a New Englander, (2) a former Whig, (3) in 1860–1861 a Republican, and (4) a senator. Other attributes of the Diarist were depicted by Professor Johnson, but those points did not seem to require attention at the moment. The four mentioned appeared to furnish a basis for testing whether Collamer was the Diarist. If Collamer met the four requirements there would be a strong case for his authorship. In fact, the case for Collamer seemed to be irrefutable unless there was some mistake as to the validity of one or more of the four points in question, or unless Collamer could be excluded upon the ground that he did not conform to other requirements in the personality of the Diarist as exhibited in the Diary.

The idea that the Diarist was a senator appeared to rest chiefly, if not exclusively, upon a passage in the Diary in which it was said, "As we sat in the senate-chamber." Indubitably such language might well have been used by a senator writing in his diary. But a spectator of proceedings in the Senate might have used the same language. I noted also that nowhere in the Diary was there any allusion to proceedings in executive session of the Senate or in fact to anything taking place in the Senate that might not have been seen or heard by somebody who was not a senator.

Further doubt as to whether the Diarist could have been a senator came from an allusion in the Diary to Senator Baker of Oregon. An uncomplimentary allusion to him in the Diary for March 2, 1861, is followed by the words, "I met the man again to-day, as I passed into the National [Hotel], and I really could hardly speak to him civilly." This appeared to be the kind of language the Diarist might well employ in regard to a man whom he disliked and met only occasionally. It could scarcely have been employed in speaking of a man he must have met almost every day on the floor of the Senate.

Fortunately there was a way, it appeared, by which the question whether the Diarist was a senator could be cleared up. It was a method that also might throw some light upon other matters involved in the question of whether Collamer was the Diarist.

The Diarist was in New York City on February 20, 1861, from quite early in the morning until late at night. He, therefore, could not have been in the Senate on that day. If Collamer was absent from the Senate on that day he conceivably might have been in New York and so might have been the Diarist, unless some circumstance should be discovered to preclude that possibility. In a word, proof that Collamer could have been in New York City that day would create a strong presumption that he was the Diarist. On the other hand, proof that he was *not* there that day would eliminate him entirely, for the Diarist was indubitably in New York.

Examination of the *Congressional Globe* and the Senate *Journal* indicated almost to a certainty that Collamer was not in the Senate on February 20, 1861. His name does not appear in any of the debates or in any of the several votes occurring on that day. Conceivably, therefore, he might have been in New York unless conclusive evidence to the contrary could be deduced. Upon investigation I found that such evidence did exist.

As already said the Diarist was in New York City late in the evening of February 20, 1861, for he relates that his "cousin V——" came to him to tell how Lincoln had appeared at the opera that evening. An examination of the railroad time tables for that period showed that he could not have left New York City for Washington until the next morning. There were no late evening trains between the two cities at that time. Examination further disclosed that the earliest train upon the morning of February 21, 1861, would not have brought a passenger to Washington until well along in the afternoon.[11] But Collamer was in the Senate that morning. His name is recorded in a roll call that occurred not later than noon.[12] It seems manifest, therefore, that he could not have been in New York City late at night on the preceding day and so could not have been the Diarist.

I found also further evidence to support the conclusion that Collamer could not have been the Diarist. One feature of it was particularly striking. The entry in the Diary for February 20, 1861, includes this statement: "Mr. Barney said that Mr. Lincoln asked about me particularly this morning, and was good enough to say that he recollected meeting me in 1848, which may have been the case; but I certainly recall none of the circumstances, and can not place him, even with the help of all the pictures I have seen of such an extraordinary-looking mortal, as I confess I ought to have been ashamed of myself once to have seen face to face, and to have then forgotten."

Could Collamer have written in that way about Lincoln in 1861? It seems impossible. In 1847–1849 the two men had been colleagues in the Thirtieth Congress as Whig members of the House of Representatives. The House at that date consisted of 226 members. The Whigs numbered about 115. These numbers were small enough to make the assumption a perfectly safe one, taking into account the general conditions then prevailing in Washington, that Lincoln and Collamer must have had some personal acquaintance at that time. The party consultations of the Whig members and the proceedings upon the floor of the House would have brought it about. Lincoln's physical appearance could hardly have failed to make some impression upon Collamer when the two men were upon the floor of the House for about ten months in the aggregate.

I found also that there was abundant evidence in the House *Journal* and in the *Congressional Globe* to indicate almost to a certainty that the two men must have known each other to some extent at that time. Collamer was chairman of the committee on public lands. Lincoln as a Western congressman was much interested in matters which commonly came before that committee and so must have been known to its chairman. Examples are not lacking to show that Collamer had had abundant opportunity to know Lincoln by sight at least. On April 3, 1848, right at the opening of proceedings Lincoln moved to suspend the rules so as to permit the taking up of a Senate resolution regarding naval contracts. There was a short but sharp colloquy between Lincoln and two other members. Then the vote was taken. Collamer was among those who voted for Lincoln's motion. On August 2, 1848, Collamer made a speech and then Lincoln immediately followed him.[13] I found that other instances of the same sort could be cited to bring to the general presumption confirming evidence that the two men must have known each other at that time.

I also took into consideration the possibility that, while Collamer must have known Lincoln to some extent in 1847–

1849, he might have forgotten him in 1861. It seemed to me too improbable for serious consideration. I recognized that in the interim between 1849 and 1861 Collamer's recollection about Lincoln might have grown dim. If so, the campaign of 1860 and the role which Lincoln was playing in the crisis confronting the country in February, 1861, must have served to revive the memory of the earlier acquaintance. Collamer could not under any circumstances have written in 1861 that with the help of all the pictures he had seen he had no recollection of ever meeting Lincoln.

# V

From all the circumstances put forth in the previous chapter, I reached the conclusion that Jacob Collamer could not have been the Diarist. Could he have been some other senator? To settle the question I employed the same method by which Collamer had been eliminated. I found that the absent senators on February 20, 1861, were George E. Pugh (Ohio), Willard Saulsbury (Delaware), John R. Thomson (New Jersey), and Louis T. Wigfall (Texas). It was clear that none of them could be the Diarist. Measured by the fourfold test drawn from Professor Johnson's pen portrait of the Diarist, none of them met the requirements. None was a New Englander; none had been a former Whig; none was a Republican in 1860–1861. Apart from that test there were conclusive reasons for holding that none of them could be the Diarist. Wigfall was a secessionist, but the Diarist was devoted to the Union. Though more could be adduced, a single count served to exclude all of the other three. The Diarist alluded to his "long experience of Washington." None of the three senators would have written in that way in a diary, for all had come to the Capital in quite recent years.[14]

It was evident that the Diarist was not a senator. I then asked myself, Could he have been a representative? To answer that question I resorted to the same method employed in the process of eliminating Collamer.

The House of Representatives in February, 1861, consisted of 204 members, those from the seven states which had seceded having withdrawn, save for two exceptions. I found that 150 had participated in a roll call on February 20. The absentees, therefore, amounted, if all who did not vote were absent, to 54. Could any of the 54 be the Diarist? Careful

32

examination for each man upon that list as to whether he met requirements—not only those involved in the fourfold test but various other indubitable requirements—satisfied me that none of them could be the Diarist. Moreover it appeared to me highly significant that nowhere in the Diary was there an account of anything that took place in the House of Representatives. A congressman keeping a diary would certainly put into it some allusion to the proceedings of the House to which he belonged.

If the Diarist was neither a senator nor a congressman, could some person be found among men with "long experience of Washington" who met requirements for the Diarist as depicted in the Diary? Before embarking upon a search for such a person, it seemed wise to look into a question that had frequently come into my mind while exploring the possibility of finding the Diarist among the senators and congressmen.

Could it be that there were other errors in the fourfold test derived from Professor Johnson's pen portrait of the Diarist? Was it certain that the Diarist was a New Englander, a former Whig, and in 1860–1861 a Republican? Careful examination of the Diary led me to entertain serious doubts in regard to all three of these points.

The idea that the Diarist was a New Englander appeared to rest chiefly upon the manner in which Charles Sumner, senator from Massachusetts, was reported to have spoken to the Diarist on March 3, 1861. Sumner is reported as having asked the Diarist what interest he or his friends could have in seeing a preponderance of the Middle States in Lincoln's Cabinet and in what way it could advance their interests "to allow the New England States, 'the cradle and spinal column of the Republican party,' to be 'humiliated and thrust beneath the salt at the board which, but for them would never have been spread,' and more to the same general effect . . ." Such language, I thought, was based upon an assumption that the Diarist would feel some sympathy with aggrieved New Englanders, but it did not necessarily indicate that he was a New Englander. Moreover, the Diarist reported that

33

on the occasion Sumner was highly excited and spoke "with an intensity and bitterness quite indescribable." Sumner was reported as appealing to the Diarist for aid in seeking to prevent the appointment of Cameron to Lincoln's Cabinet. When Sumner was not denouncing an enemy he was much disposed to assume that everybody else, if only their eyes could be opened by his argument, would share his point of view. I could not regard it as a certainty that because Sumner spoke to the Diarist as one who ought to share his point of view that mode of speaking gave evidence that the man addressed was a New Englander. At best the point seemed to be a doubtful one.

The idea that the Diarist was a former Whig appeared to rest chiefly upon his report about his conversation with Lincoln in New York City on February 20, 1861. On that occasion the Diarist reported that Lincoln was "entirely clear and sensible on the vital importance of holding the Democrats close to the Administration on the naked Union issue. 'They are,' he said to me, 'just where we Whigs were in '48 about the Mexican war. We had to take the Locofoco preamble when Taylor wanted help, or else vote against helping Taylor; and the Democrats must vote to hold the Union now, without bothering whether we or the Southern men got things where they are, and we must make it easy for them to do this, because we can't live through the case without them.' "

It appeared to me quite conceivable that the words ascribed to Lincoln might have been addressed to a former Whig, with the purpose of inducing him to share Lincoln's ideas about the importance of enlisting the help of the Democrats. But I thought the words admitted of another and to my mind a more likely interpretation. They are exactly what we would expect Lincoln to say to a Union-loving Democrat whose aid he appreciated and desired to retain. In the light of that circumstance they did not appear to me to afford satisfactory proof that the man to whom they were addressed was a former Whig. Whether he was or not seemed to me an open question.

34

The supposition that the Diarist was in 1860–1861 a Republican appeared to rest chiefly upon the fact that Lincoln consulted him about appointments to the Cabinet and various Republicans urged him to use with Lincoln the influence which they manifestly attributed to him. This did not, I thought, constitute sufficient reason for supposing that he was a Republican. Lincoln was at that time willing and even anxious to listen to the advice of others than Republicans, especially if he had a good opinion of their disinterestedness and devotion to the Union. Moreover I thought it highly significant that the Diarist always spoke of the Republican party and the Republican administration in purely objective terms. There did not appear to be in the Diary a single instance in which the Diarist alluded to the Republican party as if he belonged to it, nor one in which he spoke of the Republican administration as if he was one of its party supporters. These circumstances made it appear to me decidedly doubtful whether the Diarist could be set down as a Republican.

From the results set forth in this and the preceding chapter I came to the conclusion that the Diarist was not a senator, nor a congressman, and that search for him need not be confined to New Englanders who had been Whigs and were in 1860–1861 Republicans. Others might be included.

# VI

The whole field of prominent men who in 1860–1861 had had "long experience of Washington" needed to be searched for a man who fitted closely into the picture that the Diarist had drawn of himself. In seeking for such a man I looked into the Diary to discover every point about the personality of the Diarist which could be extracted from it and especially all those which might afford some clue as to his identity. This examination disclosed eighteen such points:

1. The Diarist must have been a man of considerable importance. This was apparent from the general character of the Diary. It was also apparent from Lincoln's attitude toward him, as shown in the intercourse between the two men. The anxiety of Charles Sumner and others to enlist the aid of the Diarist in attempts to influence Lincoln about appointments to the Cabinet also showed that he was regarded as a man of importance. His relations with William H. Seward and Stephen A. Douglas, especially the latter, would have been possible only for a man of considerable consequence.

2. He must have been a tall man. Lincoln asked him if he had ever measured backs with Sumner. As Sumner was tall, Lincoln would not have asked that question of a man of short or medium height.

3. He must have been a man who had the diary habit. The whole tone and character of the Diary indicated a practiced hand.

4. He must have been to a considerable extent a man of the world. The Diarist's description of the inaugural ball, his remarks about Mrs. Lincoln and Mrs. Douglas, his account of the dinner party he attended on February 26, 1861, and his

account of Lincoln at the opera, could have come only from a sophisticated person.

5. He must have been a man of wide acquaintance among the leading public men assembled at Washington during the winter of 1860–1861. The Diary was crowded with evidence of such acquaintance.

6. As already several times remarked, he must have known Washington for a long time. Otherwise he would not have used the expression "in all my long experience of Washington."

7. He must have been in 1860–1861 a strong Unionist. Lincoln's remarks to him in New York clearly imply it and his own often-expressed anxiety about the safety of the Union could leave no doubt about the matter.

8. He must have been a man who knew the South rather well and was free from any sectional animosity against it. This was apparent from all the Diarist's allusions to Southern matters. While regretting the precipitancy of Southern leaders and sometimes disposed to accept Northern opinions as to their shortcomings, he indulged in no denunciation of them and he nowhere exhibited any hostility to the peculiar institution of the South or to Southern points of view on any other matter than the Union.

9. He must have been a man whom Lincoln had met in 1848 and was anxious to meet again in 1861. He, however, in 1861 could not recall the 1848 meeting. In the entry for February 20, 1861, the Diarist reported: "Mr. Barney said that Mr. Lincoln asked about me particularly this morning and was good enough to say that he recollected meeting me in 1848, which may have been the case; but I certainly recall none of the circumstances, and I can not place him even with the help of all the pictures I have seen of such an extraordinary looking mortal, as I confess I ought to be ashamed of myself once to have seen face to face, and then to have forgotten."

10. He must have been a man who in 1861 was sufficiently familiar with the handwriting of Charles Sumner so he could

recognize it at a glance. Recording his interview with Lincoln at the Willard Hotel on February 28, 1861, the Diarist, after telling how Lincoln suddenly picked up a note and handed it to him, then continued, "I recognized Senator Sumner's handwriting as I took it . . ."

11. He must have been a man of considerable acquaintance with the French language and literature. The use of a few French words in the Diary entry for February 26, 1861, I thought, need not be regarded as conclusive proof that the Diarist was an accomplished French scholar. It appeared quite possible that the editor of the *North American Review*, despite disclaimer in his introductory note to the Diary, might have taken the liberty of substituting French for English words in view of the fact that the person whose remarks the Diarist was reporting was at home in French. But elsewhere in the Diary there was clear evidence that the Diarist was familiar with French political thought. Reporting a conversation with Senator Judah P. Benjamin of Louisiana on January 13, 1861, the Diarist said: "I could detect, I thought, in his views on these points, a distinctly French turn of thought, but much that he said struck me as eminently sound and sagacious."

12. He must have been a man who, in addition to general interest in business conditions had particular interest in the tariff, patents, and postal matters. His deep concern about the general effect of the secession crisis upon the business of the country was strikingly shown in the comment he made in the Diary after recording his interview with Senator Benjamin on January 13, 1861. "The chief peril seemed to me now to lie in the long period of business prostration with which we are threatened, especially if Mr. Benjamin's views are correct. I do not believe that his Confederate Government will lose the opportunity of establishing its free-trade system wherever its authority can extend while conducting negotiations for a new organization of the Union, and irreparable damage may in this way be done to our great manufacturing interests before any adjustment can be reached." Anxiety

38

about the way in which the setting up of a Confederate tariff would operate was expressed in the Diary entry for March 2, 1861. "The distress at home grows hourly and this preposterous tariff which they have assumed to establish at Montgomery points to a still worse state of things."

Fear lest Confederate refusal to recognize patents issued by the government of the United States might lead to grave results led him to say, also on March 2, 1861: "I asked ———— what these people mean to do or to attempt to do about patents, showing him some of my letters from home which clearly indicate the trouble brewing in our part of the country on that very important subject. He could give me no reassuring views of the matter, but, on the contrary, led me to think that the seceded States will try to raise a revenue by exacting heavy sums of patentees for a recognition of their rights within the territory of those States."

That he was interested in postal matters appeared from the fact that when James Guthrie, who had been secretary of the Treasury in the Pierce administration and more recently a member of the Washington Peace Conference, wished to help a fellow Kentuckian who was in a quandary over a mail contract, he sent him to the Diarist to learn "whether I thought Mr. Seward or Mr. Lincoln would give him a kind of authority to take a contract for carrying the mails for the Government at Montgomery on the same terms on which he had a contract with the Government here, so that there might be no interruption in the mail service."

13. He must have been a man who had some decided motive for frequent attendance at meetings of the Senate in the winter of 1860–1861. Several entries showed the Diarist in attendance at meetings of the Senate or following its proceedings closely.

14. He must have been a man on intimate terms with William H. Seward and Stephen A. Douglas. The Diary showed Douglas calling upon the Diarist on several occasions and talking with him in a way that would have been possible only between close friends. Seward not only called upon the Diarist

but received him in his own home, talking on occasion in a way which showed that close relations existed between the two men. The Diarist also represented that Seward made use of him in confidential matters.

15. He must have been a man who had a strong dislike for Senator Edward D. Baker of Oregon, and the Blairs. His aversion to Baker has been noted. "I met the man again to-day as I passed into the National [Hotel], and I really could hardly speak to him civilly. It is such men as he who play into the hands of the worst enemies of the country and of common sense at the South." His dislike of the Blairs was even more pointedly expressed. "I do not like any of the Blairs, and indeed I know nobody who does."

16. He must have been a man familiar with men and conditions in New York City. This appeared from the questions Lincoln put to him when they met in that city, from his contacts with prominent New Yorkers such as William H. Aspinwall, Simeon Draper, and Hiram Barney, and from his occasional comments about New York affairs and conditions.

17. He must have been the sort of man to whom James L. Orr, of South Carolina, would have turned on December 28, 1860, in seeking to secure the cooperation of William H. Seward. Orr was then in Washington as one of the commissioners sent by the South Carolina Convention to try to negotiate for an amicable transfer of the forts and other federal establishments at Charleston to South Carolina, following its secession a few days earlier. On the previous day the startling news had reached Washington that Major Robert Anderson had stolen a march on the South Carolina secessionists by transferring his garrison at night from the scarcely defensible Fort Moultrie to the supposedly impregnable Fort Sumter. In that situation the South Carolina commissioners instantly demanded that President Buchanan order Anderson to withdraw or return to Fort Moultrie. Support of such a demand by Seward, or even his silence in regard to it, would improve its chances of success. In an endeavor to get that kind of support, according to the Diarist, Orr came to him asking that he use his influence with Seward.

40

18. Finally and most decisively, he must have been a man who was in New York City on February 20, 1861, and was in Washington on each of twenty specifically indicated days lying between December 28, 1860, and March 15, 1861. Proof that a possible Diarist was anywhere else on any of those days would eliminate him.

The examination having been finally concluded, I believed that with the eighteen points as a measuring rod, it would be possible to discover the Diarist. The result of my effort to solve the mystery of the Diary by the use of that method will be set forth in the next two chapters.

# VII

In seeking for a man who met the requirements of all of my eighteen points, I sought for him first among men of national importance who had during a long period figured prominently at Washington. Such a man, I thought, need not necessarily have been in residence there in 1860–1861. His presence at Washington upon twenty particular days during the period December to March might have come about for any one of various reasons. During the Secession Winter many men who had formerly figured at Washington revisited the capital.

Three possibilities appeared. They were George Bancroft, Edward Everett, and Robert C. Winthrop. Upon examination, however, I found that all three would have to be eliminated. In each instance there was clear proof that the man in question could not have been the Diarist.

Turning to men who were indubitably at Washington during the period covered by the Diary I decided to include in the search men of less prominence, if otherwise qualified. This was done upon the theory that possibly the Diarist was not a man of as much prominence as a reader of the Diary might suppose from a good deal of what appeared in its pages. It seemed possible, though not perhaps probable, that Lincoln, Seward, and Douglas might have had the relations which the Diarist claimed for himself with some man not very prominent in the public eye.

In that thought I looked for men who had had long experience in Washington, extensive acquaintance with prominent men, and a large fund of information about public affairs. Excluding a good many such men upon the ground that they obviously lacked some of the eighteen requirements, I found four men who met a good many of them. For a time it seemed as if one of them might be found who met all of the requirements. The four men were Asbury Dickens, Henry S. Sanford, Ben Parley Poore, and John W. Forney.

A friend who possessed a large fund of information about Washington had suggested Asbury Dickens as a possibility. Aside from the fact that he had been appointed to a position in the Treasury Department early in the administration of Andrew Jackson and that at the period covered by the Diary he had been secretary of the Senate for about thirty years, I could not learn much about him. Obviously from the position he occupied he could have met many of the eighteen requirements. One consideration, however, served to eliminate him. He was an old and infirm man. The Washington correspondent of the *Springfield Republican* in March, 1861, described him as "too infirm to do the duties of the office" he held and said that the duties were performed by his chief clerk.[15] The Diarist might have been a somewhat oldish man but it was clear that he was not infirm. I concluded that Dickens was not the Diarist.

Henry S. Sanford met many of the requirements. There was much about his career, his personality, and his political and social connections to suggest that he might have been the Diarist. Early in his life he held diplomatic posts at St. Petersburg, Frankfort, and Paris. As an outcome of that experience he published several valuable reports. In a widely copied newspaper article published early in 1861, he argued that if the seceding states, as they threatened, should cut off the cotton supply for Northern textile factories, the deficiency could be supplied by cotton grown in Central America. A little later Lincoln appointed him minister to Belgium. In that capacity he rendered valuable service to the Union cause during the Civil War in counteracting the activities of the Confederate agents in Europe. Still later he rendered important diplomatic services. Always highly interested in business, he was during the later years of his life prominent among the promoters of enterprises in Florida. The city of Sanford in that state was named for him.[16]

At the period covered by the Diary Sanford was in Washington. His apparent purpose was to look after the interests of the Panama railway and to obtain a diplomatic post from the incoming Lincoln administration. He could, therefore, have kept a diary such as that published in 1879 by the *North American Review*.

In a letter to his wife written on March 9, 1861, Gideon Welles, Lincoln's secretary of the Navy, wrote after dining with Sanford several times that his host was "a very extraordinary Connecticut friend," "evidently a man of large fortune," who lived "in quiet costly English style with his French cook, costly and rare wines &c. . . . He gives dinner parties every day, I believe, but only to four or five persons at a time and they the very first persons in society. To me he is a great deal of a mystery." Writing again on the next day Welles said, apropos of still another dinner party at Sanford's table: "I told Sanford I did not rightly comprehend him or his life. He seemed pleased. Said he was fond of Washington life and of gathering as on this occasion intellectual men together. It was his passion. He preferred it even to books, or any other amusement."[17] This picture appeared to me to look much like the kind of man I conceived the Diarist to have been.

After considerable search I found that Sanford's papers had passed into the possession of the Connecticut Historical Society. An examination of them made me feel for a time quite sure that I was about to discover the Diarist. They showed that Sanford indubitably met ten out of the eighteen requirements, including several of the more important ones. He was on intimate terms with Seward and probably also with Douglas; he was a man of the world; he had an extensive acquaintance among prominent public men in Washington, including several who were mentioned in the Diary; he had a good knowledge of French and of French thought; he was much interested in business affairs. While the information I could get did not enable me to determine whether he met any of the other requirements, none of it offered any decisive reason for eliminating him on the ground that as regards a particular point he did not fit into the picture. I could not avoid some doubt as to whether Sanford at the period covered by the Diary was as prominent a man as the Diarist appeared to have been. But I reflected that a diarist is likely to exaggerate his own importance. Some notable diarists have committed that offense. One point, however, gave me pause.

Was Sanford in New York City on February 20, 1861? If not, all the points of resemblance would go for nothing. Any apparent similarity would be a matter of coincidence and could count for nothing. To my disappointment I presently discovered that on that date Sanford was in Washington, not in New York City. There were letters in the Sanford papers which showed that Sanford had written letters from Washington to a business firm in New York on February 19 and 20, 1861.[18] So he had to be eliminated.

Later the elimination of Sanford was decisively confirmed by evidence from an unexpected quarter. When the Lincoln papers at the Library of Congress were opened for examination they disclosed a letter of November 6, 1860, from Truman Smith, of New York, to Lincoln. Smith wrote: "I am this moment informed by a telegraphic dispatch from my friend the Hon. H. S. Sanford dated Chicago this day that he has seen you and mentioned a subject of great delicacy and importance . . ." A note from Sanford to Lincoln, November 15, 1860,[19] still further established the fact that they had met and become acquainted.[20] Manifestly Sanford could not have written in a genuine diary on February 20, 1861, as the Diarist did: "Mr. Barney said that Mr. Lincoln asked after me particularly this morning and was good enough to say that he recollected meeting me in 1848, which may have been the case; but I certainly recall none of the circumstances, and can not place him, even with the help of all the pictures I have seen of such an extraordinary-looking mortal as I confess I ought to be ashamed of myself once to have seen face to face, and to have then forgotten."

Ben Perley Poore was in Washington during the period covered by the Diary. He met a good many of the requirements. But it was evident that he was not the Diarist. His close and friendly relations with Charles Sumner clearly indicated that he would not have written about Sumner as the Diarist did. His dispatches to the *Boston Journal* at that time showed that he could not have been on the friendly terms with Douglas that the Diarist enjoyed. In a contribution to a volume entitled *Reminiscences of Lincoln,* which Allen Thorndike Rice edited and published in 1886, Poore stated that he knew Lincoln in 1848 well and supported the statement by convincing proof.[21] He could not, therefore, have recorded in a diary of 1860–1861 that he had no recollection that he had ever met Lincoln at an earlier date. He, too, had to be eliminated.

At first glance John W. Forney seemed a distinct possibility. Additional reason came from a report that at one time at the University of Chicago Professor Herman von Holst had suggested to some of his students that Forney might have been the Diarist. Forney unquestionably met many of the requirements. He was on intimate terms with Seward and Douglas; he had had long experience at Washington; his official and newspaper activities had brought him into contact with nearly all the prominent public men of his day; he was in Washington during the winter of 1860–1861 and had extensive personal knowledge of almost everything that happened there at that time. But he was not in New York City on February 20, 1861. On that day he sent his usual letter from Washington to his paper, the *Philadelphia Press,* over his well-known *nom de plume* "Occasional." It was, of course, possible that for that particular day Forney might have delegated the writing of the "Occasional" letter to some substitute and might himself have been away from Washington. Even so, it seemed certain that he was not in New York City on that day. The contents of his newspaper for February 21, 1861, indicate to a practical certainty that Forney could not have been in New York on the previous day. If there he would unquestionably have made use of the opportunity to send a personal account of Lincoln's visit to New York. Further

proof that Forney was not the Diarist came from an examination of his *Anecdotes of Public Men*, two volumes of reminiscent sketches which he had contributed to his newspaper and
published in 1873. None of the sketches or characterizations
in those volumes bear any resemblance to anything to be
found in the "Diary of a Public Man." If Forney had kept
such a diary he would unquestionably have drawn upon it
in his *Anecdotes*. He, too, had to be eliminated.

# VIII

The elimination of the men dealt with in the preceding chapter seemed to leave only one promising possibility. The man in question was Amos Kendall.[22]

Kendall was born in Dunstable, Massachusetts, in 1789. He attended Dartmouth College, graduated second in his class, and was awarded the valedictory honor in 1811. He then studied law in Massachusetts and in 1814 went to Kentucky. There he was for a time a tutor in the family of Henry Clay while Clay was in Europe on the negotiation of the Treaty of Ghent. Presently Kendall drifted into journalism and the remarkable talent as a writer which he exhibited all through life soon made him a factor of importance in the politics of Kentucky. Espousing the cause of General Andrew Jackson, Kendall contributed a good deal to the success of the Jackson ticket in Kentucky in the presidential election of 1828. For this service he was sent early in 1829 to Washington as the bearer of the electoral vote of that state.

Instead of returning to Kentucky Kendall remained in Washington. Early in the Jackson administration he was appointed fourth auditor of the Treasury. In that capacity and by the vigorous use of his journalistic talent he quickly became a power in the Jackson administration. He was very generally credited with occupying a leading position in Jackson's Kitchen Cabinet. It was commonly asserted that he was the real author of Jackson's most important state papers. That he at least wrote quite a number of them I found was abundantly clear, for the originals, now among the Jackson papers in the Library of Congress, were in Kendall's handwriting. In 1835 he was made postmaster general and served until 1840. He gave the department a much needed reorganization, setting up a system which provided the country with a greatly improved postal service and remained in operation with little change for many years. He was unquestionably one of the ablest and most successful administrators ever at the head of the postoffice department.

In 1840 Kendall retired from the Cabinet in order to aid in the campaign for the re-election of President Martin Van Buren. When that effort failed Kendall stayed on in Washington. During the next five years he launched several short-lived journalistic enterprises at the capital. None of them succeeded; the field was already too well occupied. To the financial hardship this entailed, Kendall added another burden by assuming personal liability in a famous lawsuit growing out of the controversies in which he had engaged with contractors for carrying the mails while he was postmaster general. He was for a time technically a prisoner for debt, at large on his own recognizance but restricted in his movements to the District of Columbia. During this period he attempted rather reluctantly to overcome his financial difficulties by acting as an agent for the collection of claims against the government. His most important activity of the sort was in conjunction with his nephew, John E. Kendall, in behalf of a portion of the Cherokee Indians. Congress finally passed a bill for the payment of the claim, but personal enemies contrived to secure the insertion of a stipulation that no part of the money should go to Kendall for his services. This left him with a claim against the government that remained pending for many years. Ultimately it was recognized as equitable and was paid.

In 1845 Kendall entered upon a new phase of his career. It was one that has attracted comparatively little attention. Even his son-in-law, William Stickney, who later strung together various products of Kendall's pen and published them as an *Autobiography*, passed over this period of Kendall's life very briefly, and the little attention he did give to it affords no real picture of the important role that Kendall played in one of the most interesting chapters in the early history of rapid communication in the United States.

This came from Kendall's activity as the business agent of Samuel F. B. Morse, the inventor of the telegraph. After Morse had attempted to sell his telegraph patents to the government of the United States for one hundred thousand dollars and had failed, he was in despair. Knowing his own lack of business capacity but realizing that only by the most capable handling could his interests be protected against the claims of rivals and the necessary capital be enlisted for pushing the invention, Morse engaged Kendall to act as his agent on a fifty-fifty basis. This was the beginning of a business relation that proved to be highly advantageous to both men and of a Damon-and-Pythias friendship between them. As Morse's agent Kendall defended or looked after the defense of Morse's interest in dozens of lawsuits involving patent rights and kindred matters. He sold or let out on royalty the right to use the patent to numerous companies operating in different parts of the country. He organized and took a hand in the management of several companies, most of them operating in the South and West. The leading one was the Washington and New Orleans Telegraph Company. He was also an active promoter in the early efforts to consolidate the numerous small companies originally formed into a few large systems.

For the first seven or eight years Kendall's labors in the telegraphic field brought only meager and very uncertain returns. But by about 1853 the initial difficulties had been so far overcome that both Morse and Kendall had become rich men, as wealth was reckoned in those days. It is important for our story to remember that these activities in the promotion of the telegraph gave Kendall a deep interest in business affairs, especially patents, and enabled him to acquire the kind of familiarity with the South and with New York City which the Diarist unquestionably had.

Kendall knew life in Washington well, as he had resided there continuously from 1829 on. In 1841 he purchased a farm of about one hundred acres just beyond the city limits at the north. On it he erected a residence which still stands, though in much altered form. To the place he gave the name Kendall Green. As soon as his wealth made it possible Kendall began, in the foundation of the Columbian Institution for the Deaf and Dumb, now Gaulladet College, the series of gifts which in the course of a few years made him one of the leading benefactors of Washington.

John W. Forney, in an illuminating pen portrait of Kendall in his *Anecdotes of Public Men,* lays stress upon Kendall's talent as a writer, "the most effective campaign writer until the star of Horace Greeley rose upon the horizon," upon his wide acquaintance, and upon his attractive personality late in life. Forney says: "As I turn my face to the past, it is difficult to reconcile the violent criminations and recriminations of 1834 and 1840 and the calm philosophy of 1860 and 1869; difficult to realize that the Amos Kendall of the first period is the same so honored and loved in the second. Such a life is a medallion—one side deeply scarred with the passions of youth and manhood; the other a lasting yet mellower lesson of magnanimity and forgiveness."

The papers of Amos Kendall, which if preserved would probably have enabled us to learn definitely whether Kendall was the author of the Diary, have not come down to us, save in very small part. At his death in 1869 they passed into the hands of his son-in-law, William Stickney. From them Stickney put together the inadequate and unsatisfactory book already alluded to, the so-called *Autobiography.* The papers themselves appear to have been destroyed in a warehouse fire, though occasionally a document turns up which at one time was among the Kendall papers. As Morse's agent Kendall carried on a voluminous correspondence. Most of his letters to Morse and letterpress copies of Morse's letters to him are in the Morse papers in the Library of Congress. They furnish considerable help in our effort to determine whether Kendall was the Diarist.

# IX

The data in regard to Amos Kendall set forth in the preceding chapter made abundantly clear that Kendall met many of the eighteen requirements for our pattern of the Diarist. In order to ascertain whether he fitted into the pattern at all points, I made careful examination all along the line.

1. The first point admitted of no doubt. Amos Kendall was in 1860–1861 a man of considerable national importance. His long career in journalism, politics, and business had made him a well-known public figure.

2. That Kendall met the second requirement was likewise beyond any doubt. Several portraits and photographs portrayed him as a tall man to whom Lincoln might naturally have put a question whether he had ever measured backs with Charles Sumner.

3. Was Kendall a man who had the habit of keeping a diary? The evidence at my disposal did not enable me to give a completely satisfactory answer to the question. It could not be said that he was a confirmed diarist after the fashion of Pepys or of John Quincy Adams. Family tradition reported that he was supposed to have kept a voluminous diary over a long period of years but the manuscript had been consumed in a warehouse fire which destroyed the bulk of the Kendall papers. That he kept a diary at times was certain. One fragment of such a diary was incorporated in the so-called *Autobiography* edited by his son-in-law.[23] Through the kindness of a granddaughter[24] I was permitted to examine another such fragment kept during his early years in Kentucky. From this meager evidence the safe conclusion seemed to be that, while proof was lacking to demonstrate that Ken-

dall was a confirmed diarist, there was enough to indicate that he ought not to be eliminated on the ground that he did not have the diary habit.

4. The Diarist was a man of the world, or at any rate a man marked by several of the qualities commonly associated with that type of person. Was Kendall such a man? At first thought I was disposed to answer in the negative. He certainly was not in the habit of going about a great deal in fashionable society. But he did move in such circles on occasion. He was among the throng which attended the grand ball given in New York in 1860 in honor of the Prince of Wales. He sojourned occasionally at Saratoga at a time when fashionable society in summer went either to Saratoga or to Newport. His family letters revealed him showing an interest in feminine beauty and making comments upon feminine attire in somewhat the same vein that the Diarist displayed in his comments about the inaugural ball and as regards Mrs. Lincoln and Mrs. Douglas. From this I concluded that, while Kendall was not a man of the world exactly, he had enough of the traits belonging to that type that he ought not to be eliminated on that account.

5 and 6. That Kendall met those requirements, wide acquaintance among public men and long familiarity with conditions at Washington, admitted of no doubt whatever. Residing at Washington for over thirty years, always active in government, politics, journalism, or business, he fitted into the pattern in perfect fashion.

7. The Diarist was a strong Unionist. Here, again, Kendall fitted into the pattern perfectly. During the presidential campaign of 1860 he had made public a correspondence with his long-time friend James L. Orr of South Carolina in which he had vigorously denied the right of secession and had endeavored to dissuade Orr from giving it support.[25] After the election, when the rising tide of secessionist sentiment was beginning to sweep the Gulf States and to make alarming progress elsewhere in the South, he contributed to the *Washington Star* a series of twelve "Letters on Secession." In these

articles, which were widely reproduced in other newspapers and a little later republished in pamphlet form, he took even stronger ground against secession.[26]

8. The Diarist appeared to have known the South well and to have been markedly free from sectional animosity against that region, despite his disapproval of the course which the Southern leaders were pursuing. In this particular Kendall fitted into the pattern exactly. Nearly all his adult life had been spent in close contact with the South. He had traveled there extensively. The telegraph companies in which he was most deeply interested, such as the Washington and New Orleans Telegraph Company, operated in that region.[27] While postmaster general he had shown decided sympathy for the South in one of the principal Southern grievances.

9. The Diarist was a man who had met Lincoln in 1848 but could not recall the circumstance when at Lincoln's desire they met again in New York City on February 20, 1861. Proof that Kendall had two such meetings with Lincoln was not available. The meeting in 1848 might very well have occurred without leaving a lasting recollection of it on the part of Kendall. Presumably it occurred at Washington while Lincoln was serving in Congress. At that time Kendall was a well-known national figure, long resident at the capital, while Lincoln was as yet almost unknown. Lincoln might well remember the occasion, while it would be equally natural that Kendall should not.

That Lincoln might have wished to meet Kendall in 1861 would also have been natural enough. Kendall had been very close to Jackson. In 1861 all Unionists were disposed to play up Jackson as a champion of the Union on account of his firm stand against the South Carolina nullifiers in 1832. Kendall's correspondence with Orr and his "Letters on Secession" had also served to call attention to him as a strong Unionist. He was the sort of man through whom Lincoln might well hope to enlist Democratic support for his own efforts to save the Union from destruction.

In the light of these circumstances the sound conclusion

54

seemed to be that while decisive, affirmative proof that Kendall met this requirement could not be adduced, there was not sufficient reason for holding that he ought to be eliminated as not meeting the requirement.

10. The Diarist was able at a glance to recognize the handwriting of Charles Sumner when Lincoln handed him a note which Sumner had written. Could Kendall have done that? At first thought it did not seem to have been possible. Kendall was not likely to have seen a great deal of Sumner's writing. I concluded, however, after some examination of the Sumner papers at Houghton Library that the matter in question was not an impossibility. Sumner's short notes were usually written in large characters of a clearly marked and decidedly individual sort, a fashion in short that might easily have been recognized by anybody who had previously seen a specimen of his penmanship.[28] Kendall could not be safely eliminated on that count.

11. There seemed to be clear indication that the Diarist had considerable familiarity with the French language and with French political thought. In this particular Kendall did not seem to meet the requirement satisfactorily. That he had some knowledge of the French language seemed likely enough. He occasionally made use of French expressions in his correspondence. But his knowledge of French apparently was not extensive. When in Paris in 1866 he bewailed his inability to understand the language sufficiently to profit by a religious service he attended.[29] I could not find any evidence to indicate that he had any particular knowledge of French political thought. I felt, however, that it would be unsafe to rule out Kendall on the basis of those supposed lacunae. It was at least possible that he had more knowledge of French political thought than could be proven from tangible evidence. It also appeared quite possible that the French words used in one passage in the Diary which seemed to indicate that the Diarist was pretty familiar with that language might have been substituted by the editor of the *North American Review*, an accomplished French scholar, for the actual words

of the Diarist. Here, as on one or two other points, Kendall did not seem to fit into the picture perfectly. But, on the other hand, I felt that the evidence as regards this point was not strong enough to warrant eliminating him. There was at least some doubt about the matter.

12. The Diarist was manifestly a man who felt deep concern over the business situation. He was particularly interested in the tariff, patents, and postal matters. Here Kendall fitted into the pattern perfectly. His recently acquired fortune, chiefly in telegraph properties, was tied up with the general business situation. Southern action about the tariff was at the moment a thing of great concern to all business interests. For fifteen years he had been almost constantly involved in litigation over patent questions. If a Southern Confederacy should be established the value of all United States patents might be seriously impaired. As a former postmaster general he was, of course, highly interested in postal matters.

13. The Diarist appeared to have been a man who had some special reason for following somewhat closely what was going on in the Senate during the winter of 1860–1861. Here again Kendall fitted into the pattern. He was at that time endeavoring to get favorable action by the Senate upon a bill for renewal of the Morse telegraph patent.[30] Activity in behalf of that measure by Kendall apparently led him to follow the proceedings of the Senate closely at that time.

14. The Diarist was on intimate terms with William H. Seward and Stephen A. Douglas. Did Kendall meet that requirement? I could not discover evidence of a documentary character to afford a completely satisfactory answer to that question. But there did not appear to be any sufficient reason for believing that such intimacies did not exist. On the contrary, they appeared not improbable. That Kendall knew Seward was certain. Seward had at one time performed legal services for Morse and thereby must have been brought into contact with Kendall as Morse's agent. Seward was at the moment piloting the bill for the renewal of the Morse patent

through the Senate.[31] This must have involved considerable contact between the two men. As many of Seward's intimacies during the winter of 1860–1861 never got into any of the documents that have been preserved, it seems quite possible that such an intimacy as existed between Seward and the Diarist could have existed at that time between Seward and Kendall.

Intimacy between Kendall and Douglas appeared even more likely than between Kendall and Seward. Both Kendall and Douglas had long been prominent in the Democratic party. During the presidential campaign of 1860 the supporters of Douglas made considerable use of Kendall's correspondence with James L. Orr. As Kendall and Douglas undoubtedly had been long acquainted, it seemed quite possible that they were on the intimate terms which the Diary represented as existing between Douglas and the Diarist.

For a time I had considerable doubt whether Kendall could have sustained the kind of relations which the Diarist appeared to have had with Seward and Douglas, for the reason that both men were represented as calling upon the Diarist at times and under circumstances which made it appear as scarcely possible that they could have gone to Kendall's home at Kendall Green. That doubt was diminished, though not entirely removed, by discovering that during the winter of 1860–1861 Kendall had rooms at the National Hotel.[32] It therefore appeared quite possible that when the Diarist said that Seward or Douglas had called upon him, he meant at the National Hotel and not at Kendall Green. Such a supposition removed a good deal of difficulty about believing that Kendall met the requirement of intimacy with Seward and Douglas. Although not entirely convinced that he did fit into the pattern in regard to that point, I did not think there was sufficient reason for eliminating him. I concluded that the proper attitude as to the point in question was to pronounce it a still open question.

15. The Diarist expressed strong dislike for Senator Edward D. Baker, of Oregon, and the Blairs, meaning thereby Francis

P. Blair, Sr., long a notable figure at Washington, Francis P. Blair, Jr., recently Republican congressman from St. Louis and the party leader in Missouri, and Montgomery Blair, soon to be postmaster general in the Lincoln Cabinet. I could not learn whether Kendall had any reason for disliking Baker. He did dislike the Blairs intensely. He had been largely responsible for bringing Francis P. Blair, Sr., to Washington in the Jackson administration to edit the newly established party organ, the *Globe*. As members of the Jackson Kitchen Cabinet the two men had worked together closely. Afterwards they had a falling out and became bitter enemies.[33] Here then as far as the evidence went Kendall again fitted into the picture.

16. The Diarist must have been a man familiar with leading men and business conditions in New York City. Kendall met that requirement. As Morse's agent he had had extensive dealings with the leading business men of New York. At the time covered by the Diary he was continuing to go occasionally to New York on business trips involving telegraphic matters. Such activity gave him opportunity to know a good deal about New York City.[34]

17. The Diarist must have been a man to whom it would have been natural for James L. Orr to have gone on December 28, 1860, for "co-operation with Mr. Seward to strengthen the hands of the President in ordering Major Anderson back at once to Fort Moultrie." The brief allusion previously made to the situation upon that day may require a little further elucidation.

James L. Orr, R. W. Barnwell, and J. H. Adams reached Washington on December 26, 1860. They came as commissioners from South Carolina to try to arrange for an amicable transfer of the Charleston forts and other United States property in South Carolina to that state, which in its own eyes had become the Republic of South Carolina by passing its Secession Ordinance on December 20, 1860. Their plan of procedure had been upset on the day after their arrival by the startling news that Major Robert Anderson had quietly and secretly transferred his little garrison from Fort Moultrie, which he could not hope to defend successfully if it should be attacked, to Fort Sumter, which presumably he could defend as long as the supply of food and ammunition lasted. Apparently the one hope for avoiding an immediate and serious clash between the government of the United States and that of South Carolina lay in the possibility that the South Carolina commissioners might induce President Buchanan to order Major Anderson to go back to Fort Moultrie. There appeared to be a good deal of reason for supposing that under the right kind of persuasion and pressure President Buchanan would issue such an order. The South Carolina commissioners and other Southerners then at Washington were engaged in exerting all the persuasion and pressure they could exert. If the Diary is to be trusted, James L. Orr sought to enlist the cooperation of the Diarist and of William H. Seward.

That James L. Orr would have gone to Amos Kendall in the hope of securing his cooperation seemed natural enough. The two men were old friends. Their recent public discussion about the right of secession had been carried on in a spirit of perfect courtesy. In the light of that circumstance, Amos Kendall seemed to fit into this requirement very well.

Before dealing with the eighteenth and final requirement a few words of explanation appear to be in order. In the paper about the Diary which I had read at the Indianapolis meeting of the American Historical Association in December, 1928, I presented the seventeen points already set forth in this chapter in substantially the same terms as here restated. I did so then in support of an argument that, if the Diary was what it purported to be, it appeared highly probable that Amos Kendall was the Diarist. I recognized and pointed out that, in order to make the argument complete, it was necessary to show that Kendall could not be excluded except upon the basis of a consideration which will here be discussed as an eighteenth point. At that time I had given considerable attention to the matter and had not as yet discovered sufficient reason for supposing that Kendall would not fit into the picture as regards that point. Later investigation raised serious doubt in my mind.

The reason for that doubt will appear in connection with the discussion of the eighteenth point. How this came about and the conclusion to which further investigation finally led me will be told in the next chapter.

# X

It will be recalled that I have put the eighteenth requirement in these words: Finally and most decisively, he must be
a man who was in New York City on February 20, 1861, and
was in Washington on each of twenty indicated days lying
between December 28, 1860, and March 15, 1861. Proof that
a possible Diarist was anywhere else on any one of those days
would eliminate him.

Doubt whether Kendall met this requirement first arose in
my mind some little time after presenting the Indianapolis
paper. It arose from discovering that Professor S. F. B. Morse,
the inventor of the telegraph, apparently left New York City
on February 19, 1861, for a visit to Washington and that he
returned on February 25.[35] The evidence indicated as probable, though not entirely certain, that while in Washington
he was a guest of the Kendalls. If so, it seemed unlikely that
Kendall would be away while Morse was there. If Kendall
was in Washington during Morse's visit he could not have
been in New York City on February 20, 1861. There was, of
course, a possibility that some urgent matter might have
taken Kendall to New York just at the moment when his
friend and business associate was coming to pay him a visit.
In the light of that possibility it became highly important to
ascertain, if possible, whether proof could be found that Kendall was in New York City at that time.

Having previously learned that when Kendall visited New
York City at that period he usually stayed at the Astor
House, I tried to ascertain whether he was there on February
20, 1861. In that endeavor my first move was to examine the
hotel arrivals in New York newspapers such as the *Herald,
Tribune, Times,* etc. None of the leading daily papers pub-

lished complete lists. So the fact that Kendall's name did not appear in any of the lists they did publish was inconclusive.

My next move was to try to discover whether the hotel register of the Astor House had been preserved. Learning that the New York Public Library was making a collection of old New York hotel registers, I sought the Astor House register there. But it was not in the collection.

Unwilling to abandon the search at that point, I inquired at the present Astor House whether anything was known there about the registers of the old Astor House. Nothing was known. I was informed, however, that the oldest employee had once served at the old Astor House and that he might know what had become of the registers. He did not know, but he informed me that the last manager of the old hotel was still living. I was further informed that possibly he might be located through a sister who was connected with the J. Pierpont Morgan Library.

I went, accordingly, to the Morgan Library to see the lady. My call was upon a hot, midsummer morning. The library was not open to the public that day. I rang the bell, however, and after a long interval the heavy bronze doors were opened to the extent of three or four inches. Through that aperture a perfect specimen of the English butler asked as to what I wanted. I began by saying, "I am a professor of history at Dartmouth College." "Ah, you are from over the water." He knew about the quite modern English naval college, but had evidently not heard of the older American Dartmouth College. Receiving the remainder of my explanation with an appearance of considerable distrust, he finally consented to look for the lady for whom I had inquired. Meanwhile I remained outside, the doors having been carefully closed. Presently the lady appeared, received my request very graciously, and promised to make known to her brother my interest in the Astor House registers of 1861. Somewhat later a nice letter from the lady informed me that her brother did not know what had become of the registers in question.

Recollection of a nearly forgotten early experience suggested another possible method of discovering whether Amos Kendall was at the Astor House on February 20, 1861. As a boy, living in a middlewestern city I distributed copies of a daily newspaper called the *Hotel Gazette*. It listed the names of all the arrivals at all the hotels of the city. I learned at that time that similar papers existed in almost all of the larger cities. Recalling that bit of information, I asked myself: Was there such a paper in New York City in 1861? After considerable search I learned that there had been such a paper and that it was called the *Transcript*.

At that time the admirable *Union List of Newspapers* had not yet been published. Some of the larger libraries, however, had published calendars or catalogues of their newspaper files. Consulting as many of those as possible, I found the *Transcript* (New York) listed in only one library, that of Yale University. As soon as possible I went to New Haven to examine that file. As often happens in old newspaper files there were gaps in the Yale file of the *Transcript*; the issues I sought were lacking. At that point I was about ready to abandon the search.

Other matter involved in the problem of the Diary took me a few days later to the library of the New York Historical Society. Knowing from previous experience that the Society had a considerable collection of newspapers and a very imperfect catalogue of them, I asked to see the catalogue. Scanning the list of entries under New York City newspapers, I looked under the letter T for the *Transcript*. It was not there. As the whole catalogue was not very extensive, I decided to make sure that the paper I was seeking was not listed under some other title. Under the letter D, I found the paper—the *Daily Transcript*.

Considerably excited by my lucky discovery, I called for the file and to my delight found that it was complete for the period in which I was interested. Turning to the list of arrivals at the Astor House for February 19, 1861, I found this entry, "J. Kendall, Washington." Once more at the end of a trail a promising lead ended in uncertainty. The printed entries in the *Transcript*, as in most newspapers of the time, gave only the initial of the first name for hotel arrivals. If "J" in the *Transcript* entry was a misprint for A—and misprints in such entries often occurred—it might well be that Amos Kendall was at the Astor House on February 20, 1861. On the other hand, it might well be that the entry was perfectly correct and that the Kendall at the Astor House was Amos Kendall's nephew, J. E. Kendall. There was also the possibility that the J might be the initial of Amos Kendall's son, John Kendall, who formerly living in Washington, had recently moved to New York. Whatever the explanation there was uncertainty instead of certainty about the matter.

Unable to determine definitely whether Amos Kendall was in New York City on February 20, 1861, I realized that it was all the more important to determine whether he was at Washington on all of the twenty days on which the Diarist was in Washington. It was scarcely to be expected that direct proof could be obtained for each and every day. Reasonable certainty in regard to the matter would appear to be attained, if proof could be found to show that Kendall was in Washington most of the time for the period covered by the Diary, that he was there upon a fair number of the days in question, and that he was not away from the capital upon any one of the twenty Diary days.

That Kendall was in Washington most of the time between December 28, 1860, and March 15, 1861, could not be doubted. He lived there and was at home except as occasionally called away on business. Such absences, which had been frequent in earlier years, had by 1860–1861 become exceptional. I found clear proof to attest his presence upon quite a number of the twenty days. The decisive issue was whether proof existed that he was away from Washington on any one of the twenty days.

Search for such evidence led to the discovery of proof that Kendall and his wife had arrived in New York City on the evening of February 27, 1861.[36] Accordingly he could not have been in Washington on February 28, one of the Diary days, unless he had for some reason decided upon an immediate return and had gone back on an early morning train. My previous study of railroad time tables left no doubt about that matter. That he would have gone back did not seem likely. It also appeared significant that if he did go back to Washington in that way, it was extremely improbable that he could have done what the Diarist appears to have done on that day. That was the day when the Diarist, according to his account, had his second interview with Lincoln. A study of what Lincoln did on that day showed that if any such interview took place it must have occurred well along in the afternoon.[37] It was, therefore, possible that Kendall, returning to Washington by the earliest train from New York and going immediately to the Willard Hotel upon his arrival in Washington, might have had an interview with Lincoln. The possibility of an interview could not be ruled out on the basis of the time element alone. But all the circumstances seemed decidedly against such an occurrence. I was obliged to conclude that Kendall was probably not in Washington on February 28, 1861.

With the discovery that there was grave doubt as to whether Kendall was in Washington on February 28, 1861, I became more than ever anxious to learn whether he was away from that city upon any other day when the Diarist was there. Such evidence did not turn up until almost the last hour of my quest. Then I found this item written by the New York correspondent of the *Philadelphia Press* to his paper on December 29, 1860:

"Among the notabilities in town today are Thurlow Weed, Francis Granger, Horatio King, First Assistant Postmaster General, and Amos Kendall."[38]

That meant that Amos Kendall was not the Diarist, for the Diarist was in Washington that day.

One other bit of evidence, also discovered late in my search, added to the certainty that Kendall was not the Diarist, despite much evidence which seemed to point to him. The entry in the Diary for February 26, 1861, is devoted mainly to a dinner at which the Diarist was present. The account indicates that the affair was a protracted one—"We were very late"—and that it must have occupied the entire evening. That Amos Kendall could not have been at that dinner, I finally discovered, did not admit of any doubt. The Washington correspondent of the *New York Commercial Advertiser*, in his letter dated February 27, 1861, reported an exhibition given by the pupils of the Columbian Institution for the Deaf and Dumb on the previous evening. In his report he said: "The liberal founder and patron of this praiseworthy establishment, Amos Kendall, was upon the platform, apparently in the enjoyment of excellent health."[39] That Kendall was at the Columbian Institution exhibition instead of at the dinner described by the Diarist thus appeared to be certain, except for one possibility. The date of the correspondent's letter might have been an error, possibly a printer's mistake, and the evening in question might not have been that of February 26, 1861. The possibility, however, disappeared a little later, when examining the Stephen A. Douglas papers at the library of the University of Chicago I discovered among them an invitation for the exhibition. The date of it was February 26, 1861. Kendall was at the exhibition given that evening by the deaf and dumb pupils. He, therefore, could not have been at the dinner described in the Diary. There could no longer be any doubt. Amos Kendall was not the Diarist.

In an Easy Chair essay apropos of F. Lauriston Bullard's edition of *The Diary of a Public Man*, Bernard De Voto, having learned that I had come to the conclusion that Kendall was not the Diarist, made the remark that I must have come to it with great reluctance.[40] He was exactly right. From my study of Kendall I had found him a man of great interest, quite a different person from that depicted in the usually accepted estimates, which have been based chiefly upon the assertions of his enemies. I had found, moreover, that in addition to the fact that he fitted almost completely into the picture of the Diarist, as delineated in seventeen of my eighteen points in regard to his personality, there were elements in the Kendall personality too subtle for exact description which made him exactly the kind of man who might have kept a diary such as that of "A Public Man." Too bad that the identification lacked the essential feature.

# XI

In giving up all thought that Kendall was the Diarist I did not think it necessary to abandon as fallacious the method I had employed. It still seemed to me possible that some person might be discovered who met all of the eighteen requirements and might therefore be regarded as almost certainly the Diarist. Further search, however, failed to disclose any such person. That result turned my attention more decidedly than in the earlier stages of my quest to the possibility that the Diary might not be what it purported to be. A searching examination as to the authenticity of the Diary seemed imperatively called for. Turning to that question, my search for the Diarist took a new turn.

In my Indianapolis paper I had stated briefly the main arguments for the authenticity of the Diary. I pointed out that the Diary met the usual tests for authenticity in an apparently convincing manner. One could not discover in it any glaring and indubitable example of an anachronism. There were no instances in which the sequence of events had been transposed. No persons were made to appear at times and places when there was evidence that the persons in question were somewhere else. There did not appear to be in the Diary any clearly manifest instance of knowledge on the part of the Diarist about anything which happened after March 15, 1861, the last day for which there was an entry in the Diary. It appeared to me almost inconceivable that anybody attempting at a later date to concoct a diary for 1860–1861 could have completely escaped letting some knowledge of later events and conditions slip into his production. Many entries in the Diary, I pointed out, showed traces of the daily newspapers of 1860–1861. A literary impostor, I argued, might and probably would have made considerable use of those papers. But such a use of them would probably not be too difficult to be detected. The Diary appeared to reflect the newspapers of its time in a way perfectly natural for one writing at the moment, but scarcely possible for anybody who wrote at a later date.

I was also much impressed at that time by the attitude of leading historians and biographers. James Ford Rhodes had shown his belief in the authenticity of the Diary by citing it seventeen times. Allen Johnson, in his *Historians and Historical Evidence* and in his life of Stephen A. Douglas, had given equally clear indication that he regarded it as genuine. N. W. Stephenson, W. E. Barton, Alonzo Rothschild, Ida Tarbell, in their books about Lincoln had accepted it. Frederic Bancroft had done likewise in his biography of Seward. George Ticknor Curtis, in his life of Buchanan, had raised some question as to its reliability in regard to certain points in which he was particularly interested, but he had not seriously questioned its authenticity. E. L. Pierce, the biographer of Charles Sumner, alone appeared to have expressed a decided belief that the Diary was not completely authentic.[41]

In the light of these considerations I then expressed the opinion that the weight of evidence was "decidedly and almost conclusively" in favor of the authenticity of the Diary. I little suspected that further investigation would put the whole matter in a different light.

Having failed after considerable effort to find the Diarist while proceeding upon the assumption that the Diary was genuine, I turned presently to a re-examination of the question of its authenticity. In that effort I looked carefully into the Diary for possible indications that it might not be exactly what it purported to be. The outcome of that examination raised serious doubts in my mind which I must now proceed to indicate.

Several of these doubts came from features of the Diary about which I was already aware but which earlier had not impressed me as raising any very serious doubt as to its authenticity. Eight of these now gave rise to serious question in my mind.

1. It appeared to me a matter of considerable significance that nearly all of the men mentioned by name in the Diary had died before its publication in 1879. In looking into the matter carefully I discovered that only three of the survivors could have raised any serious question as to the authenticity of the Diary on the ground that it attributed to them things they had not done. In each of these instances the Diarist had reported an extensive conversation which had taken place under such circumstances that the other party to it would have been likely to remember the occasion and something of what he had said.

The three men in question were Hiram Barney, Judah P. Benjamin, and Lord Lyons. Upon a subsequent page I shall show that Hiram Barney made an effort to recall the incident in which he was said to have figured and, failing to do so, quite evidently came to the conclusion that the Diarist was a mythical person. That Barney did not make public his doubt in regard to the Diarist and that we know of it only through his personal correspondence of a few years later was probably due to his age and his retired life. I could not learn whether Judah P. Benjamin or Lord Lyons ever expressed any opinion in regard to the Diary. It is not probable that either of them ever did so. Neither of them, even if appealed to, would have been likely to enter into any discussion as to its accuracy or its authenticity.

In the light of these circumstances it appeared to me that the publication of a spurious diary in 1879 ran little risk of exposure through the testimony of persons who were in a position to assert that they had never done the things attributed to them in the Diary. Therein lay a good reason, I believed, for suspecting that somebody might have taken advantage of the opportunity to palm off upon an unsuspecting public a fictitious or semi-fictitious production.

2. At numerous points the name of some person who had been mentioned by the Diarist was replaced by a dash or the

initial letter of the name. The editorial introduction explained the change from name to symbol in a manner calculated to leave the impression that the alteration had been made in order to spare the feelings of survivors. Without specifically stating that in all instances the person mentioned was still living, it gave that impression.

A study of these symbols for the purpose of identifying the individuals referred to brought out the fact that apparently the identity of about thirty-three persons was concealed by the device employed. The exact number could not be determined because in some instances the vague language of the Diary made it impossible to tell whether the Diarist was referring to a person already mentioned or was speaking about some other individual. Identification of the persons in question at that stage of my search proved to be possible in only three cases. That appeared to me to be of considerable significance. If thirty-three real persons were referred to in the way that it was done in the Diary, one ought to be able to identify a good many of them. The fact that considerable effort produced so small a result appeared to me a decidedly suspicious circumstance. Taken in conjunction with the lack of a really good reason for concealment in many instances and the vagueness of the Diary in the matter, it looked to me as if somebody might be making a studied effort to cover up the invention of imaginary persons.

One singular circumstance greatly increased my perplexity as regards this substitution of symbols for names. In several instances it seemed probable that the person designated by symbol, if a real person, would have been able to identify the Diarist upon reading the Diary in 1879. A desire to prevent such identification might well have been the reason for the use of the symbol instead of the name. But on the other hand, use of a symbol instead of the name was exactly the kind of device which the author of a spurious diary would naturally employ to cover up its fictitious character. He could safely include a good many instances in which it appeared that a person designated by symbol would have been able to

71

identify the Diarist if the person in question was an imaginary being. The fact that there were not less than fourteen instances in which capacity to identify the Diarist seemed to belong to persons who might be imaginary beings instead of real persons looked decidedly suspicious. It gave ground for suspecting that the substitution of symbols for names might have been employed to conceal a fictitious or partly fictitious production.

3. In quite a number of places in the Diary the entries were vague where one would naturally expect a diarist to be quite definite. The fact that in some of those instances a more definite statement would probably have afforded a clue which would lead to the discovery of the Diarist appeared to me a decidedly suspicious circumstance. Vagueness of that sort would naturally be employed by a literary impostor seeking to cover up all traces of the hoax he was perpetrating. A few examples of this apparently studied vagueness may serve to show the basis for the suspicion I came to feel.

Four of these examples occurred in the Diarist's report about his interview with Lincoln at New York on February 20, 1861. Mr. Barney came to see the Diarist "at the hotel." If the name of the hotel had been given it probably would have been quite possible to detect the Diarist by examining the list of persons then registered there. The Diarist explained to Hiram Barney "why I had come to New York and showed him what I thought best of Mr. Rives's letter from Washington of last Sunday." More definite information about the occasion for the Diarist's visit to New York and especially the date of his arrival, would likewise have possibly led to the discovery of the Diarist. A more explicit description of Mr. Rives's letter might well have led to a disclosure of the person to whom Rives would have sent such a letter. At the close of his account of his interview with Lincoln the Diarist "agreed to write to ———." Suppression of the name of the recipient and silence as to the contents made next to impossible the discovery of the Diarist by search for a letter of that character.

I found also in the Diary other instances of what appeared to be studied vagueness. Taken with those just mentioned, the group appeared to be exactly the sort of thing to which the fabricator of a fictitious or semi-fictitious production would resort in order to escape detection.

4. A distinguishing feature of the Diary is a considerable number of apt remarks attributed to Lincoln. They will be quoted at a later point in this story. Among remarks attributed to other persons was one by B—— apropos of Caleb Cushing, "He is the boldest man within four walls, and the greatest coward that I ever knew in my life." Another is the remark by Thurlow Weed, when asked if he knew Harris, the newly elected senator from New York, "Do I know him personally, I should rather think I do. I invented him." Still another is Douglas' remark about Lincoln a week before the inauguration in reply to an assertion that Lincoln was a weak and pliable character. "No, he is not that, sir, but he is eminently a man of the atmosphere which surrounds him. He has not got out of Springfield. . . . He does not see that the shadow he casts is any bigger now than it was last year. It will not take him long to find it out when he has got established in the White House."

These remarkably apt expressions, I thought, might well have been uttered by the men to whom they are attributed. On the other hand, their very aptness might well put them under the suspicion that they were the inventions of some clever literary man who had the advantage of a better perspective than it was possible for anyone to enjoy in 1860–1861. It also struck me as singular that the Diary should contain so many examples of such expressions. Genuine diaries are seldom so fortunate.

5. Another distinguishing feature of the Diary is the large number of good stories in it. Several relate to Lincoln and will be discussed further along in this story. One good story is attributed to Douglas who told ——— "a story of his having got a political secret out about the Kansas-Nebraska business, which he wished to propogate without caring to

propagate it himself, or having his friends do so, by the simple expedient of sending a person to tell it to the President [Buchanan], after first getting his word on no account to mention it to anyone. 'Within six hours, sir, within six hours,' he exclaimed, 'it was all over Washington, as I knew it would be.'" Others of much the same sort hit off the weaknesses and foibles of various prominent figures of 1860–1861.

These stories raised in my mind the same question that the apt sayings had done. Were they stories actually told to the Diarist or occurrences he witnessed? Did he set them down at the dates indicated in the Diary? Their very cleverness seemed to afford grounds for suspicion. They appeared to be exactly the sort of thing that a clever fabricator would invent to make a fictitious narrative interesting.

6. Readers of the Diary, if tolerably well acquainted with the situation prevailing in the United States at the period covered by the Diary, can scarcely fail to be much impressed by the exceptional shrewdness displayed by the Diarist in his appraisement of the rapidly changing situation and in his estimates of the notable men he had the opportunity to meet and observe. If actually written on the days indicated in the Diary, or even within a short period thereafter, they certainly exhibit a most remarkable insight. The Diarist was not right in every instance. But his batting average was exceptionally high. Few other men came so near to calling the turn as regards both men and events.

In a genuine diary this quality would be remarkable. It would exhibit the Diarist as an altogether exceptional man. In a fictitious or semi-fictitious diary it would appear in a quite different light. In such a production it would indicate nothing more than a fair knowledge of the history of the time covered by the Diary and a considerable degree of literary skill. It would not be in any way remarkable.

Here was a question that gave me much perplexity. Was the apparent remarkable shrewdness real or fictitious? I could not come to a definite conclusion in regard to the matter. The question could not be subjected to definite tests. I was obliged to rest content for the time being with the conclusion that there was at least some ground for suspecting that the shrewdness exhibited by the Diarist came from knowledge after the event. I could not escape having a suspicion that in this matter lay ground for questioning whether the Diary as published had been actually written in 1860–1861.

7. Diaries are valued by historians and biographers in large degree because they frequently contain information or suggest points of view not obtainable from other sources. For that reason they are often invaluable. Use of them, however, calls for caution. Many of their statements cannot be checked upon the evidence of other sources—"controlled" in the language of historical method. If a particular diary contains a good deal that cannot be "controlled"; if there is in it a good deal that other men might well have known and reported but did not; if, in a word, too much of it escapes "control," there then appears reasonable ground for distrust. Recognizing the importance of these considerations as a test for the Diary, I examined it more carefully than ever before to determine whether there was in it a particularly large amount not susceptible to "control" and whether there were in it numerous or especially significant instances in which "control" ought to be possible but in which corroboration of the Diary from other sources was completely lacking.

I found the Diary open to suspicion upon both counts. A very large proportion of it, including much that gave it particular interest and possibly high historical value, could not be "controlled." This was applicable to the Diarist's conversations with Lincoln, Seward, Douglas, James L. Orr, Judah P. Benjamin, and numerous others. Such conversations, in fact, constituted a large part of the Diary. All of them, if accepted as genuine, must rest upon the authority of the Diarist alone. Nobody else was in a position to report them or to question the accuracy of the Diarist's reports. As that circumstance lay in the nature of the case it did not necessarily count heavily against the authenticity of the Diary. But the fact that there were so many such instances did seem to afford serious ground for suspicion.

Picking out carefully instances in which the Diarist, either upon his own observation or upon the report of others to him, made record of something which could be "controlled" by the evidence of other witnesses, I found in several cases that the report in the Diary lacked confirmation or was out of line with the reports of other witnesses. Some examples of this will be pointed out further along in this story. This seemed to me a decidedly suspicious circumstance.

8. Real diaries, actually kept from day to day, even those of distinguished men of letters who have written them with a view to future publication, are usually marked by a somewhat scrappy literary style. "The Diary of a Public Man," however, is written in a smooth, flowing, and polished fashion. Its style would be remarkable if it was actually written day by day in 1860–1861. This quality, I came increasingly to feel, raised considerable doubt as to whether the Diary could be exactly what it purported to be.

# XII

All the things dealt with in the preceding chapter relate to matters found throughout the Diary. Some of them, perhaps, may admit of explanations that would show them not open to the suspicion of being devices to conceal a fictitious or semi-fictitious production. To make possible a decisive verdict it appeared necessary to find out whether there were in the Diary details of a dubious or clearly fictitious character. The Lincoln element in the Diary seemed to afford a good opportunity for applying suitable tests to determine whether the interviews and incidents related by the Diarist could have taken place in the manner described. I, accordingly, turned my attention to them.

The Diarist claims to have had three interviews with Lincoln. He also relates three striking incidents in which Lincoln is the central figure. Could such interviews actually have taken place? Would Lincoln on such occasions have said all the things attributed to him? Did Lincoln at the opera in New York really appear and act in the manner described by the Diarist? Did Lincoln actually handle, in the manner related by the Diarist, a group of Seward's friends who protested against the appointment of Chase to the Cabinet? Did Douglas hold Lincoln's hat while Lincoln delivered his inaugural address? These questions seemed to call for careful attention.

I

The first of the three interviews took place, according to the Diarist, in New York City on February 20, 1861, while Lincoln was en route to Washington. If it occurred, it must have been at the Astor House, where Lincoln stayed while in New York, for an examination of what Lincoln did that day showed plainly that there was no opportunity for such an interview at any other place. Three questions in regard to it seemed to need answer. How was it arranged? At what hour of the day did it occur? Would Lincoln have said to the Diarist all the things attributed to him?

The arrangement for the interview, according to the Diary, was made through Hiram Barney, whom Lincoln a little later appointed collector of the Port of New York. The Diary implies, though it does not specifically assert, that Lincoln sent for the Diarist. In the role of intermediary Barney brought word that Lincoln remembered meeting the Diarist in 1848, but the Diarist could not recall the meeting and was moved to express his surprise. "I certainly recall none of the circumstances and can not place him, even with the help of all the pictures I have seen of such an extraordinary-looking mortal, as I confess I ought to be ashamed of myself once to have seen face to face, and to have then forgotten."

In 1886 Barney was interrogated about his connection with the matter in question. E. L. Pierce, the biographer of Charles Sumner, wrote to him to ask about the identity of the Diarist. Barney's reply indicated that he had no recollection of playing the role attributed to him in the Diary.[42] The recollections of old men are often faulty. The correspondence between Pierce and Barney shows that Barney was no exception to the rule. He was confused as to some occurrences on the day in question. But that did not appear to me sufficient reason for rejecting his testimony as altogether worthless. On the particular point as to his own share in arranging an interview between Lincoln and the Diarist, I thought that his evidence had value. Upon such a matter his memory was not likely to have failed. The fact that Barney in later years could not recall playing the role ascribed to him in the Diary seemed to me to cast considerable doubt as to whether he did play it.

Another circumstance also cast considerable doubt upon the Diarist's account as to how his interview with Lincoln was arranged. The Diarist said that Mr. Barney came to him "from breakfasting with Mr. Lincoln at Mr. Grinnell's." Barney said in his correspondence with E. L. Pierce that he was not at any such breakfast. His recollection as to that point was abundantly confirmed by convincing contemporaneous evidence. There was a breakfast at the home of Mr. Grinnell but Mr. Barney was not among the guests.[43] The account in the Diary about what took place at the Grinnell breakfast purporting to have come from Barney could not have come from him. Here the Diary plainly appeared not to be exactly what it purported to be.

Where and at what hour did the interview between Lincoln and the Diarist take place? The Diary does not tell. It helps only by indicating that it did not take place during the morning. Where and when could it have occurred during the afternoon or evening? By close scrutiny of the accounts of how Lincoln spent that day as related in the New York newspapers of the next morning I found it possible to determine pretty definitely where Lincoln was, what he did, and with whom he talked at almost every moment of the day.[44] A study of these accounts led to the conclusion that the interview, if it occurred, must have taken place late in the afternoon. At that hour Lincoln was reported to have been resting and denying himself to all callers. It was, of course, possible that the announcement was merely diplomatic and that some callers did get access to him at that time. But that appeared unlikely. Certainly the harried President-elect needed the rest he was supposed to be taking. If anybody got access to him it escaped the argus-eyed reporters for the newspapers. Considering all these circumstances, I felt constrained to believe that there was sufficient ground for feeling decided doubt about the occurrence of the interview.

This doubt was deepened upon considering carefully the Diarist's report about what Lincoln had said to him in the interview. Unquestionably much that was attributed to Lincoln might well have come from him. The Diarist reported: "He is entirely clear and sensible on the vital importance of holding the Democrats close to the Administration on the naked Union issue. 'They are,' he said to me, 'just where we Whigs were in '48 about the Mexican war. We had to take the Locofoco preamble when Taylor wanted help, or else vote against helping Taylor; and the Democrats must vote to hold the Union now, without bothering whether we or the Southern men got things where they are, and we must make it easy for them to do this, because we can't live through the case without them.' "

Another remark attributed to Lincoln seemed characteristic of him. An allusion to the suggestion by Mayor Fernando Wood of New York that if disunion came New York City might become a sort of free city, as Hamburg was at that time, brought from Lincoln the comment: "And as to the free city business—well, I reckon it will be some time before the front door sets up housekeeping on its own account."

These remarks, I thought, have the shrewdness and piquancy that later generations have come to associate with Lincoln. Other parts of the interview which the Diarist reported in substance appeared Lincoln-like. The Diarist's own description of Lincoln's appearance—"He is not a great man certainly, and, but for something almost woman-like in the look of his eyes, I should say the most ill-favored son of Adam I ever saw"—fitted in remarkably well with generally accepted ideas about Lincoln.

Two of the remarks attributed to Lincoln, however, aroused my suspicion that no such interview actually took place.

One was the remark dealing with the Whigs, Taylor, and the Mexican War. Lincoln could scarcely have said that the Whigs "in '48" had to take the Locofoco preamble when Taylor wanted help, or else vote against helping Taylor, for Taylor had returned from Mexico in November, 1847.[45] The remark also implied that Lincoln himself had been among the Whigs who had faced that disagreeable dilemma. But Lincoln was not in Congress at the time of the occurrence. The incident in question had taken place on May 11-12, 1846,[46] whereas Lincoln did not become a member of Congress until the next year. The whole remark looked to me like the kind of blunder likely to be made by anyone who may attempt the difficult feat of concocting a spurious historical document.

The other remark was not reported by the Diarist in Lincoln's own words. He said, however, that Lincoln "owned to me that he was more troubled by the outlook than he thought it discreet to show." Would Lincoln have talked to anybody in that fashion on February 20, 1861? It seemed to me scarcely possible. So far as I could discover nobody but the Diarist became the recipient of such confidential information. It was exactly the opposite of Lincoln's general attitude as reported at the time or later by those on the most intimate terms with him. Whatever may have been his view of the situation, Lincoln was then maintaining an appearance of confidence that all would go well. In the light of that attitude it seemed to me scarcely possible that Lincoln would have made such an admission to the Diarist. If the attitude that Lincoln was then exhibiting represented his real view of the situation, he would not have spoken in the way reported. If his attitude was assumed for reasons of discretion, Lincoln was not the kind of man to make an admission of that sort to a casual acquaintance such as the Diarist. The remark looked to me decidedly like an invention of later date than 1861.

Before coming to a conclusion in regard to the interview I endeavored to give due weight to any possible explanations for the incongruities in the report of the Diarist. It was possible that in some matters the Diarist might have misunderstood Lincoln; that Lincoln might have said '46 instead of " '48"; that he did not mean to imply that he was among the Whig congressmen who had reluctantly accepted "the Locofoco preamble." But no plausible explanation seemed to account for the statement that Lincoln had admitted to the Diarist that he was "more troubled by the outlook than he thought it discreet to show." It did not appear to me possible that Lincoln would have spoken in that way. This doubt, especially when taken in conjunction with other doubtful aspects of the entry in the Diary for February 20, 1861, made me feel that there was occasion for a good deal of doubt about the first of the Diarist's three interviews with Lincoln.

## II

The second interview with Lincoln, according to the Diarist, took place at Washington on February 28, 1861. It occurred in Lincoln's quarters at the Willard Hotel, where he stayed for nine days before going into the White House after his inauguration on March 4.

Early in that nine-day period the newspaper correspondents developed the habit of recording rather minutely how Lincoln spent his time and of mentioning the names of all or nearly all of his callers, especially persons of any considerable prominence. By studying the reports of those correspondents, especially those of the leading New York newspapers and of certain other papers which had unusually good special correspondents from Washington,[47] I found that it was possible to construct a nearly complete list of the persons Lincoln saw upon any particular day and thereby to determine whether on February 28 there could have been such an interview as that described by the Diarist.

Upon examining the list of Lincoln's callers as reported by the ubiquitous correspondents it appeared that none of those who called on February 28 could have been the Diarist. All who were mentioned as among the callers lacked some of the eighteen points of personality which marked the Diarist. In every instance the discrepancy was manifest and indubitable. If the Diarist managed to see Lincoln that day he escaped the notice of all the correspondents.

I found, moreover, that the interview, if it occurred, must have come in the early afternoon, for during the morning, late afternoon, and evening Lincoln was so fully occupied that the "half an hour with Mr. Lincoln to-day" of the Diarist could not have taken place at any of those times. The time at which the interview must have taken place, in the early afternoon, made the failure of all the correspondents to take note of it appear all the more singular.

The Diarist's account of this interview is one of the most intriguing features of the Diary. The description of how Lincoln appeared and acted, the remarks attributed to him, the pen portrait of Mrs. Lincoln, and the Diarist's shrewdness as exhibited in several matters have exceptional human interest. If fanciful they are decidedly clever inventions.

The interview, as the Diarist records it, took in three different matters: a Cabinet appointment, the safety of Washington in case of attacks by disunionists, and the personality of Charles Sumner. In each instance close examination led me to feel considerable suspicion as to the genuineness of the account.

In the matter of the Cabinet appointment my suspicion sprang largely from the vagueness of the passage. The Diarist reported: "I told him [Lincoln] frankly on his own provocation to the subject what I thought would be the advantages to his Administration, and to the country, of putting ———— into the Cabinet, and gave him to understand, as plainly as I thought becoming, that he must not look on me as acting in concert with any set of men to urge that nomination, or any other nomination, upon him. I think he saw that I was in earnest; and, at all events, he advised me to write to ———— in the terms in which I wished to write to him." The vagueness of this language looked as if it could not have been accidental. Who was the man under discussion? To whom was the Diarist to write? Why should such a letter be sent? The Diary did not afford a ready answer to any of these questions.

Further suspicion arose in my mind when I examined the passage in the light of the actual status of Lincoln's Cabinet-making at the moment when the interview took place. At that time the selection of the Cabinet had been nearly completed, though public announcement had been made in regard to only two appointments, Seward and Bates. There were only two matters as to which Lincoln had not definitely made up his mind and about which he might naturally desire further advice. He was still hesitating as between Montgomery Blair and Henry Winter Davis. He was also uncertain as to whether he could include both Salmon P. Chase and Simon Cameron. If Chase was to be included he must be made secretary of the Treasury. Cameron, however, aspired to that post and was extremely reluctant to be content with any other portfolio. Both men had strong support and in each instance there was powerful opposition.

If Lincoln asked the advice of the Diarist about any Cabinet matter as the Diarist alleged, it would appear to have been about the Chase-Cameron imbroglio. That it could not have been about a choice between Blair and Davis would seem to be assured. The Diarist reported that he told Lincoln about the "advantages . . . of putting ——— into the Cabinet." That the Diarist would not have seen any "advantages" of putting either Blair or Davis into the Cabinet was abundantly clear. His dislike and distrust of the Blairs has already been noted. Davis would manifestly have been equally objectionable to him, for that brilliant but erratic man was closely identified with influences that the Diarist disliked.

In view of the circumstances just set forth it appeared clear that the Cabinet question about which Lincoln sought the advice of the Diarist, if he did seek it, must have been the Chase-Cameron imbroglio. If that was the case, why should Lincoln have asked him to write to anybody about the matter? There was no occasion for writing to either Chase or Cameron, for both men were in Washington. Either man could be reached in person. If some other man than Chase or Cameron was to be the recipient of the letter, why was there any occasion for a letter? The announcement of the Cabinet appointments would be made only five days later. The recipient of a letter dealing with a Cabinet matter would scarcely be able to make advantageous use of any information it might contain.

This examination, in sum, led clearly to the conclusion that the Diarist's story in regard to his discussion with Lincoln about a Cabinet appointment appeared decidedly suspicious. It looked like a clever ruse to create an impression that the Diarist was a man of considerable importance.

From consultation about the Cabinet the interview turned, according to the Diarist, to discussion in regard to the danger that Washington might be attacked by disunionists. "I was sorry," the Diarist said, "to find him [Lincoln] anxious about the safety of Washington and he asked me some questions about Captain Stone, which surprised me a little and annoyed me more." Thereupon the Diarist, according to his account, told Lincoln what he knew about Stone, who was in charge of the District of Columbia militia, and in so doing told a story for the accuracy of which he said he could vouch. According to this story the appointment of Stone to the post he occupied had been opposed by Floyd, Buchanan's former secretary of war, who desired that the position should go to his nephew "Charley Jones." Floyd, the story said, had then tried to get Jones to pick a quarrel with Stone and shoot him. Upon hearing the story, the Diarist said Lincoln remarked, "That was not such a bad idea of Floyd's . . . Of course, I'm glad Stone wasn't shot, and that there wasn't any breach of the peace; but—if the custom could be generally introduced, it might lubricate matters in the way of making political appointments!" Here, it appeared to me, as in several other places, that the Diary had a good story and a salty remark attributed to Lincoln which bore the appearance of being clever invention, the sort of apocryphal anecdote highly relished in later times.

One feature of this story particularly aroused my suspicion. Floyd resigned as secretary of war on December 29, 1860. After that date he was completely estranged from President Buchanan and was not in a position to exert any influence in regard to a military appointment. But Stone was not appointed to the post he occupied until January 2, 1861. The creation of the position and the selection of Stone for the post were parts of a new policy inaugurated at the instance of General Scott after Floyd left the War Department. Here it was clear that the Diarist's story was out of line with what had recently taken place, so recently in fact that neither Lincoln nor the Diarist could have forgotten the circumstances. The story told by the Diarist looked to me like a good story invented to provide occasion for the quaint remark attributed to Lincoln.

At the close of the Diarist's commendation of Captain Stone, Lincoln suddenly picked up a note and handed it to him to be looked at. The Diarist, according to his own account, recognized as he took it that it was in the handwriting of Charles Sumner and was not surprised to find it "alarmish and mysterious in tone, bidding Mr. Lincoln, for particular reasons, to be very careful how he went out alone at night." Discussion of the note led Lincoln to tell how Sumner had evaded a challenge to measure backs with him and had insisted upon making "a little speech" to the effect that "this was a time for uniting our fronts and not our backs before the enemies of the country." Lincoln pronounced the little speech "very fine," but added, "I reckon the truth was, he was—afraid to measure!" All of this, according to the Diary, led up to a characterization of Sumner by Lincoln, describing in piquant fashion one conspicuous trait of the man, which has been often quoted. "I have never had much to do with bishops down where we live; but, do you know, Sumner is just my idea of a bishop."

The picture of Sumner portrayed in the remark attributed to Lincoln seemed to me lifelike. It looked like the kind of characterization that might have come from Lincoln. But on the other hand, I could not avoid a suspicion that it might be a clever fabrication which aimed to put Lincoln in a familiar light and at taking a sly dig at Sumner.

The Diarist's account of the interview closes with a pen portrait of Mrs. Lincoln. His description of her, while not wholly unfavorable, is far from flattering. "She is not ill-looking, and, though her manners are not those of a well-bred woman of the world, there would be nothing particularly repulsive about them, were it not for the hard, almost coarse tone of her voice, and for something very like cunning in the expression of her face." Admitting that his opinion might be influenced by what he had previously learned from Mr. Douglas about the relations between Mrs. Lincoln and her husband and also by the contrast between Mrs. Lincoln and the beautiful wife of Douglas, the Diarist recorded that Mrs. Lincoln "made a most disagreeable impression" upon him, pronounced her "dowdy" and "a most unprepossessing little woman." "I think," he said, "if the wives had been voted for, even by the women, Mr. Douglas would be President-elect to-day."

Was this spicy delineation of Mrs. Lincoln written and entered into a diary in February or March, 1861? It looked to me much more like one drawn at a later date to meet the conception of her that had become prevalent about 1879. Most of the descriptions of Mrs. Lincoln drawn in early 1861, even those coming from unfriendly sources, were distinctly more favorable to her.[48] I found in this contrast grounds for suspicion that the Diary was not written in its entirety in 1861.

Putting together all of the doubts just set forth as regards the second interview between Lincoln and the Diarist, I felt forced to a conclusion similar to that I had reached as to the first interview. While recognizing that there might be explanations that would lessen or even remove the suspicious aspects belonging to various features of the Diary entry about the interview, I could not see how all doubt in regard to it could be overcome. There appeared to be a dubious air about the whole matter. The account of the interview looked like a clever invention of a date later than 1861. It seemed designed to lay stress upon the importance of the Diarist and to play up to the conception which had come to be prevalent about Lincoln, Mrs. Lincoln, and Charles Sumner.

### III

The third interview, according to the Diary, took place at the White House on the afternoon of March 7, 1861. It was arranged at the solicitation of the Diarist in consequence of a call upon him on the previous day by a recent visitor to Montgomery and Charleston.

The fact that the Diarist did not give the name of his

caller made any attempt at identification extremely difficult. He was described as having come directly through Montgomery, stopping only a day at Charleston, where he saw and had a long conversation with Major Anderson, who was "a connection by marriage of his wife, and with whom he had long been on terms of particular good will." Such a man obviously might be in possession of important information in view of the critical state of the country, particularly as regards Fort Sumter. The entry in the Diary for March 6, 1861, showed that the Diarist was alive to that possibility.

The caller, the Diarist declared, astonished him "by his statements, which I can not doubt, as to the real status of things at Fort Sumter. . . . He tells me Major Anderson has no expectation whatever of the re-establishment of the Government over the seceded States, and that he intends to be governed in his own future course (military considerations and the question of subsistence of course apart) by the course of his own State of Kentucky. He does not sympathize at all with the States which have now seceded, but he thinks that the provocation given them in the action and attitude of the Northern abolitionists an adequate provocation; and assures me that in his opinion Major Anderson would unhesitatingly obey the orders of a Confederate Secretary of War were Kentucky to withdraw from the Union and join this new and menacing organization."

The full significance of the information which the Diarist's caller brought to him, if the Diary may be trusted, can be appreciated only if the situation on the morrow of Lincoln's inauguration is kept in mind.

When South Carolina seceded on December 20, 1860, Major Anderson was at Fort Moultrie with a garrison of only about seventy men. The other forts in the Charleston harbor were unoccupied. His position at Fort Moultrie was decidedly precarious. He could not reasonably expect to hold that fort if the South Carolina authorities demanded its surrender or if it were attacked by a mob. Believing that he was in serious danger from one or the other of these possibilities, Anderson escaped from the dilemma by a cleverly contrived and secret removal of his little force from Fort Moultrie to Fort Sumter during the night of December 26, 1860.

The critical situation brought about by this move had been unexpectedly prolonged and still endured when Lincoln became President on March 4, 1861. A continued occupation of Fort Sumter by Major Anderson and his garrison had upon several occasions come close to precipitating the conflict which did come a little later. South Carolina had assembled several thousand troops and erected powerful batteries to back up her demand for the evacuation of the fort. Strong desire both North and South to avoid civil war had served to prolong the crisis over possession of the fort. The language of Lincoln's inaugural, in which he had announced his intention to "hold, occupy, and possess" the forts and other United States property which had been taken over by the seceding states, had been denounced in the South as a virtual declaration of war. In that situation there was obvious danger that at almost any moment war might come over the Sumter question.

In the light of this situation it is easy to understand the anxiety of the Diarist to bring his caller into personal contact with President Lincoln. A difficulty arose at first from reluctance on the part of the caller to comply with a suggestion for that purpose. After some urging, however, his consent was obtained. The Diarist then wrote a note to the President requesting an appointment for the next day. A favorable answer having come in the morning, the interview took place at the White House on the afternoon of March 7, 1861.

In the interview, as the Diarist recorded it, the talking was done by the man from Montgomery and Charleston. He reported to President Lincoln what he had told the Diarist the day before. Lincoln did not appear much surprised and did not ask many questions, though he did inquire several times whether his informant was quite sure "about Major Anderson's ideas as to his duty in case of any action by Kentucky." Assured that his caller felt no uncertainty about the matter, Lincoln astonished the Diarist and the man from

89

Montgomery and Charleston by remarking: "Well, you say Major Anderson is a good man, and I have no doubt he is; but if he is right it will be a bad job for me if Kentucky secedes. When he goes out of Fort Sumter, I shall have to go out of the White House."

Lincoln's callers, according to the Diary, were still further astonished by another remark he made just as they were taking their leave. "You haven't such a thing as a postmaster in your pocket, have you?" In response apparently to the looks of astonishment which this remark excited, Lincoln continued: "You see it seems to me kind of unnatural that you shouldn't have at least a postmaster in your pocket. Everybody I've seen for days past has had foreign ministers, and collectors, and all kinds, and I thought you couldn't have got in here without having at least a postmaster get into your pocket!"

The actual occurrence of this interview, I knew, had already been called in question. E. L. Pierce, the biographer of Charles Sumner, in a paper read before the Massachusetts Historical Society in March, 1896, had argued that it could not have taken place, because on the afternoon in question there was a reception for the diplomatic corps at the White House.[49] Such a conclusion I found untenable. The diplomatic reception came at two o'clock.[50] In a brief ceremony the dean of the diplomatic corps read a short address in behalf of the assembled diplomats and the President made a short reply. A little sociability followed from the entrance on the scene of Mrs. Lincoln and the Cabinet, who happened to be at the White House. The whole affair occupied so short a time that there was abundance of opportunity later in the afternoon for such an interview as that described in the Diary.[51]

I found, however, good reason for believing that no such interview did occur. Proof in support of this belief came from an examination of what had been happening at Fort Sumter.

Our knowledge in regard to what went on comes in large degree from Samuel W. Crawford's *Genesis of the Civil War.*

Crawford was the surgeon with Anderson's garrison at Sumter. The account of the Sumter episode as related in his book was based upon a diary which he kept while at the fort. A manuscript copy of that diary is in the Manuscript Division of the Library of Congress. Its entries include the names of all visitors to the fort. An examination of the diary for the period in which the man from Montgomery and Charleston must have made his visit to the fort, if he really made one, showed that there were only two visitors during that time. Neither of them could have been the man from Montgomery and Charleston as delineated in the Diary.

One of the visitors was J. W. White, a druggist from Nashua, New Hampshire. I found it possible, or even probable, that White did visit Washington about March 6–7, 1861.[52] Although direct evidence was lacking, I could not believe that White had "long been on terms of particular good will" with Major Anderson or that the Major was "a connection by marriage of his wife." From the available evidence it was plain that White visited Sumter, not for the purpose of seeing Major Anderson, but in order to see Captain Foster, a member of the garrison, whose mother lived at Nashua. Neither of two newspaper accounts of White's visit to Fort Sumter, for which he furnished the information, made any claim that he had even seen Major Anderson.[53] Manifestly White could not have been the man from Montgomery and Charleston who figured in the Diary.

The other visitor mentioned in the Crawford diary was Joseph R. Anderson, the head of the Tredegar Iron Works at Richmond. In certain respects he appeared to fit into the Diarist's description of the man from Montgomery and Charleston. For a time I thought that he must have been that man. He was at Fort Sumter on March 1, 1861, for the purpose of seeing Major Anderson.[54] The two men had been long acquainted and might well have been close friends, for Joseph R. Anderson had been a senior cadet at West Point while Robert Anderson was an instructor in artillery at the Academy. I was prepared to believe that there might have been "a connection by marriage" between Major Anderson and the wife of Joseph R. Anderson, although considerable investigation along genealogical lines failed to disclose any such connection.

On the other hand it did not seem to me that Joseph R. Anderson would have consented to go to the White House on March 7, 1861, in the manner described by the Diarist. In Virginia he was among the advocates of secession and he was at the time busily engaged in supplying heavy ordnance to the states which had already seceded. Presently I discovered conclusive proof that he could not have been at Washington on March 7, 1861. On that day he was at Montgomery. I found the proof in the shape of a contract which he signed on that date with the Confederate Secretary of War.[55] Manifestly Joseph R. Anderson was not the man from Montgomery and Charleston of the Diary.

From these considerations it seemed to me clear that the account of the interview at the White House on March 7, 1861, was fictitious. No such interview took place. Somebody had concocted a good story.

Looking at the Diarist's accounts of his three interviews with Lincoln in the light of the evidence adduced and the reasoning set forth in this chapter, I felt obliged to conclude that there was decided doubt about the first and second and that the third was clearly fictitious. That conclusion naturally raised doubt in my mind as to the three striking incidents in the Diary in which Lincoln had appeared as the central figure. They also seemed to call for close scrutiny.

# XIII

The first of the three incidents, according to the Diarist, happened in New York City on February 20, 1861. While there on that date Lincoln attended the opera. The Diarist was not present, but later that evening obtained an account of the occasion from his "cousin V——," who sat in a box opposite that occupied by the President-elect. The Diarist's informant related "a most amusing account of the President-elect at the opera in Mr. C——'s box, wearing a pair of huge *black* kid gloves, which attracted the attention of the whole house, hanging as they did over the red velvet box-front." He also related how a lady, sitting in a box opposite, "first told a story of Major Magruder of the army, a Southern man, who took off his hat when a procession of Wide-awakes passed his Broadway hotel last year and said, 'I salute the pall-bearers of the Constitution'; and then rather cleverly added 'I think we ought to send some flowers over the way to the undertaker of the Union.'"

The Diarist's informant also reported that during "one of the *entr'actes*," he had gone to the "directors' room," where Lincoln, coming in shortly afterwards had met a troop of gentlemen anxious to be presented to him. "V—— said Mr. Lincoln looked terribly bored, and sat on the sofa at the end of the room with his hat pushed back on his head, the most deplorable figure that can be imagined, putting his hand out to be shaken in a queer mechanical way." The Diarist added by way of remark: "I am afraid V—— has a streak of his sarcastic grandmamma's temper in him."

Here was a good story. It was, in fact, so good that it appeared open to suspicion. Such stories are often inventions. In this instance I found that there were special reasons for suspecting the whole incident, as related in the Diary, apart from the fact that Lincoln did attend the opera on the occasion in question.

The newspapers of New York City and the New York correspondents of newspapers of other cities furnished numerous accounts of the occasion, some of them entering into a good deal of detail.[56] In an examination of more than a dozen such accounts I failed to find anything to confirm the story and I did find a good deal to discredit it. None of these accounts said that Lincoln wore "*black* kid gloves." If his huge gloves "attracted the attention of the whole house, hanging as they did over the red velvet box-front," they apparently escaped the notice of all the journalists who reported the occasion. This seemed all the more singular in that several of these accounts appeared in papers that seldom missed an opportunity to poke ridicule at Lincoln.

Cousin V——'s account of what took place in the "directors' room" also looked incredible. None of the contemporaneous newspaper accounts confirmed the report that Lincoln visited that room. They did say that Lincoln entered his box at the Academy of Music, where the opera was performed, during the progress of the first act; that in the interval between the first and second acts he bowed repeatedly to the applause bestowed upon him by the audience and afterwards joined in a patriotic demonstration when the opera company appeared upon the stage and sang the "Star Spangled Banner"; and that he left after the second act. From this it appeared clear that if Lincoln visited the "directors' room," as stated by cousin V——, it must have been just before leaving the building. His visit there, if it occurred as related, must have consumed some little time. That it did occur appeared highly doubtful in view of the fact that only a very short interval elapsed between the time when the second act of the opera must have come to a close and the time at which he arrived at the Astor House upon his return there.

The statement that Lincoln "sat on the sofa" while shaking hands with the "troop of gentlemen" who were presented to him also looked incredible. As a shrewd politician anxious to create a favorable impression among influential men Lincoln could have scarcely failed to stand erect for such an occasion, however unwelcome it might have been. No other account in regard to any of the incidents attending the long journey from Springfield to Washington reported any similar failure on Lincoln's part to act in a manner befitting the President-elect.

In the light of all these circumstances the account of Lincoln at the opera as related by "cousin V——" looked to me decidedly like an invention devised in order to add spice to a fictitious or partly fictitious production.

II

The greater part of the entry in the Diary for March 2, 1861, is devoted to an episode of remarkable interest. If an actual occurrence it is a splendid example of Lincoln's aptitude in the handling of men and of thorny situations. If an invention it is an amazingly clever fabrication. As the story is rather long and has already been reproduced in the first chapter, the reader should turn back to that point, pages 9–12, and read it again.

After doing so, the reader, I think, will readily consent to join the writer in asking, Could such an episode have actually occurred?

I found reason for doubt in the fact that the incident is known to historians and biographers only from the pages of the Diary. I could not find any confirmatory evidence for it. Apparently none of the many enterprising journalists who were following closely the final stage of the fierce conflict over the formation of Lincoln's Cabinet heard about the affair. As far as I could ascertain, none of the participants ever related the incident to anybody else. Such omissions appeared to me significant. It seemed scarcely conceivable that a gathering such as that described by the Diarist could have escaped the notice of all the newspapers that were hostile to Seward and critical of his followers. It seemed to me that if the incident occurred Thurlow Weed must have been among the delegation that conferred with Lincoln, according to the Diary. If Weed did receive such a rebuff at the hands of Lincoln, knowledge of the matter, I thought, would almost certainly have reached some of Weed's numerous enemies, who would have made haste to proclaim their delight over his discomfiture. In particular, it seemed singular that in subsequent years, when many men who had known Lincoln were making their contributions to the growing fund of stories about him, none of the participants in the alleged conference, as far as I could discover, ever told or confirmed the intriguing story related by the Diarist.

Another reason for doubt lay in the difficulty of fitting such an incident into the day of March 2, 1861. A careful study as to how Lincoln spent his time on that day indicated that he was kept busy, morning, afternoon, and evening.[57] Could it have happened on that day? The answer appeared to be, possibly but not probably. Such a conference as that described in the Diary would have required at least an hour. On that busy day, when so many individuals and delegations were clamoring for an opportunity to get in a last word with Lincoln before his final decision as to the Cabinet, the use of so long a period by any one delegation could scarcely have escaped notice. But none of the newspapers made mention of a call upon Lincoln by a delegation such as that described by the Diarist. No newspaper, so far as I could discover, reported that Lincoln spent an exceptionally long period with any one group of callers. In a word, it appeared to me next to impossible that such a conference could have taken place and have escaped notice.

Still another reason for doubt arose in connection with a point of detail involved in the Diarist's story. The place where the conference took place is not mentioned in the Diary. It is clear, however, that if it occurred it must have been in Lincoln's reception room at the Willard Hotel. Lincoln is said during the course of the conference to have "opened a table-drawer" and to have taken out a paper, saying: "I had written out my choice here of Secretaries in the Cabinet after a great deal of pains and trouble; and now you tell me I must break the slate and begin all over!" Could such a thing have occurred? Would Lincoln have put such a paper in a table drawer in a room through which a stream of callers was constantly passing, not all of whom could be safely trusted to refrain from opening table drawers?

While careless in some things Lincoln was careful about matters he desired to keep to himself. That trait had been particularly marked as to two things, the inaugural address and the Cabinet. Upon both matters, aside from an announcement that Seward and Bates were to be in the Cabinet, he was still preserving the utmost secrecy. Premature disclosure in regard to the inaugural address had been narrowly averted a few days earlier through the recovery of a valise containing the document, which had been carelessly lost by Bob Lincoln, the "Prince of Rails."[58] That experience, if anything were needed, would have made Lincoln more than ever cautious in regard to his list of intended members of the Cabinet.

Putting together all the dubious aspects of the Diarist's account of a conference alleged to have taken place on March 2, 1861, between Lincoln and a group of Seward men, I found it impossible to escape decided doubt about the whole matter. It looked to me much more like an invented good story than a historical fact.

### III

The third incident is of exceptional interest. As told by the Diarist, Douglas held Lincoln's hat while Lincoln delivered his inaugural address on March 4, 1861. The dramatic and human interest involved in such an occurrence have not escaped notice. Scores of writers have incorporated it in their accounts of the ceremony by which Lincoln became President of the United States. Nearly all who relate it have derived it directly or indirectly from the Diary.

The incident as related in the Diary comes just after the Diarist had remarked that the arrangements for the inauguration had been badly handled and that none of the principal figures, Lincoln, Buchanan, or Chief Justice Taney, had appeared at ease.

"I must, however, except Senator Douglas, whose conduct can not be overpraised. I saw him for a moment in the morning, when he told me that he meant to put himself as prominently forward in the ceremonies as he properly could, and to leave no doubt on any one's mind of his determination to stand by the new Administration in the performance of its first great duty to maintain the Union. I watched him carefully. He made his way not without difficulty—for there was literally no sort of order in the arrangements—to the front of the throng directly beside Mr. Lincoln, when he prepared to read the address. A miserable little rickety table had been provided for the President, on which he could hardly find room for his hat, and Senator Douglas, reaching forward, took it with a smile and held it during the delivery of the address. It was a trifling act, but a symbolical one, and not to be forgotten, and it attracted much attention all around me."

I asked myself the question: Did this actually take place as the Diarist described it? The question, I thought, was highly important, because a satisfactory answer to it might well be regarded as a nearly decisive test as to the character of the Diary. Here was a place where the Diary could be "controlled." If the incident, as related by the Diarist, actually took place, there ought to be discoverable a considerable amount of confirmatory evidence. Thousands witnessed the inauguration ceremonies. Many of them put on record what they saw. Their testimony would sustain or contradict the story related by the Diarist. An examination of all the available evidence was clearly in order.

The evidence seems to fall into six classes:

1. Private letters written on March 4, 1861, or within a day or two thereafter, by persons who had witnessed the inauguration.

2. Spot-news descriptions in the newspapers of March 5 and 6, 1861.

3. Follow-up incidents about the inauguration reported in the newspapers of the next few days.

4. Recollections told or written within a short period after the inauguration by persons who had witnessed it.

5. Descriptions of the inauguration in books and in magazines and newspaper articles appearing considerably after the event but not later than July, 1879, when "The Diary of a Public Man" was published.

6. Recollections long after the event by persons who had been present at the inauguration.

Keeping in mind the varying value of these six different kinds of evidence, I set to work to examine all the evidence of each sort, so far as available, in order to determine, if possible, whether the Diarist had reported an incident that he had actually witnessed or whether his account was an invention, or perchance a story picked up somewhere and then told as something he had himself seen.

1. Private letters, written on March 4, 1861, or within a day or two thereafter, by persons who had witnessed the inauguration.

Letters of this kind, written while the occasion was still fresh in mind and usually to members of the writer's family or to close friends, are evidence of the highest value. The writers of such letters usually had no special motive for coloring or distorting their accounts of what they had actually witnessed.

Unfortunately I could find only a few such letters. Among them, however, was one from Gustave Koerner of Illinois to his daughter. At one time a close personal and political friend of Douglas, Koerner had broken with Douglas politically but continued to maintain friendly personal relations with him. An active and enthusiastic supporter of Lincoln in the campaign of 1860, Koerner had gone to Washington for the inauguration. On that occasion he occupied a point of exceptional advantage for observing any striking incident involving Lincoln and Douglas that might occur. In a letter written to his daughter at five p.m. that day, Koerner said, "I stood close to his [Lincoln's] chair; next to me stood Douglas."[59]

That Koerner under such circumstances made no mention of any incident such as that described by the Diarist, I felt obliged to regard as significant. The omission, considering the circumstance, appeared to me to cast considerable doubt upon the account given by the Diarist.

Similar letters from other witnesses failed to include any mention of the incident in question. The number of letters available, however, was so limited that I did not feel warranted in reaching a decisive conclusion on the basis of such evidence.

2. Spot-news descriptions of the inauguration in the newspapers of March 5 and 6, 1861.

Here I had at my disposal a vast amount of most valuable evidence. Almost all of the leading newspapers of that day had their own special correspondents at Washington. The general practice was that such correspondents sent each day a special dispatch by telegraph, the length varying considerably from day to day. On an important occasion, such as the inauguration of a president, the dispatches often amounted to several columns and entered into a good deal of detail. In addition each correspondent within a day or two usually wrote a follow-up letter which supplemented the dispatch sent by telegraph. These letters frequently contained additional details, especially as to points of human interest likely to appeal to readers of newspapers.

Much of the spot news contained in the dispatches and letters of the Washington correspondents of that day must be handled with caution. The correspondents often played up to the point of view of the papers which employed them. But in the main their news was fairly accurate, especially as to incidental matters. It is to be remembered that the writers on such an occasion as the inauguration had abundant opportunity to see and hear what took place and that they were alert to observe everything likely to be of interest to their readers.

I examined the spot-news dispatches describing the inauguration in upwards of twenty-five newspapers. Among

100

them were the leading papers of New York, Boston, Philadelphia, Baltimore, Cincinnati, Cleveland, Chicago, and Detroit. I also included the descriptions in the Washington papers, the *National Intelligencer*, the *Evening Star*, and the *States and Union*. Some of the dispatches published in these papers were duplicates in whole or in part. There were, however, fully twenty independent accounts.

In none of this plethora of spot news and follow-up letters did I discover mention of any such incident as that related by the Diarist. Such an incident would have fitted admirably into the accounts written by many of the experienced journalists who reported the inauguration. This silence appeared to me all the more impressive because quite a number of these accounts paid particular attention to Douglas and his behavior on the occasion. They told where he stood, what he said or was reported to have said *sotto voce* while Lincoln was speaking, and the remarks he made at the close of the address. Other details in regard to him were also given. It scarcely seemed possible that if Douglas held Lincoln's hat during the address it could have gone unreported by any of the vigilant journalists who described the inauguration scene in great detail. That not one of them did report it appeared to me to argue strongly that it did not occur.

3. Follow-up incidents about the inauguration reported in the newspapers of the next ten days.

Nearly all of the more important newspapers of 1861 supplemented their spot news in regard to the inauguration by additional incidents a few days later. For that reason I thought it possible I might find a report that Douglas had held Lincoln's hat during the delivery of the inaugural address among reports of that kind. I sought, accordingly, to ascertain whether there had been any such report.

An extensive search in the newspaper files for March, 1861, yielded a singular result. For six days after the inauguration no newspaper among the many consulted made mention in its follow-up items that Douglas held Lincoln's hat. Then one and only one account somewhat similar to that reported by the Diarist did appear. It was published in the *Cincinnati Commercial* for March 11, 1861. As there reported it read as follows:

"One of the Representatives of this State in Congress reports an interesting and rather funny incident of the Inauguration, which, not having seen in print, we record. On approaching the platform, where he was to take his oath and be inducted into the office of Chief Executive, Mr. Lincoln removed his hat as he took the seat assigned him. The article seemed to be a burden. He changed it awkwardly from one hand to another, and finally despairing for it any other easy position, deposited it upon the platform beside him. Senators and Judges crowded in, and to make room for them he removed nearer the front of the stage, carrying his tile with him. Again it was handled uneasily, and as Senator Baker approached to introduce him to the audience he made a motion as if to replace the tile on the stage under the seat, when Douglas who had been looking on quietly and apparently with some apprehension of a catastrophe to the hat, said 'Permit me, Sir,' and gallantly took the vexatious article and held it during the entire reading of the Inaugural. Douglas must have reflected pretty seriously during that half hour, that instead of delivering an inaugural address from that portico, he was holding the hat of the man who was doing it."

One of the most singular things about this item was the way in which it was handled by the other newspapers of the day. It was widely reproduced.[60] Occasionally there was a slight change of wording or typography, but otherwise there was no material alteration in any reproduction I could discover. Not one of the papers that reproduced the item added anything to confirm or to deny the story. Many of the reproductions did not give the name of the paper in which the item had originally appeared, simply crediting it to "a Cincinnati newspaper."

From the foregoing it plainly appeared that strictly contemporaneous confirmation of the Diary in the spot news and in the follow-up items of the newspapers of the day, as far as there was any confirmation, was limited to one account. Was that one account an unquestionable confirmation? After careful consideration I felt obliged to hold that it was not.

The incident, as related by the *Cincinnati Commercial*, was told upon the authority of "one of the Representatives of this State in Congress." His name was not given. There was no claim in the report that he had witnessed the incident. It may have been hearsay on his part. It may have been invention. Newspapers of that day indulged rather freely in the practice of concocting spurious incidents for the edification of their readers and especially for the purpose of poking jibes at their political opponents. Republican papers—the *Cincinnati Commercial* was Republican—delighted in anything calculated to present Douglas in a ridiculous light. In view of these circumstances, it seemed to me not unlikely that the item in the *Cincinnati Commercial* was an invention designed to please its readers by a bit of spoofing aimed at Douglas. That the item should not be regarded as satisfactory corroboration of the Diary would appear from the fact that it did not include any statement such as that in the Diary, that the act ascribed to Douglas excited much favorable comment on the part of those who saw it.

4. Recollections told or written within a short period after the inauguration by persons who had witnessed it.

Evidence of this sort has high value. The lapse of time has not seriously affected it. Unless distorted by the influence of subsequent events, it has almost equal value with strictly contemporaneous evidence. While momentous events did happen shortly after the inauguration of Lincoln, there does not appear to be any good reason for supposing that those events affected any of the evidence now to be considered.

I found several pieces of evidence belonging in this category. All came from a time not more than four months after the day that Lincoln was inaugurated.

John W. Forney witnessed the inauguration of Lincoln, standing only a few feet from where Douglas stood.[61] Any evidence coming from him, I felt, would have special value in view of his relations with Douglas and Lincoln. In 1860–1861 Forney was clerk of the House of Representatives and also proprietor and Washington correspondent of the *Philadelphia Press*. In the campaign of 1860 he had worked zealously for Douglas to whom he was deeply attached by ties of personal and political sympathy. Sharing Douglas' strong devotion to the Union, Forney began almost immediately after the election to gravitate toward the Lincoln camp. By inauguration day his support of Lincoln had become hardly distinguishable from that given by rock-ribbed Republican journalists. The difference lay in his often repeated praise of Douglas for lending support to Lincoln in his effort to save the Union.

On July 2, 1861, at the Smithsonian Institution in Washington, Forney delivered a memorial eulogy upon Douglas,[62] who had died a month earlier. The occasion offered him a good opportunity to pour forth praise for Douglas and to plead for support of Lincoln in the cause of the Union. It was exactly the sort of occasion for the use of any such incident as that related by the Diarist, if it had occurred and if Forney had seen it or had even heard of it, as he had had good opportunity to do. There were, moreover, several points in Forney's address at which mention of the incident would appear to have been almost inevitable, if Forney was familiar with it. There was, however, no mention of any such incident anywhere in the address. Silence, under the circumstances, I thought, cast considerable doubt as to whether the incident had really taken place.

On July 9, 1861, both houses of Congress listened to numerous speakers who pronounced eulogies upon Douglas.[63] At least five of the six senators and five of the ten representatives who spoke had witnessed the inauguration on March 4, occupying places upon the platform. In several instances there were passages in their addresses whereat some mention of an incident like that related by the Diarist must almost certainly have been made if the speakers had witnessed the occurrence or had heard the favorable comment which the Diarist said it had aroused among those near at hand. None of them did mention it.

This omission appeared particularly singular in the case of the address of Congressman Isaac Arnold of Illinois. Arnold was a former Democrat who had broken with Douglas politically but had remained upon friendly terms with him. His address praised the conduct of Douglas at the time of Lincoln's arrival in Washington as "in the highest degree graceful and magnanimous." It then continued in a striking paragraph:

"None who witnessed it can ever forget the scene on the eastern portico of the Capitol when Mr. Lincoln in the presence of the representatives of the people assumed the sublime prerogatives of Government, and swore by the eternal God that he would faithfully support the Constitution and enforce the laws of the country. Douglas, not by accident, stood by his side; and, in the midst of scowling traitors, whispered in the ear of the President that come what might in the dark and bloody future darkening before him, he would stand by the Government and strengthen its arms to crush treason and rebellion."[64]

Here, it seemed to me, the speaker must almost necessarily have introduced the incident related by the Diarist if he had witnessed it or had heard the favorable comment it was said to have excited. Silence at such a point seemed decidedly significant. It appeared to argue strongly that Arnold had not witnessed any such incident and thereby cast considerable doubt as to whether it actually occurred.

The *Atlantic Monthly* for August, 1861, contained an article entitled "Reminiscences of Stephen A. Douglas." Although unsigned it was written by a newspaperman named Howard, "Howard of the *New York Times*."[65] The publication date indicated that it must have been written not later than the early days of July. Howard had occupied a point of advantage at the inauguration of Lincoln. "It was my good fortune," he said, "to stand by Mr. Douglas during the reading of the Inaugural of President Lincoln." Howard was the kind of reporter who would have been most likely to have observed and reported such an incident as that related by the Diarist. In his reporting for the *New York Times* at that period there was a large element of what is known in newspaper circles as "H. I.," i.e., human interest stuff. His reports were widely reproduced by other papers for that reason. At the inauguration, as his spot-news reports and his *Atlantic* article clearly show, Howard paid close attention to Douglas. It was he who had chiefly reported what Douglas had said on that occasion. That he failed to make any mention of the hat incident in his account of Douglas at the inauguration in his *Atlantic* article, where it would have been particularly appropriate, must almost certainly have been because he did not see it. Here again the argument from silence seemed entitled to considerable weight.

Douglas died on June 2, 1861. During the next few days almost every newspaper in the country had an obituary article and an editorial in regard to him. There were also many follow-up articles. In the expectation that I might find mention of the incident in some of those articles I examined a large number of them, especially in the more important newspapers. None of them mentioned it.

It is sometimes said that the argument from silence is never conclusive. The point is in general well taken. But under some circumstances silence may be almost conclusive. Silence in the cases just examined seems to me highly significant. It added to the doubt I had come to feel in regard to the story told by the Diarist.

5. Descriptions of the inauguration in books and magazine or newspaper articles appearing considerably after the event, but not later than mid-July, 1879, when the first installment of "The Diary of a Public Man" was published.

Evidence of this kind, while of some value has not a value equal to that of any of the four classes of contemporaneous or nearly contemporaneous evidence already considered. I included it for two reasons. Some of the writers did witness the inauguration; others may have done so; still others may have derived their information from persons who were present on the occasion. Moreover, evidence of this kind will tend to show whether the story in question was widely known and accepted before publication of "The Diary of a Public Man."

I found that at least four writers of books that belong in this category had been present at the inauguration, Horace Greeley, Henry Wilson, Isaac Arnold, and L. O. Gobright, the Washington representative of the Associated Press.[66] None of the four, except Arnold, make any mention of the alleged incident. Arnold did mention it, but in a way to leave doubt as to whether he actually saw it.

The mention of it in his book, *Lincoln and the Overthrow of Slavery* (1866), came in a footnote. "The author is reminded of the following incident: As Mr. Lincoln removed his hat before commencing the reading of his 'Inaugural,' from the proximity of the crowd, he saw nowhere to place it, and Mr. Douglas, by his side instantly extended his hand and held the President's hat while he was occupied in reading the address."[67] Arnold said that he was "reminded" of it. The use of that word "reminded" and the fact that the incident was put into a footnote instead of into the text looked singular to me. It looked like a last minute addition put in at the suggestion of somebody else. I could not regard Arnold's mention of the matter as a statement that he had witnessed the incident.

Three other books published prior to 1879 made mention of such an incident as that described by the Diarist. These books were by E. A. Pollard (1863), J. G. Holland (1866), and Benson J. Lossing (1866).[68] None of them indicated the source from which their information came. All of them probably derived it directly or indirectly from the *Cincinnati Commercial*.

I also examined a large number of other books published between 1861 and 1879, especially biographies of Lincoln and the numerous popular histories of the Civil War. In none of them did I find any mention of the incident.

My search also included a large number of magazine and

newspaper articles of the period 1861 to 1879 which described or touched upon the inauguration of 1861. In only one of them did I find any mention of the incident or alleged incident. An editorial in the *St. Louis Republican* for February 5, 1873, said:

"Those who witnessed Lincoln's first inauguration will not soon forget one little scene which then transpired. The President-elect came forward upon the platform prepared at the east front of the Capitol, with his natural awkwardness increased by the momentous circumstances of the occasion, and the gorgeous wardrobe, in which it was evident he felt exceedingly uncomfortable. The stiff dress coat, vest and pantaloons of black broadcloth were enough of themselves to disturb his mental and physical equanimity, but to these were added other incumbrances in the shape of a brand new silk hat and a handsome gold-headed cane. The cane he managed to put away in a corner, but the disposition of the hat perplexed him greatly. It was too good to throw away, too nice, as he thought, to rest upon the rough boards, so, for a minute at least, poor Lincoln stood there in the gaze of assembled thousands, grasping the hat desperately and seeking in vain for a safe place to deposit it. Douglas who sat immediately in the rear, saw the embarrassment of his rival, and rising took the shining beaver from its sorely bothered owner and held it during the delivery of the inaugural address. It is doubtful whether Stephen A. Douglas ever dreamed that he was destined to hold the hat of Abraham Lincoln while that individual was appearing for the first time as president of the United States."

At first reading this striking paragraph looked like an account of a real incident recalled after twelve years by a man who had witnessed it. If I had found the account, along with several contemporaneous reports to the same general effect by actual witnesses of the inauguration, I should have accepted it as a substantial confirmation of the Diary. Two considerations, however, led me to doubt whether it was entitled to that degree of confidence.

(a) While the opening words seemed to imply that the man who wrote the article had witnessed the incident he described, he did not say that he had done so.

(b) The account contained manifest errors not likely to have been made by an actual witness. Douglas did not sit behind Lincoln at the inauguration. He stood at Lincoln's right.[69] Lincoln did not put his cane away in a corner. He put it upon the table near which he stood.[70]

In the light of these circumstances, after giving to the article from the *St. Louis Republican* all the weight to which it appeared entitled, I could not regard it as an adequate confirmation of the account in the Diary. It looked like an editorial elaboration of the *Cincinnati Commercial* item.

6. Recollections long after the event by persons who had been present at the inauguration.

If recollection long after the event could be accepted as good evidence, the Diarist's account of the incident in question would appear to be abundantly confirmed. Not less than seven men who witnessed the inauguration have left accounts of that event which state specifically or clearly imply that they witnessed the incident. The seven were Henry Watterson, Carl Schurz, Isaac Arnold, Ben Perley Poore, Clark E. Carr, George Williamson Smith, and Charles Aldrich.[71] All of these men were veracious men who would not deliberately have made a false statement. They undoubtedly believed that they had witnessed the incident.

Two considerations, however, led me to reject their testimony as unreliable. One was that it was given long, long after the event. The earliest of the seven wrote twenty-five years later. None of the others wrote earlier than forty-four years after the event. The other consideration was that "The Diary of a Public Man" was published before any of the seven gave their testimony. It has frequently happened that men writing or speaking after a long interval about an important event they had witnessed have fallen into the error of incorporating into their own recollection details about the event which they did not actually see or hear but had derived from the report of some other witness or reputed witness. Memoirs and reminiscences afford numerous examples of such mistakes. In this instance, I felt obliged to believe that all of the seven had derived their knowledge from the Diary, or from some writer who had drawn upon the Diary, and had then afterwards unconsciously come to believe that they had witnessed the incident. All seven were well-read men, much interested in everything concerning the Civil War. It seemed to me not unlikely that all of them had read the Diary at the time of its publication in 1879. All of them must have read numerous books and articles that related the incident, deriving it from the Diary.

One significant circumstance in regard to the testimony of these seven witnesses gave me added reason for rejecting the evidence as unreliable. If the accounts of the seven were in close agreement about the inauguration and were in line with those written at or close to the time by other witnesses, there might be considerable reason for accepting their recollections as accurate, despite the late date at which they were put on record. But that is not the case. They do not agree about the inauguration in general or as to the incident in question. One would have it that Lincoln took the oath before delivering his inaugural address.[72] In fact he took it after the address had been delivered. There is no agreement among them as to the time at which Douglas took Lincoln's hat. One puts it definitely at the time when Lincoln came upon the platform;[73] four with equal definiteness put it at a later point, when Lincoln was about to deliver his address;[74] the other two are silent or a little obscure about the matter. There is also contradiction as to where Douglas sat or stood. In a word, the seven accounts exhibit the defects as evidence usually displayed in recollections written long after the event. Any confirmation which they may seem to bring to the support of the Diarist must be at best of a very dubious character.

It is also to be noted that numerous other equally veracious men who were present at the inauguration, including John G. Nicolay, John Hay, John Sherman, C. C. Washburn,

George W. Julian, Granville Dodge, Gustave Koerner, and Henry Villard, failed to include any mention of the episode in accounts of the inauguration which they wrote at various dates subsequent to 1879. All of these men were stationed upon the platform and had better opportunity to see what was done by Lincoln and Douglas than did most of the seven men whose accounts give some support to the Diarist. Four of the other group were in the crowd on the ground and could therefore have had only an imperfect opportunity to observe details about what took place upon the platform. Silence on the part of Nicolay, Hay, Sherman, and the others of that group appeared to me of considerable significance. By the time they wrote their accounts the hat incident had become widely accepted as historic fact. Silence on their part, while not amounting to contradiction, rather offsets the testimony of the other group.

Completing my examination of all the evidence I could discover that has any bearing upon the incident in question, five things seem to stand out clearly.

1. The account of the incident as related by the Diarist cannot be corroborated by any strictly contemporaneous evidence of unquestionable value. Only one contemporaneous account, the highly dubious item which appeared in the *Cincinnati Commercial* on March 11, 1861, gives any support to the Diary.

2. Failure to observe any such incident by any of the others who were at the inauguration and who put upon record within a short time what they saw ought to be regarded, under the circumstances, as nearly conclusive proof against the report of the Diarist.

3. The only real support for the Diarist comes from men who witnessed the inauguration in 1861 but gave their evidence after the publication of the Diary. While such witnesses were fairly numerous and were men whose intention to tell the truth there is no occasion to question, their evidence must be appraised as not a satisfactory corroboration. Those men gave their testimony from recollection long after the event.

111

An even larger number of equally reliable men who had also witnessed the inauguration and wrote about it after the publication of the Diary failed to offer any similar corroboration. The historical canon against acceptance of recollections long after the event, unless abundantly confirmed, appears clearly applicable in this instance.

4. The fact that mention of the hat incident seldom occurred in any publication prior to the publication of the Diary in 1879 indicates that the story had little acceptance until the Diarist gave it currency.

5. It seems clearly evident that when the story at an auspicious moment came to the attention of a wide audience by its appearance in the Diary it made a strong appeal to the minds and the hearts of its readers. Repeated from the Diary by scores of writers in subsequent years, it has entered into the folklore of the American people by its appeal to their dramatic instinct and their admiration for good sportsmanship. As folklore it deserves the place it occupies. But from the standpoint of the historian, consideration of the evidence upon which it rests requires that it be pronounced almost certainly a myth.

# XIV

The Diarist represents himself as having been on intimate terms with William H. Seward. His pages abound in passages recording such an intimacy. Seward is represented as talking to him with remarkable freedom, imparting information and divulging intended future action in a way that would be employed only in highly confidential relations with a man of considerable importance. On one occasion the Diarist called upon Seward shortly after dinner and engaged in a long discussion with him. Two days later Seward called on the Diarist, "not long after breakfast," to ask a favor. This confidential and friendly attitude on the part of Seward appeared to me all the more notable in that the Diarist had only a rather qualified admiration and respect for Seward. He was, moreover, not at all favorably impressed with many of Seward's friends and followers.

On the evening of March 7, 1861, if the Diary is to be believed, the Diarist called upon Seward. "After dinner I went in to see Mr. Seward, determined, if possible, to get some satisfactory statement as to the outlook of the immediate future from his point of view, and anxious also to ascertain what he knows, if he knows anything, either to confirm or to contradict the story of —— as to Major Anderson and Fort Sumter." In this instance the blank referred to the man from Montgomery and Charleston, who that afternoon in company with the Diarist had talked with Lincoln at the White House.

"I found Mr. Seward," the Diarist reported, "in a lively, almost in a boisterous mood, but I soon induced him to take a more quiet . . . tone." Then there follows in the Diary a detailed account of an interview which, if it actually took place, must have consumed a large part of the evening. In that interview, according to the Diarist, Seward expressed opinions and announced intentions which I found it hard to believe that he could have uttered at that time, while the Diarist himself exhibited shrewd doubt as to the optimistic expectations of Seward. At the close of the interview the Diarist went to his own home "discouraged and depressed."

On looking into the matter I found that almost certainly no such interview could have taken place. On the evening of March 7, 1861, Seward was a sick man in no condition to have engaged in any such discussion as that described by the Diarist. On the next day Seward wrote to his wife: "I went to the office [at the State Department] on Wednesday [March 6] and for two days have attended at the department nine hours each. Last night [i.e., March 7] I broke down and sent for Dr. Miller. I have kept my chamber to-day except for an hour, when I went on a necessary errand to the White House."[75] Quite evidently the report in the Diary about the interview on the evening of March 7 was either an invention or possibly the recollection of things which Seward might have said on some other occasion but could not have said at the time stated in the Diary.

Two days later, according to the Diarist, Seward stopped to see him, "not long after breakfast," in order to give him a piece of information and to ask a favor. It appeared clear to me, however, that Seward's illness was still continuing at that time to a degree that would have precluded any such occurrence. On that day Alexander Rives, a Virginia Unionist who was in Washington for the purpose of conferring with Seward, being unable to get access to him, wrote: "I desired to present the enclosed letter to you in person; and to that end, called upon you at the Department and your residence; and was sorry to learn that you were too unwell to receive visitors."[76] Moreover, Seward wrote to Lincoln that day: "I am yet kept indoors, but I could muffle up and ride to your house if necessary at any time today."[77] Here again it seemed almost a certainty that the talk with Seward on March 9

114

which the Diarist reported could not have taken place at the time and place indicated.[78] It appeared to have been either an invention or a misplaced and confused recollection.

I also came to feel a considerable degree of doubt about a number of passages in the Diary in relation to Seward and as to the whole picture the Diarist presented of that enigmatical statesman. My reason for distrust, I recognized, did not rest upon such clear and tangible evidence as in the two instances just discussed. There appeared, nevertheless, sufficient reason for feeling a good deal of doubt in the matter. In particular I felt doubt about some of the stories which the Diarist told as having been reported to him. To me they looked like good stories invented for the purpose of adding spice to the production in which they appeared and to aid in rounding out a definitely conceived pen portrait of Seward.

One story of the kind was that Seward, while at Richmond on a visit, when taken to task at a dinner party for the truculence of his tone in regard to the rendition by New York of runaway slaves from Virginia, had replied: "Is it possible you gentlemen suppose I believe any such ——— nonsense as that? It's all very well, and in fact it's necessary, to be said officially up there in New York for the benefit of the voters, but surely we ought to be able to understand each other better over a dinner-table!" Another was that Seward had assured one of his anxious followers that "all he had to do to insure a peaceful settlement of the whole business [of secession] was to be sure and buy a lot of tickets to the inauguration ball and make it a grand success; that would satisfy the country, and lead to peace."

Other stories and numerous remarks seemed calculated to give the impression that the Diarist in 1860–1861, observing Seward in action at close range, had detected in him a somewhat shady politician whose shrewdness was overrated and who would be likely to make a mess of his effort to save the Union by intrigue and dubious methods. The Diarist also appeared to be at considerable pains to make it appear that the Seward influence at Washington was not in fact as potent

115

as was commonly supposed. He seemed particularly anxious to put on record that Seward did not possess the confidence of Lincoln and would not be able to determine the action of the Administration to anything like the degree expected of him. In a word, the picture of Seward as presented in the Diary has a close resemblance to the conception of Seward that had come to prevail in the years shortly after his death in 1872, when he and the role he had played, particularly in relation to the Civil War had been much under discussion. The picture of Seward in the Diary looked to me much like something written at a later date than 1860–1861 and antedated to that period. It also looked to me like an extremely clever effort to make the Diarist look like an uncommonly shrewd observer.

Some of the Diarist's reports in regard to his conversations contained expressions of opinion and alleged disclosures that I found it difficult to believe could have come from Seward, especially at the time when they were said to have been uttered. On February 24, 1861, the day after Lincoln arrived at Washington, the Diarist recorded his chagrin over the "most unfortunate night-trip of Mr. Lincoln's from Harrisburg here." The allusion was to the manner in which Lincoln had by-passed Baltimore, at the instigation of Seward and General Scott, who feared that the President-elect might be assassinated if he went openly through that city. Calling the affair "a most distressing and ill-advised thing," he added, "Mr. Seward feels about it as I do, though he affects, with his usual and rather exasperating assumption of levity, to laugh it off." While recognizing Seward's propensity, especially at the period, to laugh off things that could not be easily explained or well defended, I found it difficult to believe that he would have said anything on February 24, 1861, which could have been construed as agreeing with the Diarist that the affair was "a most distressing and ill-advised thing." Such an opinion was exactly the opposite of that which Seward on that date seems to have entertained.

# XV

It would appear from the Diary that the Diarist was upon terms of particularly close intimacy and friendship with Stephen A. Douglas. If the Diary is to be trusted the Diarist had at least five long and several shorter exchanges of conversation with Douglas during the Secession Winter. From express statement or clear implication it would appear that four of these conversations took place at the home or quarters of the Diarist. In all of them Douglas talked with great freedom, expressing his opinions vigorously and divulging important information to the Diarist. The reports in regard to these conversations, I felt, called for close scrutiny.

The earliest of the conversations, according to the Diary, occurred on December 28, 1860. On that occasion Douglas brought to the Diarist "a story, the origin of which he would not give me, but which, he believed: that Anderson's movement [from Fort Moultrie to Fort Sumter] was preconcerted with one Doubleday, an officer, as I understood him, of the garrison, with 'Ben Wade,' and was intended to make a pacific settlement of the questions at issue impossible." Douglas further said, "Wade and that gang are infuriated at Seward's coming into the Cabinet, and their object is to make it impossible for Lincoln to bring him into it. I think, as a friend of Seward's, you ought to understand this."

Could such "a story" as that which Douglas was said to have brought to the Diarist have been in circulation at Washington on December 28, 1860? It seemed scarcely possible.

The "story," I found, involved three assumptions: (1) that the suitability of Captain Doubleday for the role attributed to him was well known at the time in Washington; (2) that Wade and his "gang," i.e., the radical Republicans

117

already knew and had known for some time that Lincoln intended to put Seward into his Cabinet; (3) that there had been time after the arrival of such knowledge for Wade and his "gang" to preconcert with Doubleday the action he was supposed to have brought about.

None of these assumptions seemed to be well founded. Doubleday was not yet known at Washington as the kind of man likely to preconcert with Wade and the radical Republicans any kind of action; Lincoln's decision to offer a place in his Cabinet to Seward was not definitely made until December 8[79] and could not have become known even in senatorial circles until several days later; accordingly the time required for preconcerting with Doubleday at Fort Moultrie was too short for anything of the kind to have been done. I could well believe that such a "story" as that which the Diarist said had been brought to him by Douglas might have been circulated in Washington at a later date, but not as early as December 28, 1860. Its inclusion in the Diary under that date indicated, I thought, either invention or antedating. In either case it cast considerable doubt upon the authenticity of the Diary.

The Diarist reported that he had a call from Douglas late on the evening of February 28, 1861. His record of the conversation included a statement, both on his own authority and on that of Douglas, that down to that time Lincoln had not yet let Seward know what he proposed to say in the inaugural address. The alleged omission filled the Diarist with alarm. "How is it possible that Mr. Lincoln can intend to put Mr. Seward at the head of his Administration, if he leaves him thus in the dark as to the purport of the first great act of his official life, now only four days off! I can not even reconcile Mr. Seward's acquiescence in such a course with the respect I would like to feel for him as a man; and it seems to me absolutely discouraging as to the outlook for the country."

The statement that Lincoln had not yet shown the inaugural address to Seward was inaccurate. Lincoln had already shown the address to Seward.[80] The inclusion of the erroneous statement looked to me like an invention put in to lay a foundation for the apparently sagacious comment just quoted, a comment which in itself had the appearance of belonging to some date subsequent to 1861.

Another feature of that conversation appeared to me even more surely to indicate that the Diary record of it could not have been entered in a diary written in 1861. The Diarist said: "Before going, Senator Douglas had a word to say about President Buchanan and the South Carolina Commissioners. He tells me that it has now been ascertained that the President nominated his Pennsylvania Collector at Charleston on the very day, almost at the very moment, when he was assuring Colonel Orr, through one of his retainers, that he was disposed to accede to the demands of South Carolina if they were courteously and with proper respect presented to him. They rewrote their letter accordingly, submitted it to the President's agents, who approved it and sent it to the White House. This, Senator Douglas says was on January 3d, in the morning. The Commissioners spent the afternoon in various places, and dined out early. On coming in, they found their letter to the President awaiting them. It had been returned to them by a messenger from the White House, about three o'clock P.M.; and on the back was an endorsement, not signed by any one, and in a clerkly handwriting, to the effect that the President declined to receive the communication! They ordered their trunks packed and left for home by way of Richmond on the four o'clock morning train, feeling, not unreasonably, that they had been both duped and insulted."

While this account had in it several errors which might suggest that it had been written from imperfect recollection at a later date, I did not think the errors of any great significance, except as to one matter. Douglas was speaking about things that had happened nearly two months earlier and his recollection in regard to them might well have gone astray as regards some points. There was, however, one blunder that Douglas could hardly have made. Traveling from Washington to Richmond in January, 1861, one did not begin by taking a train. There was, moreover, no "four o'clock morning train" out of Washington. The journey from Washington to Richmond on the route usually employed began with a boat trip to the mouth of Acquia Creek. There the boat made connection with the Richmond, Fredericksburg and Potomac Railroad for Richmond. I found it easy to believe that Douglas might have made the other errors involved in the account given by the Diarist, but I could not believe that he would have made the mistake of saying that the South Carolina commissioners "left for home on the four o'clock morning train."[81] It appeared to me almost a certainty that the passage in the Diary must have been written at a later date by somebody who had never known or had forgotten the transportation situation of 1861.

The Diarist had another conversation with Douglas on the evening of March 3, 1861. In his report of it he said: "He [Douglas] says that since Mr. Lincoln reached Washington he had inserted in the message [i.e., the inaugural address] a distinct declaration that, while he regards it as in his duty to 'hold, occupy, and possess' the property and places belonging to the Government and to collect the duties, he will not attempt to enforce the strict rights of the Government where hostility to the United States is great and universal. I then told him that Mr. Seward, some days ago, had assured me that he believed he would be able to induce Mr. Lincoln to take such a position as this, and that it would suffice, he thought, as a basis of negotiation with the seceded States, and give the people breathing-time to recover their senses at the South; and we came to the conclusion, which I was very glad to reach, that Mr. Seward's counsels must have brought Mr. Lincoln to this stand, in which I have no sort of doubt, and Mr. Douglas has none, that the great majority of the Northern people of both parties will support him."

The words "hold, occupy, and possess," which Lincoln did utter in his inaugural address were not inserted after his arrival at Washington. They were in the draft prepared before he left Springfield.[82] That Douglas could have known about them, i.e., the exact words, and could have quoted them to the Diarist on the evening before the inauguration appeared to me scarcely credible. Douglas had talked with Lincoln a number of times after Lincoln's arrival at Washington. Lincoln well understood the desirability of getting as much support as possible from his erstwhile rival for the presidency. Even so, I could not believe that Lincoln would have imparted to Douglas a secret which he had carefully guarded from all except a few trusted friends and supporters. Even on the assumption that Lincoln had seen fit to share the secret of his inaugural utterance with Douglas, it seemed to me scarcely possible that Douglas could have repeated the exact words of Lincoln to the Diarist and that the Diarist in turn could have put them down in his diary without the slightest variation. The Diary included even the quotation marks. Such exactitude looked decidedly suspicious. It suggested that the passage in the Diary was almost certainly written at a later date, when the words in question had come to have their deep historical significance.

On March 11, 1861, the Diarist had another "long conversation" with Douglas. It related mainly to Fort Sumter, a circumstance easily comprehensible, as apparently authoritative announcements had just appeared that the new Lincoln Administration had decided to evacuate Fort Sumter. In reporting the conversation the Diarist said: "He [Douglas] is entirely of my mind that the fort ought to have been abandoned already, and that much valuable prestige has been lost by the new Administration, which might have been secured had orders been sent at once to Major Anderson to that effect. . . .

"Mr. Lincoln has assured Mr. Douglas positively, he tells me, that he means the forts shall be evacuated as soon as possible, and that all his Cabinet whom he has consulted are of the same mind excepting Mr. Blair, which is precisely what I had expected. Mr. Douglas says that the President sent for him after his speech of Wednesday [March 6] to assure him that he entirely agreed with all his views, and sympathized with its spirit. All he desired was to get the points of present irritation removed, so that the people might grow cool, and reflect on the general position all over the country, when he felt confident there would be a general demand for a National Convention at which all the existing differences could be radically treated. Meanwhile he did not see why the Executive should attempt to dispossess the seceded States of the forts occupied by them unless Congress insisted that he should, and gave him the means necessary for the work. 'I am just as ready,' he said to Mr. Douglas, 'to re-enforce the garrisons at Sumter and Pickens or to withdraw them as I am to see an amendment adopted protecting slavery in the Territories or prohibiting slavery in the Territories. What I want is to get done what the people desire to have done, and the question for me is how to find that out exactly.' "

Upon examining closely into the situation at the time that Lincoln was reported to have spoken to Douglas in the fashion thus attributed to him, I found it impossible to believe that Lincoln could have done so or that Douglas could have so reported to the Diarist. I could believe that Douglas might have construed something that Lincoln had said into a general endorsement of the speech which Douglas had made on Wednesday, March 6, in the Senate, but I could not believe that Lincoln had said that Sumter would be evacuated as soon as possible. Such an avowal of intention Lincoln was at that time carefully avoiding. Many of the men who surrounded him advised and desired that he should give such an order. Lincoln listened to their counsel, but he kept complete silence as to what he intended to do. Whether this silence was because he had not made up his mind as to what he ought to do or whether he was awaiting the proper moment for announcing his decision may be open to question. But there should be no doubt as to one point: he was not telling anybody what he finally intended to do. In the light of that circumstance, the statement in the Diary that Douglas said Lincoln had told him that Fort Sumter would be evacuated appeared to me as almost certainly an invention of subsequent date.

After discovering the suspicious-looking features of the Diarist's accounts of his relations with Seward and Douglas, as set forth in this and the preceding chapter, I reviewed once more all that the Diary contained in relation to Seward and Douglas. As a result of this examination I came to feel quite certain that the pen portraits were not the accidental result of entries made in a diary from day to day, but were the result of conscious design. The portrait of Seward appeared to be one drawn by a man who saw in his subject an enigma for whom he could have only a qualified and restricted admiration. That of Douglas, on the other hand, appeared to be the portrait of a man who commanded his personal sympathy and admiration. Both portraits appeared to me to show the marks of a perspective of later date than 1860–1861.

# XVI

In the five preceding chapters I have set forth in considerable detail the results of a critical examination of the Diary undertaken after the failure of my attempt to discover its authorship while proceeding upon the assumption that it is a genuine diary actually kept in 1860–1861. To me the cumulative effect of the examination appeared to leave no room for reasonable doubt. The Diary as published by the *North American Review* in 1879 was not an actual diary kept in 1860–1861. As already indicated at an earlier point, page 16, there appeared to be two possibilities. (1) It might be mere fiction. If so, it appeared likely to have been the work of some exceptionally clever literary man who had considerable personal knowledge about Washington during the Secession Winter and who had in addition made some use of contemporaneous materials, especially the newspapers of 1860–1861. (2) It might be that the Diary had as a nucleus a genuine diary, probably of a rather meager character which had been re-written and to which a good deal had been added from recollection and from invention. Such embellishments in the way of good stories, striking incidents, vivid pen portraits of well-known public figures, and shrewd, ostensibly contemporaneous comments upon the passing scene of 1860–1861 would naturally enhance the interest that a genuine but meager diary would not have produced.

The first of these possibilities I had already considered to some extent in my Indianapolis paper. The treatment I then gave it consisted largely in an examination of the reasoning put forth by E. L. Pierce, the biographer of Charles Sumner, in a paper read before the Massachusetts Historical Society in March, 1896. He argued that the Diary was "a fiction—nothing more nor less."[83]

Pierce's dislike for the Diary was clearly manifest. He did not like the ridicule the Diarist cast upon Charles Sumner. Pierce's arguments, aside from questioning the apparent knowledge and importance of the Diarist, were confined to two matters, both of which have already been mentioned. He reproduced, in extract or paraphrase, his own correspondence with Hiram Barney in 1886 about Barney's part in arranging for the interview which the Diarist claimed he had with Lincoln in New York City on February 20, 1861. It appeared clearly that Barney could not recall having played the role on that occasion which the Diarist ascribed to him. His inability to do so, I thought, might well be regarded as casting considerable doubt upon the authenticity of the Diary, for the incident in question was of a sort not likely to have been forgotten even after a lapse of twenty-five years. All the attendant circumstances seemed to me to make almost compulsory the recognition of an exception to the general rule against the acceptance of the testimony of very old men speaking from recollection long after the event. I found it difficult to believe that if Barney had actually arranged for a meeting between Lincoln and the Diarist at the time of Lincoln's visit to New York in 1861 he could ever have forgotten about the incident.

Pierce also asserted that the visit to the White House by the Diarist and the man from Montgomery and Charleston on the afternoon of March 7, 1861, could not have taken place on account of a reception for the diplomatic corps, an affair that he supposed to have been "a protracted ceremonial." As I have already tried to show, Pierce had good reason to question whether Barney did play the role attributed to him by the Diarist, but was quite mistaken in supposing that the diplomatic reception on March 7, 1861, precluded the possibility that the Diarist and the man from Montgomery and Charleston did see Lincoln later that afternoon at the White House.

Pierce's contention that the Diary is "a fiction—nothing more nor less" would appear to have called upon him to give the name of the man to whom he attributed it. He did not do so, or at least he did not include it in the printed proceedings of the Massachusetts Historical Society. Instead he put forward but did not discuss the "latest theory," apparently his own, that the Diary was the work of "an adventurer, recently deceased, who had much to do with newspapers and magazines, who had a career both in this country and in England, and who late in life figured in a scandalous trial in London." That man, he contended, "was able, by a general knowledge of social occasions and of the presence of public men in the two cities [Washington and New York] to give an air of probability to his production."

Believing that any satisfactory discussion of the theory that the Diary is merely fiction would require an attempt at the identification of the man who had produced it, I tried to identify the man Pierce had in mind. At the time of my Indianapolis paper I thought I had done so. I thought he referred to Henry Wikoff, "Chevalier Wikoff" as he was generally known during much of his life. From my study of Wikoff's career and character [84] I recognized that he did not fit exactly the thumbnail description given by Pierce, but finding a general resemblance and thinking that Pierce's information about the man he believed had concocted the Diary might have been meager and inexact, I thought that probably Wikoff was the man. What I learned about Wikoff, moreover, made me think that if the Diary was merely fiction Wikoff might well have been the man who produced it. I, accordingly, described the man and his strange career in my paper.

John W. Forney in his *Anecdotes of Public Men* has given a striking description of Wikoff.[85] "You might travel a long way before meeting a more pleasant companion than the cosmopolite Wikoff. He has seen more of the world than most men, has mingled with society of every shade and grade, has tasted of poverty and affluence, talks several languages fluently, is skilled in etiquette, art, and literature, and, with-

out proclaimed convictions, is a shrewd politician, who under-
stands the motives and opinions of others. . . . Ranging
through all society, he can talk of love, law, literature, and
war; can describe the rulers and thinkers of his time, can
gossip of courts and cabinets, of the *boudoir* and the *salon,*
of commerce and the Church, of the peer and the pauper, of
Dickens and Thackery, of Victor Hugo and Louis Blanc, of
Lamartine and Laboulaye, of Garibaldi and the Pope, of
Lincoln and Stanton, of Buchanan and Pierce, of the North
and the South, of the opera and the theatre, of General
Sickles and Tammany Hall, and of the inner life of almost
any capital in the world. With such gifts, aided by an air
*distingué,* a fine address and a manner after the English
model, Wikoff has the *entrée* in many circles which higher
intellect and deservings can never penetrate."

His career was as singular as his personality was exceptional. He was born into a wealthy family at Philadelphia in
1813. He wanted to go to Princeton but was sent to Yale by
his guardian. He was expelled from Yale about the opening
of his senior year. He then went to Cambridge and tried to
get into Harvard but was refused admittance. Union College
opened its doors to him, as in that day it did for a good
many men in similar plight, and so he graduated. After that
he studied law in Philadelphia but never practiced. For a
time he traveled considerably in the United States, especially
in the South, and then went to Europe in 1834. From that
time on he went back and forth to and from Europe so frequently that it was said of him late in life that he had crossed
the ocean more than eighty times. For some years he did
nothing in Europe but have a good time. He first attracted
public attention in 1840, when he brought Fannie Elsler, the
dancer, to the United States. Over her he and James Gordon
Bennett, of the *New York Herald* had the first of several
quarrels which mark the checkered relations of the two men,
at times close friends and fellow workers and again bitter
enemies. In 1845 he got an opportunity to interview Prince
Louis Napoleon Bonaparte while the Prince was a prisoner

of the July Monarchy in the fortress at Ham. Afterwards in the early days of the Second French Republic he used this as a starting point for a small book upon the life of the Prince.

Meanwhile he had drifted into journalism at Paris. Some of his articles, according to his own account, attracted the attention of Lord Palmerston, who sent for him. At Breadlands Palmerston made him an offer of employment *sub rosa* by the British Foreign Office. His job was to influence the Parisian and American press in a manner favorable to British interests. He was, according to his own account, remarkably successful on the Parisian side of the business and was just getting into action on the American side when he made the unpleasant discovery that Downing Street wanted to get rid of him. He was offered pay he had not yet earned to terminate the arrangement. This offer he declined. Instead he went to London and tried to get an interview with Palmerston. But Palmerston would not see him.

About this time Wikoff, always according to his own account, fell in love with a wealthy woman, the ward of Joshua Bates, the American-born manager of Baring Brothers and Co., the London bankers. The lady seems to have been a good deal of a coquette. One day she was willing to marry him, but the next day she was not yet ready. This state of affairs often repeated led Wikoff to follow her when she went to travel on the Continent. At Genoa, late in 1851, he conceived the madcap design of enticing the lady and her maid into some rooms he had rented and of holding them as prisoners until the lady would consent to marry him. She consented but upon release reported the matter to the British consul, who had Wikoff arrested on a charge of abduction.

The arrest and subsequent trial created a sensation. Wikoff was or professed to have been convinced that Lord Palmerston was at the bottom of his tribulation and that the Piedmontese government proceeded as it did for fear of losing British good will, which at that time was of great importance for Piedmont. Whatever the explanation, Wikoff was put on trial for abduction, convicted, and spent fifteen months in prison. After his release Wikoff, during the next few years, related his experiences in love and diplomacy in a series of books, published with slight variations and under different titles in England and the United States. The first of the series, *My Courtship and its Consequences*, attracted a great deal of attention in the United States and was among the best-sellers of the day. The English editions also excited some discussion. Wikoff particularly resented a *Times* editorial which called him a spy. But the English do not appear to have taken as much interest in Wikoff as his own countrymen did.

At intervals Wikoff was at Washington in the late 1850's. He appears to have been the man who served as intermediary between Buchanan and James Gordon Bennett when the *New York Herald* swung over to the support of Buchanan late in the presidential campaign of 1856. He was a friend of Dan Sickles and sat beside him when Sickles was on trial for the killing of Francis Barton Key, the nephew of the author of "The Star Spangled Banner." Late in 1860 Wikoff returned from a trip to Europe and published in February, 1861, a large-sized pamphlet dealing with slavery and secession under the title, *A Letter to Lord Palmerston*.

In my Indianapolis paper I expressed a pretty confident belief that E. L. Pierce looked upon Wikoff as the author of the Diary. Not being entirely sure about the matter I was anxious to arrive at certainty. My first effort yielded no result. The *Proceedings* of the Massachusetts Historical Society indicated that at the time Pierce's paper was read it was discussed by several members. Only one of them, my former teacher at Harvard, Albert Bushnell Hart, was still living. I went to him in the hope that he would be able to recall the discussion and could tell me whether Pierce had given the name of the man he suspected of concocting the Diary. But Professor Hart had no recollection of the discussion.

Several years later I did discover, partly by accident, the name of the man Pierce had in mind. In the manuscript division at Widener Library I found a small collection of E. L. Pierce papers. It at once occurred to me that they might enable me to discover the name of the man that Pierce had in mind. I figured that Pierce might have had separates of his paper made for distribution among his friends and that correspondence in regard to them might disclose the name of the man he suspected. I figured that in sending the separates he might in some instances have accompanied them with letters, that in some of those letters he might have mentioned the name of the man he suspected, and that some of his correspondents in replying might have alluded to the man by name.

On putting my conjecture to the test I found that Pierce had sent out separates, that at least seventeen of the recipients had written him in acknowledgment, and that their replies constituted a neat, alphabetically arranged bundle in the Pierce papers. Going through those replies in their alphabetical order disappointment grew as I proceeded. Toward the end I all but abandoned hope, for as yet none had said anything to indicate that Pierce had given any clue to the identity of the man I was seeking. The last letter was from Horace White. He gave the name. It was not Henry Wikoff. It was William Henry Hurlbert.[86]

At the moment I knew little about Hurlbert. It did not take me long to discover that, like Wikoff, he had had a singular career and that he had been a decidedly exceptional personality. Considerable attention to the man brought out the details of a career as singular and a personality as hard to comprehend as that of any man of his day. Much of his story reads more like fiction than fact. The main facts, however, are not open to question.[87]

Hurlbert was born at Charleston, South Carolina, in 1827. He graduated from Harvard College in 1847 and from the Harvard Divinity School in 1849. After two years spent in travel in Europe he became a Unitarian minister, serving a church for a short time. In that period he wrote several hymns that were afterward widely used. Turning from the ministry to literary pursuits he published in 1854 a book, *Gen-Eden or Pictures of Cuba,* wrote dramatic criticisms for the *Albion,* and was upon the editorial staff of *Putnam's Magazine.* During those years he appeared to be a decided opponent of slavery, criticizing the Southern institution sharply.

In 1857 he became an editorial writer on the *New York Times.* In that capacity he acquired considerable reputation for the brilliancy of his style and the extent of his widely varied information. Popular report attributed to him an ability to write simultaneously editorials upon three different subjects, writing a few words for each article in turn, while the copy boy carried the sheets from the editorial desk to the composing room as each was written. He also got a reputation for convivial habits. The popular impression in regard to him appeared to find confirmation when the *New York Times* on July 16, 1859, published its famous editorial, "The Defensive Square of Austrian Italy." In that once famous article Hurlbert, after an amazing display of topographical information about the theater of the war then raging in Northern Italy, in the latter part of the article mixed in sentences and parts of sentences intended for two other articles, the whole making up a jumble of nonsense that aroused the hilarity of rival editors.[88]

In 1860 Hurlbert left the *New York Times.* At about the same time his opinions seem to have undergone a decided change. He became a defender of slavery. It was reported that he was about to become the editor of the *New York Daily News,* then about the most virulent anti-Republican newspaper in New York City. Shortly after the fall of Fort Sumter he paid a visit to Charleston, apparently relying upon his recently expressed opinions and his connections there to protect him from molestation. While on the return journey, however, he was arrested by the Confederate authorities and for about a year was held as a prisoner at Richmond. In July, 1862, he contrived to escape and made his way to Washington. The method by which the escape was effected was never satisfactorily explained. There was some suspicion that bribery or belief on the part of some Confederate authorities that the cause of the Confederacy would be better served by his release than by his detention might have been the real explanation.

During the remainder of the Civil War Hurlbert was active in various ways, almost all of them marked by hostility to the Lincoln administration. He translated the Comte de Paris' first publication in regard to the war. He wrote and campaigned for McClellan in 1864. About that time he became an editorial writer on the *New York World*. In 1877 he became its editor-in-chief and held that important post until its purchase by Joseph Pulitzer in 1883.

In the *Galaxy* for January, 1869, Eugene Benson described Hurlbert, as he appeared to many observers at that period, in the first of a series of articles dealing with the leading editorial writers for the New York press, a series which included Park Godwin, George William Curtis, E. L. Godkin, and Theodore Tilton. According to Benson, Hurlbert was "the prince of persifleurs," "the Heine of our press." "Mr. Hurlbert," he said, "is a Théophile Gautier in a democratic society, where the political interests are dominant, and call the most unscrupulous and available talents. Being in New York he writes leading articles on politics and piety instead of art criticisms." Hurlbert's articles Benson described as alike exuberant, unscrupulous, and remarkable. The resonance of Hurlbert's style Benson found "equalled only by the fluency of his conversation."

After his separation from the *World* by Pulitzer Hurlbert went to Europe. Apparently he aspired to some diplomatic appointment. When disappointed he took his revenge upon Secretary of State Thomas F. Bayard, a former friend, in the first of a series of articles, "Letters to Prominent Persons," which began to appear in the *North American Review* in January, 1886. In 1888 he published a book, *Ireland under Coercion*, which pleased British Tories and displeased British Liberals. In like manner his *France and the Republic*, 1890, pleased the French monarchists and displeased the French republicans.

In 1891 Hurlbert got into serious difficulty in England. A suit was brought against him, *Evelyn vs. Hurlbert.* The plaintiff, a young woman, alleged that Hurlbert had seduced her under promise of marriage. She sought monetary damages. When the suit came to trial Hurlbert presented an amazing defense. He claimed that he had had in his employ a secretary who had cultivated the art of imitating his handwriting so successfully that the imitation could scarcely be distinguished from the original. The letters which the plaintiff presented in proof of her contention, many of them of a decidedly obscene character, Hurlbert contended were written by that secretary, who had somehow disappeared and could not be found. It is to be supposed that the jury, if permitted to examine the letters along with examples of Hurlbert's handwriting, must have been skeptical about Hurlbert's defense, for his writing was of a sort that would have defied close imitation.[89] In rendering its verdict the jury did not pass upon the validity of Hurlbert's defense. It gave a verdict in his favor on the ground that the evidence submitted by the plaintiff did not show that there had been any promise of marriage.

Shortly after the trial of *Evelyn vs. Hurlbert* Hurlbert left England for the United States. The apparent reason for his hurried departure was a decision of the British government to have him arrested upon a charge of perjury. After his return to the United States Hurlbert remained only a short time. Upon legal advice he left for Italy, where he remained until his death in 1895.

Hurlbert was unquestionably a man of great ability and of varied accomplishments. To many of his contemporaries, including a large number who were disposed to be friendly to him, he appeared to be decidedly unscrupulous. That he deserved the questionable reputation he bore during his lifetime would appear open to little doubt.

When I had before me pretty full information in regard to

133

Wikoff and Hurlbert I recognized in them the type of man who might well have attempted to perpetrate a literary and historical hoax in the form of a bogus diary purporting to have been kept in Washington and New York during the Secession Winter. Both had been in those cities much of the time during that period. Both had many personal contacts with the leading public men of that day. Both were experienced and exceptionally clever literary men. I accordingly asked myself the question: Could either Wikoff or Hurlbert in 1879 have concocted such a thing as "The Diary of a Public Man"?

After careful consideration my answer to the question was, No. Two considerations in particular influenced me in reaching that conclusion. One of the major difficulties encountered by anyone attempting to concoct a fraudulent diary is that at some points he will unconsciously allow to slip into his production some knowledge of matters which a genuine diarist writing at a given date could not possibly have had. The utmost precaution on the part of a talented concoctor can seldom, if ever, escape that pitfall. Unconsciously he refers to some event that has not yet happened; or he alludes to some state of affairs that has not yet come about; or he employs some form of expression that has not yet come into use.

Repeated examinations of the Diary failed to disclose any indubitable instances of such blunders. I did find two or three places in which it seemed possible that the Diarist had used a form of expression a little ahead of the time at which it came into common use. But none of them constituted a perfectly clear case. Apart from those possible exceptions the Diary appeared to be entirely free from the kind of error into which the concoctor of a fictitious diary would almost certainly fall. I recognized that if either Wikoff or Hurlbert had attempted to get up a fictitious diary he would undoubtedly have been as careful as seemed possible to avoid the pitfalls just indicated. But I could not believe that either of them, or anybody, could have been completely successful in the case of a diary purporting to belong to the Secession Winter. The difficulties of doing it for that momentous period were too great to be overcome.

My other reason for thinking that neither Wikoff nor Hurlbert could have concocted the Diary came from the way in which the Diary reflected the newspapers of 1860–1861. If either man had attempted to produce a fictitious diary purporting to have been kept during the Secession Winter he would undoubtedly have made some use of the newspapers of that day. But neither man was of the sort who would have spent the long hours required for the kind of detailed examination of newspapers that would have been necessary to make his production reflect the newspapers of 1860–1861 in the way that the Diary has done. One of the distinguishing features of the Diary, I had found, was that it reflected the newspapers of the day in a manner scarcely possible except for one who was reading them from day to day as they came from the press.

While continuing to recognize that various other arguments, pro and con, could be advanced as regards the supposition that the Diary might be mere fiction, I regarded the two tests just applied as acid tests. Neither Wikoff, nor Hurlbert, nor anybody else, I thought, could have produced it as a mere piece of the imagination. The Diary was not, as Pierce characterized it, "a fiction—nothing more nor less."

I also took into consideration some suggestions as to other possible authors of the Diary, upon the supposition that it is purely fictitious. One of the most interesting came from Bernard De Voto. He suggested that Allen Thorndike Rice, the editor of the *North American Review* might have written it. I found that suggestion of particular interest and gave it careful consideration.

Allen Thorndike Rice was born in Boston on June 18, 1851.[90] His parents were members of wealthy and leading families. Their marriage, which had occurred in 1850, turned out badly. Not long after Allen's birth his mother left her husband, taking the child with her. Three or four years later the husband obtained a divorce and after a long legal battle secured the custody of the child by a decision of the Massachusetts Supreme Court.

The determined mother, however, was not daunted by that decision. The boy, then nine years old, had been placed in a school at Nahant by his father. She contrived to get possession of him through a sensational episode. Details in regard to the affair, as reported in the newspapers at the time and in the recollections of his schoolmates, Henry Cabot Lodge and Robert Grant, are conflicting. It is clear, however, that the boy was abducted by a negro coachman, or a white man disguised as a negro, and delivered to his mother. She apparently put to sea with him, headed for Europe. For some unknown reason she returned to land, made her way to Canada, despite hot pursuit by detectives as far as the border, and ultimately reached Europe.

During four or five years spent in France and Germany with his mother, young Rice acquired so good a knowledge of French and German that he was reputed to speak both languages as well as he did his native tongue. In 1870 he was in Paris on the fourth of September and was an eye witness of the overthrow of the Second Empire. A little later he matriculated at Oxford, where he seems to have made an unusual impression upon his tutors and fellow students at Christ Church College. In 1873 he obtained a bachelor's degree and a few years later, but without further residence, a master's degree.

Returning to America after leaving Oxford, he quickly became a prominent social figure in New York, Boston, and Newport. His birth, wealth, attractive personal qualities, and keen enjoyment of social activities, secured for him immediate admission to the highest social circles. For a time he seemed destined to a career of prominence in smart society, but not in the least degree for that in which he subsequently figured.

Some time during 1877 he acquired control over the *North American Review* by purchase of the property. At that time the *Review* was continuing to maintain the form and preserve the character which had marked the previous sixty-two years of its existence. It was a quarterly published at Boston by James R. Osgood & Co., the leading publishing house, the successor of Ticknor and Fields. It was edited by a distinguished board of editors of which Henry Adams was the chief. Its contents consisted mainly of forty- or fifty-page articles written by members of the editorial board, or persons closely associated with them. Its appeal was exclusively to the scholarly interest of the intellectual élite of the country. Matters of current popular interest were seldom touched upon in its pages.

An article that appeared in the October, 1876, number of the *Review* seems to have paved the way for the opportunity which Rice seized upon shortly afterward. The article in question was entitled "The 'Independents' in the Canvass." By implication it advised Independents to vote for Tilden for president. That the article had led to a rupture between the editors and publishers was made plain in a publisher's notice. "The editors of the 'North American Review' having retired from its management, on account of a difference of opinion with the proprietors as to the political character of this number, the proprietors rather than cause an indefinite delay in publication, have allowed the number to retain the form which had been given it without committing the Review to the opinions expressed therein."

Soon after taking control of the *Review* Rice transformed it completely. He converted it into a monthly, removed it to New York, and began the publication of articles upon topics of current interest contributed in the main by persons whose knowledge or whose opinions were calculated to excite widespread interest. His list of contributors during the next decade included an amazingly large number of people of prominence. Among the many were Gladstone, Huxley, Renan, Emerson, Parkman, Froude, De Lesseps, Oliver Wendell Holmes, and nearly all of the prominent surviving generals of the Civil War. Nearly all the articles were upon topics that Rice had himself selected and then by personal solicitation had persuaded the contributors to write. The amount of editorial work that went into the *Review* was enormous. Rice fully earned the appellation of "hard-working editor." The efforts he put forth brought quick response. Almost at a bound the *North American Review* reached a circulation reported to be the largest enjoyed by any American monthly periodical.

Rice died in May, 1889, shortly before his forty-eighth birthday. He was just about to sail for St. Petersburg, having been appointed minister to Russia by President Benjamin Harrison. By his contemporaries he was always described as a man of exceptional talent and industry. Gladstone was said to have characterized him as the most fascinating young man he had ever met.

Recognizing that Rice had talent and interests that might have enabled him to become a highly successful writer of historical fiction and that there was a short period immediately after his return to America in which he could have been trying his hand at that kind of writing, it seemed to me, nevertheless, that four considerations ruled out the possibility that he actually did write the Diary.

Successful writing of historical fiction involves long and careful preparation. It can usually be accomplished only by writers of experience who have taken the time to delve deeply into large bodies of historical material. As a young man who could have had no personal knowledge about matters dealt with in the Diary, the period of preparation which Rice would have needed could not have been compressed into a short period. In the time between his return from Europe and his acquisition of control over the *North American Review* he could not possibly have undergone the needful preparation for writing the Diary.

Emphasis has already been placed upon two features of the Diary which seem to preclude the possibility that it could be altogether a piece of fiction. It reflects the newspapers of 1860–1861 in a way that could scarcely have marked the work of a writer of fiction, however long and careful his preparation. Anachronisms, the pitfall of historical fiction, are almost completely absent. If Rice at the period in question had attempted to concoct the Diary he might have used the newspapers to some extent but scarcely enough to have reflected them as the Diary did. He also would have blundered into more anachronisms than are to be found in the Diary.

A third consideration clearly indicates that Rice could not have written the Diary. If he had possessed in 1879, when the Diary was published, the large fund of information about the Civil War which he undoubtedly had in later years it is conceivable that he might have been able to concoct such a production as the Diary. But that information in the main came to him at a later date. It was acquired through his activities in procuring and editing the long series of Civil War articles which appeared in the *North American Review* while under his management. The Diary, however, was one of the earliest of the series.

The supposition that Rice concocted the Diary and then published it as authentic material for history would seem to involve a serious indictment against his moral integrity. Such action could scarcely be excused as the perpetration of an innocent literary hoax. It would have been a deliberate fraud. Nothing that I could learn in regard to Rice gave any occasion for believing that he was to that degree lacking in moral integrity. I could believe and had come to believe that on occasion he allowed himself some editorial license. But I could not believe that it reached the extent of actual fraud. Caution, moreover, i.e., the danger of getting caught, would have restrained him from personal participation in a fraudulent transaction.

Another interesting suggestion was that possibly John Hay might have written it. At about that period Hay was trying his hand at fiction. He had large knowledge about all Civil War matters, though his residence at Washington did not begin until shortly before the close of the period covered by the Diary. One consideration, however, seemed decisive against a possible Hay authorship. The hero of the Diarist was Stephen A. Douglas. John Hay would never have made a hero out of Douglas even in a work of fiction.

# XVII

Having come to the conclusion that neither the first nor the second of the three alternatives already mentioned was a tenable solution for the problem of the Diary, I came perforce to adopt the third alternative. In doing so, I recognized, however, that a final and definitive conclusion would not be possible unless I could find a man who had been in Washington during the Secession Winter and who, either by himself or with the aid of others, could have transformed a meager diary kept at that time into "The Diary of a Public Man."

Proceeding upon the search for such a man I decided to use a method analogous to that I had employed while trying to find the author of the Diary upon the basis of the first alternative. Now I would look into the Diary for the portrait of a man who had kept a meager genuine diary in 1860–1861 and had afterwards set himself to embellish it through recollection and the invention of good stories and striking incidents.

In adopting this method I recognized that the Diarist would doubtless have made a determined effort to conceal his identity. But I believed it could be discovered, for in the process the Diarist would almost inevitably have drawn two portraits of himself. One would be drawn primarily to make the Diary appear genuine. It would not correspond closely with the real self of its author. Much of it would be inserted mainly for the purpose of concealing his identity. The other portrait would be put into the Diary unintentionally and unconsciously. It would be done in the same way that writers of fiction almost invariably draw their own portraits in the stories they write. Sometimes such portraits are delineated in clear and distinct fashion. Sometimes the lines are vague and shadowy. But the portrait is there and can often be distinguished.

The method called for a new examination of the Diary to disclose the portrait that the Diarist had unintentionally and unconsciously drawn of himself. The striking features of this portrait could then be examined and set forth. After that had been done, search could be made for a man who fitted into the pattern. If such a man could be found the identity of the Diarist would be established.

Looking into the Diary for this portrait, it seemed to me that there could be little room for doubt in regard to thirteen points in the personality of the man I was seeking.

1. He must have been at Washington during the Secession Winter. This would have enabled him to keep an actual diary, probably of a meager character, which had served as the basis for the Diary.

2. He must have been a man of extensive personal acquaintance among the public men then at Washington. Hearsay or subsequent reading would not have enabled anyone without considerable personal acquaintance to fashion the pen portraits which make the Diary fascinating reading.

3. He must have been a man who had the diary habit. The Diary seems indubitably the work of a practiced hand.

4. He must have been a man of the world of wide experience. The comments of the Diarist in regard to Mrs. Lincoln and Mrs. Douglas, the inauguration ball, the shabby furnishings at the White House, could have come only from a man of the world of long experience.

5. He must have been a man who was conversant with the French language and literature. That the Diarist had such knowledge of the French language seemed unquestionable from the entry of February 26, 1861, wherein his report of a dinner-table conversation indicated that he had a ready knowledge of that language. That he was also familiar with French literature appeared scarcely less certain. Reporting the views expressed to him by Judah P. Benjamin on January 13, 1861, he remarked, "I could detect, I thought, a distinctly French turn of thought, but much that he said struck me as eminently sound and sagacious." Less tangible but neverthe-

less convincing evidence to the same effect appeared in the tone and atmosphere of the Diary taken as a whole. It has a distinctly French cast with a marked resemblance to French memoires of the post-Napoleonic period.

6. He must have been a man who was in 1860–1861 a strong Unionist in sympathy, but not antagonistic to the South on sectional or anti-slavery lines.

7. He must have been a man of considerable knowledge and interest in politics, but not a decidedly party man. As already pointed out the Diarist always spoke of the parties, Republican, Whig, or Democratic, in purely objective terms, never in a way to indicate that he identified himself with any of them. Even his account of how Lincoln consulted him as to Cabinet appointments did not exhibit any indication of a party allegiance.

8. He must have been a man decidedly interested in business affairs. The Diarist exhibited this aspect of his personality in his report about his interview with Lincoln in New York on February 20, 1861. Allusion having been made to Fernando Wood's idea that if disunion came New York City should become "a free city" after the fashion of Hamburg, the Diarist then characterized such suggestions as "visionary plans" and told Lincoln that "the only importance I attribute to them was that they illustrated the necessity of getting our commercial affairs back into a healthy condition as early as possible." On another occasion, even before the Confederate government had been formally organized, he expressed fear that it would establish "its free trade system" and thereby do "irreparable damage" to the "great manufacturing interests of the country." A little later he wrote: "The distress at home grows hourly worse and worse. And the preposterous tariff which they have assumed to establish at Montgomery points to a still worse state of things." He was also much concerned lest Confederate action in regard to patents and the coasting trade would be highly injurious to the material interests and prosperity of the country.

9. He must have been a New Yorker or at any rate a man

well conversant with the leading men and with conditions in New York City. The questions Lincoln addressed to the Diarist in the interview at New York would have been propounded only to one who knew the city well. The Diary is replete with mention of prominent New Yorkers in a way that implies personal acquaintance. Many are mentioned by name, e.g., W. H. Aspinwall, Moses Grinnell, Simeon Draper, and Hiram Barney. Others are indicated by symbol, e.g., "Mr. Aspinwall's lawyer," "S——, with a face as long as his legs," who was anxious over patent matters, "Mr. C——," who was Lincoln's host at the opera, and the Diarist's own "cousin V——," who reported how Lincoln appeared and acted on that occasion.

10. He must have been a man who felt a strong dislike for the Blairs, for Senator Edward D. Baker, of Oregon, and for Edward M. Stanton. "I do not like any of the Blairs, and indeed I know nobody who does," the Diarist recorded on February 25, 1861, a remark he repeated as if for emphasis, on March 4. His dislike for Baker was expressed by calling him "that noisy and vulgar cockney, Orator Puff" and by saying, "I met the man to-day as I passed into the National [Hotel] and I really could hardly speak to him civilly." His dislike for Stanton was reflected in his report of a conversation on February 25, 1861: "as I was crossing Fourteenth Street, I met the Attorney-General, who stopped me to ask if I had seen the President-elect since he 'crept into Washington.' It is impossible to be more bitter or malignant than he is; every word was a very ill-suppressed sneer, and it cost me something to keep my temper in talking with him even for a few moments."

11. He must have been a man who distrusted and feared the influence of extremists on both sides of the crisis over secession. His disapproval of Southern fire-eaters, such as Toombs and Wigfall, was scarcely more pronounced than for radical Republicans, such as Sumner, the Blairs, and Ben Wade. His marked dislike for extremists on both sides was accentuated by a manifest preference for moderate men,

143

whether Southerners such as James L. Orr, John Bell, and W. C. Rives, or Northerners such as Seward, Cameron, Douglas, and Thurlow Weed.

12. He must have been a man who would have taken personal satisfaction in casting ridicule upon Caleb Cushing, Pierre Soulé, and especially upon Charles Sumner. On December 29, 1860, the Diarist wrote: "B—— has seen Cushing since he got back from Charleston and tells me that he never saw a man who showed clearer traces of having been broken down by sheer fright. 'He is the boldest man within four walls, and the greatest coward out of doors,' said B——, 'that I ever knew in my life!' " The anecdote about Soulé, told with evident relish by the Diarist in his entry for February 26, 1861, was manifestly reported for the purpose of casting ridicule upon that bombastic and wily individual. The desire of the Diarist to make Sumner appear ridiculous is clearly manifested in the Diary entries for February 28 and March 3, 1861. In them he tells, in a way to make Sumner appear highly ridiculous, how Sumner wrote a note to Lincoln "alarmish and mysterious in tone, bidding Mr. Lincoln, for particular reasons, to be very careful how he went out alone at night," how Lincoln characterized Sumner as "just my idea of a bishop," and how Sumner, in an effort to enlist the assistance of the Diarist for the fight against the appointment of Cameron to a place in Lincoln's Cabinet, exhibited in striking fashion his vehemence, pomposity, and assumption of superior moral rectitude.

13. He must have been a man who in 1860–1861 was upon at least fairly intimate terms with Seward, for whom he had a qualified admiration, and with Douglas, for whom his admiration was in every respect deep and sincere.

# XVIII

My endeavor to find a man who would meet the requirements set forth in the preceding chapter began before I had fully formulated them. Starting upon the basis of a few of the more obvious ones, I was fortunate enough to discover a possibility after only a short search. But turning possibility into reasonable certainty proved difficult and time consuming. The evidence was not easy to get at; much of it was in private hands; at all stages of the endeavor there appeared to be a prospect that a little further investigation in another direction might bring to light some document that would be decisive for the whole problem of the Diary.

My start came through an instance of "serendipity," a word coined by Horace Walpole. He defined it as "the faculty of making happy and unexpected discoveries by accident."[91] While engaged upon a quite different pursuit I happened upon a man who had been in Washington during the Secession Winter and upon intimate terms with William H. Seward. As he was quite a different sort from any I had thought of as possibly the Diarist, it was with decided skepticism that I began my scrutiny as to whether he might be the man I was seeking.

The first step in the process of determining whether this possibility was the man in question or only another must-be-excluded took the form of a journey to Auburn to examine the Seward papers, now in the possession of a grandson, who kindly permitted me to examine them. The result was not particularly encouraging. I did find a few things that confirmed what I had already discovered about the intimacy between Seward and the man in whom I was interested. I did discover evidence upon one important matter which gave additional reason for belief that I might be upon the right track. But none of the new evidence served to remove the doubt I still felt. That doubt had been somewhat diminished but not removed.

My next step was to look more fully than hitherto into the family connections of the man I had in mind in order to see if among his descendants and relatives I could find any of his papers, especially those of 1860–1861 and 1879. That process, pursued as opportunity offered over a period of fifteen years, finally brought a decisive result. I became convinced that the man I had at first regarded as only a doubtful possibility was in fact the Diarist.

The man in question was Samuel Ward. To the general public in 1879 he was known chiefly through his appellation, the King of the Lobby, a title that concealed rather than revealed a unique figure in the life of the day. Almost forgotten by the present generation, his memory was recently revived through the publication of *Uncle Sam Ward and his Circle* by his niece Mrs. Maud Howe Elliott, the Grand Old Lady of Newport. By good fortune I met that remarkable woman about the time that she began to assemble the materials from which she afterwards wrote her fascinating book. Appreciating the reason for my interest in her uncle, she kindly permitted me to examine all of the many letters she gathered from her uncle's numerous relatives for use in preparing her book, a favor I was able to repay only in part by aiding her somewhat in gathering materials from outside of her family circle.

Samuel Ward,[92] fourth of the name, was born in New York City on January 27, 1814. He sprang from distinguished lineage. His paternal great grandfather had been governor of Rhode Island and a member of the Continental Congress; his grandfather was a lieutenant-colonel in Washington's army. His own father, also Samuel Ward, was head of the banking firm of Prime, Ward and King, a firm which played a role in the banking circles of the 1830's and 1840's somewhat similar to that played fifty years later by J. P. Morgan and Co.

Brought up in a family circle that included three sisters, all of whom grew to be distinguished women in their generation and one of whom, Julia Ward Howe, by her "Battle Hymn of the Republic," was to become a beloved national and international character, Sam Ward at an early age began to exhibit those qualities of mind which in later life astonished and delighted those of his contemporaries included in the wide circle of his friends.

At nine years of age he was sent to the famous Round Hill School at Northampton, Massachusetts, which had recently been established on the lines of a German gymnasium by George Bancroft, later the distinguished historian, and Joseph Cogswell, whose long service at the Lenox Library blazed the trail for the New York Public Library of today.

At fourteen he entered Columbia College, now Columbia University, graduating in 1831. While there, or in the year following, he developed a decided aptitude for mathematics and a liking for literature. Numerous contributions along mathematical lines for Robert Walsh's *American Quarterly Review* and a chance opportunity to display his mathematical prowess as examiner for the Board of Examiners at the West Point annual examinations led Sylvanus Thayer, the Father of West Point, to offer him a post as assistant professor of mathematics at the Academy. This offer Ward declined on the ground that while equal to the task along some lines he was deficient as regards engineering mathematics. He made good use of the offer, however, to persuade his father to send him to Europe for further study. Thither he went in the fall of 1832 with letters of introduction from Albert Gallatin to some of the most distinguished French scholars of the day, among them Arago, the Perpetual Secretary of the *Académie des Sciences.*

Except for a short visit home Ward remained in Europe four years. The first two were spent mainly at Paris. During the first of them he paid close attention to his studies in mathematics and literature, adhering closely to his puritanical bringing up, except as to music and the theater, and making the acquaintance of distinguished scholars. At that time

147

he purchased from Madame Legendre the mathematical books of her famous husband which he afterwards gave to the Astor Library and which are still consulted by mathematicians at the New York Public Library. During his second year at Paris his manner of life changed. Without forsaking his intellectual interests he participated somewhat in the convivial life of the traditional *bon vivant* student at Paris and began to develop that delight in good dinners, good wine, and good company for which he later became famous. At the same time he began the practice he constantly followed of spending money freely whenever it was available for the satisfaction he took in giving pleasure to friends and interesting acquaintances.

The third and fourth years were spent largely in Germany. At Berlin Henry Wharton made him an attaché of the American embassy and enabled him to make interesting acquaintances. At Dresden, in company with the Ticknors, he moved much in court circles. While at Heidelburg he met Longfellow, who was then making his second sojourn in Europe in further preparation for his professorship at Harvard. The close friendship between the two men which then began continued until Longfellow's death nearly fifty years later. Their frequent exchange of visits was interspersed by a prodigious correspondence, at times carried on almost daily.[93] Despite his absorption in other pursuits Ward contrived to get a Ph.D. in mathematics at Tübingen, writing his dissertation in Latin. Toward the end he passed a short time in England, where he began to develop the friendships among notable English people that were later to become an important element in his life.

During all of those four years Ward traveled extensively, everywhere contriving without apparent effort to meet scores of celebrities and to participate in the social life of the most exalted circles. Whether he was at Paris, Berlin, or Dresden, in England, Italy, or Spain, he somehow managed to meet socially and intellectually important people to an extent that would appear astonishing if related in a work of fiction.

Among the many he met were Joseph Bonaparte, Ole Bull, Paganini, Rachel, the Duchess of Abrantes (Madame Junot), Jules Janin, Vogelstein the painter, Lindenea the astronomer, John Murray the publisher, Ludwig Tieck, Baron Stroganoff, and Friedrich Gauss, a mathematician whom Ward later pronounced the Newton of the nineteenth century.[94]

Returning to New York in 1836 Ward there led for a few years a life of mingled pleasure and dissatisfaction. His bent for mathematical, literary, and artistic pursuits found expression in occasional public addresses, contributions to magazines, and in considerable literary brokerage. Among the beneficiaries of his mediation was his friend Longfellow, who was as yet quite unknown to most editors. He was able to place a good many of Longfellow's early poems at prices which now seem ridiculously low, but were at that time well above the prevailing rates. A gratifying recognition of his standing as an intellectual came in the form of election to Phi Beta Kappa by the Harvard chapter. In affairs of the heart he was likewise fortunate, marrying in January, 1838, Emily, the daughter of William B. Astor, then the richest man in the United States.

The fly in the ointment came from "irksome avocations" forced upon Ward by his father, the banker, who insisted that the young man should prepare for future responsibilities by entering the employ of Prime, Ward and King. Required to devote long hours to business details that did not interest him, he chafed under the compulsion and longed for freedom.

The death of his father in 1839 was the first in a series of misfortunes that marked the next decade in Ward's life. Not really interested in banking and adversely affected by the situation of the times he allowed the family fortune to slip away. Before financial catastrophe finally fell other misfortunes came upon him. In 1841 his wife died. A second marriage two years later brought about estrangement from the Astor family and the surrender of his young daughter to the control of her mother's family. His second wife, née Medora Grymes, a dazzling Southern beauty, met Ward's financial reverses with equanimity for a time. But presently a change came, estrangement followed, and she departed for Europe with the two young sons of the couple. At the end of the decade the brilliant prospects of his earlier years had disappeared; for Ward there was apparently no future in New York.

In that situation Ward joined the gold rush to California. His life there is the obscure period of his career, for he wrote few letters at that time and those that have been preserved tell little about what he did. Some of the obscurity has been removed for a portion of the period through an interesting discovery recently made by Dr. Carvel Collins of Harvard who found in an obscure New York newspaper a series of letters by an anonymous writer describing some of his California experiences. Careful study of the letters disclosed convincing evidence that they were written by Ward. The Stanford University Press has just issued them under the title *Sam Ward in the Gold Rush*.

These letters, however, cover only one phase of Ward's California career. For other parts of it, in the absence of reliable information, rumor has been busy. According to rumor, he made a new fortune and then lost it; living for a considerable time among the Indians and exercising his remarkable linguistic talent, he learned a fabulous number of Indian dialects. The one sure thing about this period in Ward's life appears to be that he returned to the East about 1854–1856 no better in fortune than at his departure in 1849.

During the next few years Ward tried without much success a brokerage business in Wall Street. At one time he engaged in a romantic journey to Mexico in a vain endeavor to save the life of a Californian adventurer who had participated in an unsuccessful attempt to bring about one more revolution in that then distracted country. On another occasion he accompanied as secretary the diplomatic mission to Paraguay which, backed by American warships, "negotiated" a satisfactory settlement of an American claim against that country. In 1860 he went to Washington to look after the interests of some claimants in the disputes then raging over the land titles to highly valuable mining properties in California. In that capacity he appears to have been the author of an anonymous pamphlet which criticized severely the course pursued by Edward M. Stanton as the representative of Attorney General Jeremiah S. Black.[95] On a visit to London in 1859 or 1860 Ward made the acquaintance of William H. Russell, the famous war correspondent of the *Times*. Writing many years later Russell recalled the circumstances of their first meeting:

"One night in the summer of 1860, I think, I was sitting alone in my study, when I heard a ring at the front door, and as it was past 10 o'clock, and as I was not expecting visitors, I said to the servant, 'Not at home.' But the door was already open and a voice I loved dearly cried: 'Only five minutes, William; I have brought an American friend who desires above all things to see and know you.' It was Thackery who spoke, and he was always welcome. Taking my hand and putting it in the palm of his companion's he said: 'This is Mr. Sam Ward, of New York, nominally a citizen of the world—the rest you will find out for yourself.' It was near 2 o'clock ere the visitors left."[96]

When Russell came to the United States on the eve of the Civil War, in order to report for the *Times* upon the crisis over secession and upon the war, if war should come, Ward performed friendly services for him in New York and at Washington. A little later he accompanied Russell on the famous tour of the Southern Confederacy upon the morrow of the fall of Fort Sumter which Russell reported in his dispatches to the *Times* and in his book, *My Diary, North and South*. During the war Ward was frequently in Washington but apparently spent most of his time in New York. Hostile witnesses accused him of engaging in stock speculations of which they did not approve.

Shortly after the close of the Civil War Ward entered upon that part of his career by which he came to be most widely known among his contemporaries. Within a short time he became the King of the Lobby. That title came to him in large degree because as a lobbyist he got results for his clients by methods which no other lobbyist could employ with anything like equal success. Acquainted with everybody of importance at Washington and on intimate terms with many of the most influential men of the day, he exercised the art of persuasion through his engaging personality. His dinners became famous for good food, rare wines, distinguished company, and the sparkling wit of their host. That he did not conform in all particulars to the usual type of lobbyist is attested by his letter of February 27, 1874, to Longfellow.

"When I see you again I will tell you how a client, eager to prevent the arrival at a committee of a certain member before it should adjourn at noon, offered me $5000 to accomplish his purpose which I did, by having his boots mislaid while I smoked a cigar and condoled with him until they would be found at 11.45! I had the satisfaction of a good laugh, a good fee in my pocket, and of having prevented a conspiracy."[97]

As a lobbyist Ward was a unique figure.[98] His success lay in the persuasive power of his unusual personality. Operating at a time when there was much corruption in legislative matters at Washington and when lobbyists were commonly regarded as its chief agents, he escaped any serious imputation as to the honesty of the methods he employed. Not all of his activities as a lobbyist were exerted in behalf of private interests. When Secretary of the Treasury Hugh McCulloch was endeavoring to induce Congress to pass legislation for the restoration of specie payments he was reported to have employed Ward's services. William M. Evarts, while secretary of state, solicited and obtained his help in seeking to fathom De Lesseps' designs as regards Panama.[99] One of Ward's proudest assertions in later years was that he had aided in preventing the impeachment of Andrew Johnson by an early discovery of the plans of the anti-Johnson leaders, by carrying that news to the White House, and by the advice he gave as to the selection of counsel for the trial.[100]

In the intervals between his lobbying activities at Washington Ward did considerable traveling at home and abroad and spent much time at New York, Newport, and Boston. While so engaged he constantly played a role most congenial to him. As occasion offered he performed valuable services for many of his friends. An example was afforded by the skillful manner in which as a "lyrical broker" he obtained the payment of four thousand dollars from Bonner, of the *New York Ledger,* for Longfellow's "Hanging of the Crane."[101] Many foreigners of distinction or of exalted social position renewed former acquaintance with him or brought letters of introduction to him and he in turn saw that they met the right people. The young Lord Rosebery on several visits to America was much in Ward's company.[102] That he found Ward stimulating and congenial he attested in some verses published at the time. An editorial note which accompanied them called the picture they presented "a very good portrait of the far famed uncle."

> No more shalt thou approach my bed,
> A bandit's hat upon thy head,
> Beneath whose brim there beams an eye
> That puts to shame the brilliant tie;
> Beneath one arm a trout, alack!
> The other holds a canvas-back;
> The pockets bulge with products rare,
> French novels, prints, and caviare,
> Two manuscripts of odes and bets,
> Old bills of fare and cigarettes,
> Two thousand-dollar notes—ye gods!
> Welcker's accounts, green pepper-pods
> And pressing calls to various duties
> From railways, Senators, and beauties.
>
> And then, perhaps, thy bursting brain
> Reveals the treasure room again,
> And recollections, lightly move
> With tales of horror and of love,
> Carry the listener swiftly through
> From Cochin China to Peru

And further yet, as in a trance
From memory slightly to romance,
He hears thee clothe the arid fact
And scorns the fools who are exact,
He's borne aloft from Picadilly
To California—willy nilly—
He sees thee change without a creak
To banker, sportsman, or casique.
He sees thee read with deep emotion
The burial service in mid-ocean
Or play with one hand on thy knife,
A ruined miner for thy life.
By Tennyson or "Longo" sought,
Probing a jockey's inward thought,
Counselling statesmen on finesse,
Counselling ladies on their dress,
A wit, a scholar, and a poet,
A rake, we fear, a friend we know it;
It is the lion and the lamb,
And there's your portrait, Uncle Sam.[103]

Amid his many activities at this time Ward did not entirely forget his own literary aspirations. A volume of his poems, *Lyrical Recreations,* which was published in England in 1865, was re-issued in a revised and enlarged form in 1871, and again in 1883.

About 1880 Ward terminated his career as a lobbyist and removed the scene of his principal activities to New York City. There in a short time he made a new fortune, said to have amounted to about $750,000. This came from successful speculation in stocks, an occupation in which he was aided by the advice, and perhaps at times by the financial assistance, of James R. Keene, then in the full tide of his astonishing career as a stock speculator. In his California days Ward, as often during the course of his career, had on one occasion played the part of a good Samaritan by nursing Keene through a serious illness.

With plenty of money at his disposal and no clients to serve, Ward now had opportunity to indulge to the full his propensity for entertaining his friends and for showering gifts upon them and his numerous relatives, especially his sisters and nieces. As sponsor and adviser he was in large degree responsible for launching his nephew, F. Marion Crawford, upon his career as a novelist. In the character of Mr. Bellingham, Ward appeared in Crawford's *Doctor Claudius*.[104]

Early in 1882 Ward met with his final financial disaster. His recently won fortune was swept away through the failure of a Wall Street firm in which he had become a silent partner. In order to protect himself against threatened litigation he went to Europe. In England and in Scotland he lived for some months as the welcome guest of Lord and Lady Rosebery. Under their urging he began his autobiography with Lady Rosebery acting as amanuensis. The manuscript, mainly in her handwriting, recounts his career down to about 1840. While with the Roseberys at London Ward mingled freely in London society and according to some reports was the lion of the social season. Late in the summer of 1883 he went to Italy to be with his sister, Mrs. Terry. He died at Pegli in May, 1884.

A man of many talents, Ward's most unusual talent was perhaps his capacity for friendship. Intimate friendships bound to him large numbers of men and women of many different sorts. Included among the many were Longfellow, Washington Irving, Thackery, William H. Russell, James A. Garfield, William M. Evarts, S. L. M. Barlow, Thomas F. Bayard, Lord and Lady Rosebery, Emperor Don Pedro of Brazil. All of them found in him a congenial spirit and freely acknowledged a debt of gratitude for his friendship.

In the quality of his mind and in the scope of his intellectual and artistic interests Ward was an exceptional man. Henry Adams in his *Education* said: "Few figures on the Paris stage were more entertaining and dramatic than old Sam Ward, who knew more of life than all the departments of the Government together, including the Senate and the Smithsonian."[105] Highly proficient in mathematics at an early age he maintained in later years a considerable interest in that subject and in kindred fields. The extent and character of his attainments in language and literature were a constant surprise and delight to his friends. He spoke fluently French, German, Spanish, and Italian and was well versed in the literature of those languages. Throughout life he read for pleasure the Greek and Latin poets, especially Horace. His letters to Garfield were often written in Latin.[106] His acquaintance with English poetry enabled him to form critical judgments which commanded the respectful attention of his friend Longfellow, who frequently submitted his own poems for advance criticism and not infrequently adopted the suggestions Ward made. A prodigious memory enabled Ward to quote instantly not only little bits but long passages from his favorite writers. William H. Russell wrote in his diary: "What a wonderful man Sam Ward is! Today I was trying to find a passage in Dante's 'Inferno' which I remembered but vaguely. In came Sam Ward, and I mentioned my difficulty. He quoted the passage in Italian out of his head, and others as well which he thought might be useful."[107]

From the foregoing sketch the reader will readily perceive that Sam Ward was a man who might have produced "The Diary of a Public Man." In the following chapter I shall endeavor to answer the question whether he did do so.

# XIX

From what has been said my readers will understand how I reached the conclusion that Sam Ward must have been the Diarist if he fitted perfectly into the pattern formed by the thirteen points in the personality of the Diarist as set forth in chapter seventeen. While other arguments might have a bearing upon the matter, I felt that the acid test would be the degree in which he conformed to those points. Failure to meet satisfactorily any one of them would cast grave doubt about his connection with the Diary. Perfect conformity, on the other hand, would be decisive. So believing, I proceeded to make the test.

1. He must have been at Washington during the Secession Winter. About that matter there could be no doubt. Notes and letters from Ward to Seward and Barlow show conclusively his presence in Washington at that time.[108]

2. He must have had an extensive acquaintance among public men at Washington. Ward's flair for getting such acquaintances wherever he might be and the contents of his notes to Seward indicate clearly his conformity to that point.

3. He must have been a man who had the diary habit. That Ward was at least an intermittent diarist would appear to admit of no doubt. Three diaries kept by him at different times have been preserved.[109] It seems highly probable that others were among the papers destroyed after his death by his nephew-in-law, David Prescott Hall. Late in his life rumor reported that he had kept a diary for many years and that, when published, it would make him an American Pepys. If any such diary ever existed it probably disappeared along with the bulk of his papers.

4. He must have been a man of the world of wide experi-

ence. That Ward met this requirement the sketch of his career in the preceding chapter fully attests.

5. He must have been a man thoroughly conversant with the French language and literature. That Ward met this requirement also admits of no doubt.

6. He must have been a man who in 1860–1861 was a strong Unionist in sympathy, but not antagonistic to the South on sectional or anti-slavery lines. Here again Ward exactly conformed. While strongly opposed to secession, he did not share the anti-slavery views of his friends in the North. His attitude at the time covered by the Diary appears to have been exactly that which he maintained during the Civil War, when he was regarded by many as a Copperhead.[110] He thought that the South, in rushing into secession, was acting precipitately and unwisely, but that its action was only natural in the face of what he regarded as Northern disregard of Southern rights.

7. He must have been a man of considerable knowledge and interest in politics, but not a decided party man. Here too Ward conformed. In early life he had usually voted Whig, but without any pronounced party feeling. By 1860 he had become a Democrat but, as before, without strong party spirit. His party label did not at any time prevent him from cooperating with men of other parties or from enjoying the friendship and confidence of their leaders.

8. He must have been a man decidedly interested in business affairs. While less interested in business than in literature and in his friendships, Ward was by no means oblivious to the importance of business even before entering upon his career as a lobbyist. Business matters such as those about which the Diarist was especially apprehensive—the tariff, the coasting trade, patents, and postal affairs—would have interested him at any time.

9. He must have been a New Yorker, or at any rate a man who was conversant with leading men and with conditions in New York City. That Ward was such a man was obvious. He was a New Yorker who knew his city well.

10. He must have been a man who felt a strong personal dislike for the Blairs, for Senator Edward D. Baker of Oregon, and for Edward M. Stanton. Here again Ward fitted into the pattern. While concrete documentary evidence about his feeling as to the Blairs was lacking, the presumption that he did dislike them I found was overwhelmingly strong. They represented exactly the type to which Ward was hostile, radical Republicans intent upon no compromise with the South on any issue and bent upon coercion.

In the case of Baker, as in that of the Blairs, documentary evidence to show a dislike on the part of Ward was lacking. That he did dislike Baker would appear, however, to admit of no doubt. Baker's general attitude was distasteful to him. As a former Californian, who sympathized with the political and personal enemies that Baker had made during his California career, Ward must have shared their distaste for Baker and his florid oratory.

That Ward at about the time when the Diary was put into shape for publication did feel an intense dislike for Stanton would seem to admit of no possible doubt. The manner in which Stanton, as the representative of Attorney General Black, had acted in the legal disputes over California land titles in 1860 aroused intense resentment on the part of claimants for whom Ward had acted at Washington. At a later date Stanton had behaved with his characteristic meanness toward Ward's friend, William H. Russell. Still later Stanton had been among the most virulent and unscrupulous of the men who tried to bring about the impeachment of Andrew Johnson, to whom Ward, at least in his own opinion, had given invaluable support.

11. He must have been a man who had distrusted and feared the influence of extremists on both sides in the crisis over secession. In that crisis Ward, as nearly always throughout his life, occupied a middle position. By temperament, too, he disliked extremists of all sorts. Fire-eating secessionists such as Wigfall and Toombs, despite his sympathy with the South on the broad general issue between the sections, did not

command any of his sympathy. Anti-slavery men of the virulent sort, such as Sumner, Wade, and the radical Republicans in general, were equally distasteful to him.

12. He must have been a man who would have taken personal satisfaction in casting ridicule upon Caleb Cushing, Pierre Soulé, and especially Charles Sumner. Documentary evidence to show the precise reasons why Ward should have desired to ridicule Cushing and Soulé was not available. But he knew the men or knew enough about them to understand how readily they laid themselves open to ridicule. Pictures of them in terms of ridicule would add spice to almost any literary production.

That Ward would have taken keen delight in concocting the picture of Charles Sumner that appears in the Diary admitted of no doubt.[111] As young men Sumner and Ward had seen a good deal of each other. They moved in the same circles and friendly letters passed between them. After Sumner entered upon his political career their friendly relations continued, despite Ward's dislike for Sumner's views and attitude and Sumner's dislike for nearly everybody who did not share his own opinions. But thereafter there was a difference. Each looked upon the other as in part personal friend and in part political enemy. Knowing Sumner thoroughly well, appreciating to the full how naturally Sumner laid himself open to ridicule, and feeling strong dislike for the views and policies which Sumner represented, Ward would have welcomed and utilized to the full such an opportunity as the Diary offered to make Sumner appear in a ridiculous light.

13. He must have been a man who in 1860–1861 was upon at least fairly intimate terms with Seward, for whom he had a qualified admiration, and with Douglas, for whom his admiration was in every respect deep and sincere. Ward met this requirement as regards both men.

Proof that Ward was upon intimate terms with Seward during the Secession Winter can be found in the notes Ward wrote to Seward at that time.[112] The Gwin Memoirs, to be cited presently, add further proof.

The proof of intimacy between Douglas and Ward in 1860–1861, I found not so ample but enough to indicate at least friendly relations. When Douglas gave a dinner in honor of William H. Russell for a small group of friends Ward was one of the guests.[113]

Finding that Ward fitted into the pattern for all of the thirteen points and that the proof was overwhelmingly convincing as to nearly all of them, I felt bound to conclude that, except for one possibility, Ward must have been the Diarist.

The one possibility was that some other person might be found who also fitted into the pattern. If so, it might be argued that he rather than Ward might have been the Diarist. Looking into this possibility with great care I could find only one person who might have been such a man.

Henry S. Sanford, already mentioned at an earlier point, met many of the thirteen points of the pattern. At about the time the Diary was published in the *North American Review* Sanford was in the habit of visiting Newport frequently. There he might have met and come to be upon intimate terms with Allen Thorndike Rice, the editor of the *Review*, who was also a frequent visitor at Newport. Together they might have transformed a genuine diary which Sanford had kept while at Washington during the Secession Winter into "The Diary of a Public Man."

After careful consideration I rejected that possibility as untenable. Sanford conformed to many but not to all the points of the pattern. In regard to one of them he manifestly did not fit into the picture. Indebted to Seward for his appointment as minister to Belgium in 1861 and on terms of devoted friendship with him, Sanford would never have drawn the portrait of Seward that the Diarist drew.

Having found that Ward fitted into the pattern at all thirteen points and that nobody else I could discover did likewise, I came to the conclusion that indubitably Ward must have been the Diarist.

This conclusion I found further sustained by several other striking and convincing considerations. They will be set forth in the following chapter.

# XX

Why did the Diary stop with the entry for March 15, 1861? No satisfactory answer appeared in sight until I got on the trail of Sam Ward. Then the answer presently became plain. Ward was away from Washington, save for possibly two or three days, for a considerable period right after the date when the Diary terminated. When William H. Russell, the *Times* correspondent, landed in New York on March 16, 1861, Ward met him there.[114] Shortly afterwards he joined Russell at Charleston and accompanied him upon his famous trip through the Confederate States.[115] That the Diary stopped just at the time when Ward was no longer constantly in Washington did not look to me like a coincidence. On the contrary, that circumstance appeared to afford strong additional reason for believing that Ward must have been the Diarist.

In the Diary as published by the *North American Review* the names of persons mentioned were often concealed by the use of dashes or initial letters. As previously indicated an early endeavor to discover the identity of these persons yielded little result. Despite considerable effort, satisfactory identification appeared to be possible only in three out of the thirty-two or thirty-three instances in question.

After turning to the view that Sam Ward was probably the Diarist, but before reaching a definitive conclusion, I went into the matter again. In doing so I argued that if Ward was the Diarist he would almost certainly have put into the Diary in the fictional portion some of his personal friends and acquaintances, concealing their identities in a variety of ways. The discovery of several of Ward's personal friends or acquaintances among the concealed identities would constitute a strong argument that Ward was the Diarist. The argument would become all the stronger if in some instances the persons in question were upon intimate terms with Ward but were not likely to have been mentioned in similar fashion by any other diarist.

My new examination disclosed the highly significant fact that in at least five instances a concealed identity seemed to stand for a friend of Sam Ward. In four out of the five cases the evidence appeared to be conclusive. The fifth appeared highly probable though perhaps not quite decisive.

1. The Diary entry for January 13, 1861, presented a particularly interesting opportunity, inasmuch as it contained two cases so related to each other that discovery of one of the identities would point almost unerringly to the other identity. The opportunity appeared all the more important as the Diarist himself was one of them.

The entry for January 13, 1861, reads in part: "A very long and interesting conversation with Senator Benjamin. . . . After a while I told him what I had heard yesterday from Mr. Aspinwall, whom it seems he knows very well, and offered to read him the remarkable letter from Mr. Aspinwall's lawyer, a copy of which Mr. Aspinwall, at my request, was so good as to leave with me. It illustrates Benjamin's alertness and accuracy of mind that before he had heard six sentences of the letter read he interrupted me with a smile, saying: 'You need not tell me who wrote that letter, Mr. ———. I recognize the style of my excellent friend Mr. B——, of New York, and I can tell you what he goes on to say.' Which he accordingly proceeded to do, to my great surprise, with most extraordinary correctness and precision. In fact, I inferred necessarily that the views expressed by Mr. Aspinwall's counsel must have been largely drawn from Mr. Benjamin himself, so completely do they tally with his own diagnosis of the position, which is, curiously enough, that the leaders of the inchoate Confederacy are no more at one in their ultimate plans and purposes than, according to my best information, are the leaders in South Carolina."

Who was "Mr. B—— of New York"? The clue for an answer to that question I found in a note which Sam Ward wrote to William H. Seward, now in the Seward papers at Auburn. The note read:

"My dear Sir: The following extract from a letter I have just this moment received from New York may interest you.

" 'I wish I could think there would be no fight at Pickens, but I am skeptical as to the possibility of preventing it. Benjamin writes Barlow (recd yo A.M.) [i.e., yesterday morning] in the most emphatic manner as to the dissatisfaction of the Govt at Montgomery with things in Washington and their intention not to await events.' "[116]

This note, though undated, was obviously written within a month or two after the date at which the Diarist depicts himself as talking to Senator Benjamin in Washington. The Barlow mentioned in the note was manifestly S. L. M. Barlow, the distinguished New York lawyer. That Barlow was "Mr. Aspinwall's lawyer" seemed manifest, as shortly before he had brought about an amicable settlement of a bitter dispute between Aspinwall and William H. Vanderbilt. That Ward would have taken a Barlow letter to Benjamin appeared an obvious thing for him to have done, as he was at least tolerably well acquainted with Benjamin and was an intimate friend of Barlow. That Benjamin could and would have recognized a letter written by Barlow after hearing a few sentences from it appeared likely enough, for the two men were close friends and were at the time carrying on a lively correspondence.[117] These circumstances when taken together, I felt bound to conclude, pointed clearly to Ward as the Diarist. Whether the incident actually took place and was recorded in 1861, or whether it was a recollection of perhaps dubious authenticity, or whether it was pure invention, it appeared to be exactly the sort of thing Sam Ward would have written —a thing, moreover, which could scarcely have come from anybody else.

2. The Diarist's account of Lincoln at the opera in New York City on February 20, 1861, was reported as coming to

him later that evening from his "cousin V——," who had been in attendance at the performance. It depicted Lincoln as "wearing a pair of huge *black* kid gloves, which attracted the attention of the whole house, hanging as they did over the red velvet box-front" and as exhibiting a decided lack of sophistication during an entre-act visit to the "directors' room." It also included a spritely remark made by a lady who sat in a box opposite that occupied by the President-elect. At the conclusion the Diarist remarked, "I am afraid V—— has a streak of his sarcastic grandmamma's temper in him." Here again lay a good opportunity to detect a concealed identity. Moreover, detection of "cousin V——" would almost certainly indicate the identity of the Diarist.

Upon investigation I found that Sam Ward had a "cousin V——," Valentine Mott Francis. He resided in New York at the time of Lincoln's visit to the opera there. As the son of Dr. John W. Francis, the Nestor of the literary and artistic lights of New York City for the period of about 1830 to 1860, he was likely to have attended the opera frequently and to have known about the "directors' room" at the Academy of Music where the opera was held. Whether he had a sarcastic grandmother I could not learn, but I did discover that his mother, Eliza Cutler Francis, was noted for her sharp and sarcastic tongue.[118]

In the light of this combination of circumstances I felt that there was little room for doubt that "cousin V——" of the Diary was Valentine Mott Francis. Except as to the point about his grandmother, which was perhaps altered for the purpose of concealment, he fitted perfectly into the picture drawn by the Diarist. Here again was a friend of Sam Ward put into the Diary. His presence there constituted a further indication that Ward was the Diarist. Who but Sam Ward could have put him into the Diary as his "cousin V——"?

3. The first entry in the Diary contains a long account of a conversation which the Diarist claimed to have had on December 28, 1860, with James L. Orr, who was then in Washington as one of the commissioners from South Carolina. "He

assures me," said the Diarist, "that he and his colleagues received the most positive assurances to-day from President Buchanan that he would receive them and confer with them, and that these assurances were given them by Mr. B——, who certainly holds the most confidential relations with the President, not only as an editor of the official paper but personally."

Identification of this "Mr. B——" presented no real difficulty. He was obviously William M. Browne, at that time editor of the *Constitution,* the official newspaper of the Buchanan administration. That he was a friend of Sam Ward, I found clearly established by a diary kept in 1860 by Senator Latham of California. The diary showed Browne as a dinner guest of Ward upon two occasions.[119] Here again it appeared practically certain that Ward had made use of a personal friend to play a role in one of the fictitious passages by which he embellished a meager diary.

4. In recording the conversation he claimed to have had with James L. Orr on December 28, 1860, the Diarist represented himself as expressing doubt whether President Buchanan could be induced to order Major Robert Anderson to evacuate Fort Sumter and return to Fort Moultrie, the post from which he had removed his garrison two days earlier. The Diarist then continued: "He [Orr] hesitated a little, and finally told me that Mr. Seward had given him reason to think the decision could be brought about through the influence of Senator ———, whose term expires in March, but who has great personal weight with the President, and, as a Southern man by birth and a pronounced Breckenridge Democrat, no inconsiderable hold upon the more extreme Southern men, particularly of the Gulf States. Mr. Seward, in fact, told him that this subject had been discussed by him with this gentleman last night pretty fully, and that he thought Mr. Buchanan could be led to see that the crisis was an imminent one, and must be dealt with decisively at once."

Identification of the "Senator ———" mentioned in this passage did not prove difficult. He was obviously Senator

William M. Gwin of California. Gwin fitted into the picture at all points.[120] His term expired on March 4, 1861; he was Southern born; his personal relationship with President Buchanan was exactly the one described; he had been a Breckenridge Democrat; he had considerable hold upon the Southern extremists, particularly those of the Gulf States. No other senator of 1860–1861 corresponded to this description. Moreover, Gwin was exactly the man Seward would have been most likely to suggest for the operation in question, as Seward and Gwin, despite political differences, were at that time good personal friends and were actively cooperating in an effort to prevent the disruption of the Union. In the role of intermediary Gwin acted as a channel of communication between the Southern senators who had withdrawn from the Senate, especially Jefferson Davis, and Seward and the conservative Republican leaders at Washington.[121] In playing the role, he tells us in his Memoirs, a time came when he could no longer have interviews with Seward without exciting remark. To overcome the difficulty "a mutual friend" was selected as go-between. "He secured rooms next door to Seward's residence and messages were thus passed between us." This "mutual friend" was Sam Ward.[122]

Here again I found reason to believe that Ward had put a personal friend into the Diary, for at the time it covered he stood in close personal relationship to both Seward and Gwin.

5. The Diary entry for March 9, 1861, includes this passage: "A letter from ———, at Augusta. She writes in good spirits, but is evidently much impressed with the awkward situation and with the feverish state of feeling all about her in Georgia. Certainly there is nothing bellicose or savage in her mood, but she tells me that her husband is disturbed and disquieted by what he thinks the imminent peril of great business disasters at the South, and especially in Georgia. He may well feel in this way, with the investments he has made in factories sure to be ruined by the policy of his 'Confederated' brethren at Montgomery."

The lady in question here, I found reason to believe, was

almost certainly Mrs. Eve, of Augusta, Georgia. The Latham diary showed that she had been at Washington in May, 1860, that while there she had moved in the same social circle as Ward, and that he must have met her on at least one occasion.[123] As Ward had a gift for friendship and the habit of correspondence with many of his numerous friends, receipt of a letter from Mrs. Eve could have been a fact recorded in an actual diary. It could also quite as well have been a bit of fiction suggested by a recollection of an earlier acquaintance. In either case its appearance in the Diary seemed to indicate that Ward had put it there.

Discovery that at least four and probably five friends of Sam Ward were among the concealed identities of the Diary naturally suggested that there might be still more among those for whom specific identification could not be made out. One circumstance contributed to make such an inference appear highly probable. Nearly all of the concealed identities are to be found in passages of the Diary that clearly appear to be fictitious and of the sort that point to Ward as the Diarist. In several instances the persons in question were New Yorkers of considerable business or social importance and therefore likely to have been among Ward's numerous friends or acquaintances.

# XXI

In this final chapter, I desire to remove from the mind of the reader any doubt, if any there be, about the real character of "The Diary of a Public Man" and the identity of the Diarist. In attempting to do so I shall perhaps repeat things already sufficiently set forth and emphasized. The repetition, however, seems necessary to avoid leaving any uncertainty as to the main point and because some of the things already said need to be connected with other matters not yet brought into the story.

I am thoroughly convinced that the Diary, as published in the *North American Review* in 1879, is not what it purports to be. It is not a genuine diary actually kept in 1860–1861. It is, on the contrary, in part genuine and in part fictitious. It includes as a core a genuine diary, probably rather meager, actually kept by Sam Ward at Washington during the Secession Winter of 1860–1861. Attached to this genuine core there is a large amount of embellishment added at a later date. This added increment is in part recollection and in part pure invention. The genuine core, the recollection, and the invention have all been skillfully blended with a polished literary style.

A number of questions will instantly occur to the reader. Who did the job of putting the parts of the Diary together? When was it done? How could the *North American Review* have accepted such a production? How could the fabricator or fabricators of the Diary have for so long deceived not only the general public but critical historical scholars as to the real character of their production? Why did Allen Thorndike Rice and Sam Ward see fit to keep the authorship of the Diary a profound secret? Can the various parts of the Diary

169

—genuine core, recollections, and inventions—be satisfactorily distinguished, one from the others?

Completely satisfactory answers to all these questions cannot be given upon the basis of any evidence I have been able to discover. In the future somebody may be able to answer some of the questions conclusively through the use of evidence not now available. It seems quite likely, however, that some of them never can be answered in a way to remove all doubt. As far as I am able to answer the questions, the answers will be found in the remainder of this chapter.

It seems almost certain that Sam Ward, utilizing his well-trained memory and his lively imagination, did the job. He certainly had the requisite ability and he would have delighted in doing such a job. A good many aspects of the Diary aside from those already mentioned, little touches here and there, point to him. If he did not do the job unassisted, he must have cooperated closely with the man or men who did.

If Ward did not do the transforming job alone it seems to me quite likely that it was done by collaboration on the part of Ward and William H. Hurlbert. The two men were cronies for many years.[124] When Lord Rosebery came to New York the three formed what they called "The Mendacious Club." In a collaboration Ward's recollections about Washington during the Secession Winter would have served well, while Hurlbert's lively imagination would have been equal to the task of supplying inventions so plausible that they could pass for historical facts. The literary style of the Diary has a good deal of the pungency characteristic of almost everything that Hurlbert wrote. If Ward and Hurlbert worked together in the manner supposed, I think it quite possible that Allen Thorndike Rice, the editor of the *North American Review*, may have assisted in the process to some extent. The three men were upon intimate terms at the time the Diary was published.

The date at which the Diary was put into the shape in which it was published cannot be definitely determined. The presumption would seem to be that the job was done only a short time before publication. There appears to be additional reason for believing that the date was not long prior to 1879 in the fact that in some of the apparently fictitious portions of the Diary the ideas about various persons appear to be those prevailing in the late 1870's rather than those of 1860–1861.

The question as to how the *North American Review* could have accepted the Diary for publication, in view of its actual character, presents a puzzling problem. It is, of course, conceivable that its editor, Allen Thorndike Rice, may have been as thoroughly deceived as scores of historians and biographers have been since that time. But such a supposition is hard to accept. Editors of leading magazines are supposed to and commonly do scrutinize closely any anonymous productions which they publish in order to make sure that their readers are not deceived. It seems likely that Rice did know more about the character of the Diary than he saw fit to tell the readers of his publication.

My belief that in all probability Rice did know the real character of the Diary is fortified by his decided reticence in regard to its authorship, by his attitude in 1879 as to all expression of doubt about its accuracy, and by the singular character of the editorial note prefixed to the Diary.

In the only known instances wherein Rice was asked to reveal the identity of the Diarist he refused to comply with the request. The refusal may have been due to general editorial policy. But such an explanation would not seem to explain satisfactorily Rice's refusal in the instance of George Ticknor Curtis, the biographer of Buchanan. If required, Curtis would have treated the information as confidential.

So far as I have been able to discover, Rice never paid any attention to any impeachment of the reliability of the Diary by its readers in 1879, save in one instance. One reader questioned it on the basis of the story about Seward's conduct at a dinner given for him at Richmond as told in the Diary. The reader having mistakenly assumed that the episode was represented to have taken place shortly before the date on

171

which the incident was recorded in the Diary, February 8, 1861, and having questioned it by pointing out that Seward did not go to Richmond at that time, Rice wrote a letter to the *New York World* calling attention to the error on the part of the reader about the date and pointing out that Seward had been entertained at dinner in Richmond at an earlier date.[125] It was the kind of editorial reply to criticism that appears intended not only to silence one critic but to discourage other possible critics.

Rice's editorial note prefixed to the Diary is a singular thing. It omits information one would expect to find in such a note and it puts in cryptic words several points about which a critical reader would particularly desire that the editor should be clear and specific. It read:

As a contribution to what may be called the interior history of the American Civil War, the editor of the "North American Review" takes pleasure in laying before his readers a series of extracts from the diary of a public man intimately connected with the political movement of those dark and troubled times. He is not permitted to make public the whole of this diary, and he has confined his own editorial supervision of it to formulating under proper and expressive headings the incidents and events referred to in the extracts which have been put at his service. When men still living, but not now in the arena of politics, are referred to, it has been thought best to omit their names, save in two or three cases which will explain themselves; and, in regard to all that is set down in the diary, the editor has a firm conviction that the author of it was actuated by a single desire to state things as they were, or at least as he had reason at the time to believe that they were. Those who are most familiar with the true and intimate history of the exciting time covered by this diary will be the most competent judges of the general fidelity and accuracy of this picture of them; nor can it be without profit for the young men of the present generation to be thus brought face to face, as it were, with the doubts, the fears, the hopes, the passions, and the intrigues through which the great crisis of 1861 was reached. It is always a matter of extreme delicacy to decide upon the proper moment at which private memorials of great political epochs should see the light. If there is danger by a premature publicity of wounding feelings which should be sacred, there is danger also in delaying such publications until all those who figured on the stage of political affairs have passed away, and no voice can be lifted to correct or to complete the tales told in their pages. In this instance it is hoped that both of these perils have been avoided. While many of the leading personages whose individual tendencies, ideas, or interests, gravely and decisively affected the cause [course?] of American history just before and throughout the Civil War are now no more, many others survive to criticise with intelligence and to elucidate with authority the views and judgments recorded in this diary from day to day under the stress of each day's crowding story.—EDITOR.

Rice in this note did not tell his readers that he had seen the manuscript from which the Diary was derived. He said nothing about the source from which he had obtained the extracts that he published. He gave no reason why only extracts were published, why the entries for only twenty-one out of the seventy-eight days of the Diary period were included. He did not give any explicit certification that the Diary was a genuine diary. Upon all these vital points Rice observed complete silence. While that silence may have been accidental, I find it hard to accept such a supposition. It looks to me like a studied attempt to conceal information to which readers of the Diary were entitled. It also looks like an attempt to lay the foundation for an editorial retreat if the real character of the Diary were discovered.

The editorial note described the Diary as "extracts from the diary of a public man intimately connected with the political movement of those dark and troubled times." Unless I am entirely mistaken about the real character of the Diary, these are cryptic words. They appear to me carefully selected to give the reader an idea that the Diarist was quite a different sort of man from what he was in fact. The words "intimately connected with the political movement" naturally suggest a man of some political prominence. Speculation as to the identity of the Diarist has usually been based upon the assumption that he should be sought among politically prominent men. As a description of Sam Ward in 1860–1861

173

they are deceptive. Somewhat later in his career Ward had at times an "intimate" connection with public affairs, but he was never a prominent political figure.

The words "When men still living, but not now in the arena of politics, are referred to, it has been thought best to omit their names, save in two or three cases which will explain themselves" are surely cryptic, if the Diary is what I have concluded it must be. Those words convey the impression that persons referred to by initials or dashes were in all cases persons actually living in 1879 who might in some way be embarrassed by disclosure of their identity. Such was surely not the case in all instances. The words appear to have been employed for the purpose of concealing the real character of the Diary.

A third example of cryptic words is afforded in the expression "the editor has a firm conviction that the author of it [the Diary] was actuated by a single desire to state things as they were, or at least as he had reason at the time to believe that they were." Here again the editorial note seems carefully phrased to convey the idea that the Diary as presented was actually written in 1860–1861, but no assertion to that effect is actually made.

That the Diary as published by the *North American Review* in 1879 won acceptance as a genuine diary written during the Secession Winter, that its authenticity went unchallenged for another generation, that the first challenge by E. L. Pierce did not seriously impair confidence in it, and that its authorship and real character have remained undetermined until today, sixty-nine years after the date of its publication, are indeed proof that the work of all those who shared in its preparation and publication was cleverly done.

How could such a deception have gone so long undetected, especially in view of the extensive use of the Diary by numerous critical historical scholars? The answer to this question has been indicated in part at least at earlier points in this story. The Diary as published meets in satisfactory fashion the test by which spurious historical diaries can usually be detected. While not entirely free from anachronisms, there are none of a glaring character. Nowhere in the Diary is there an instance wherein a person is put at a place on a given day and hour when there is convincing proof that he was somewhere else at that time. In the few instances in which the Diarist seems to have possessed knowledge or to have used forms of expression which a genuine diarist could not have done at the date in question, the blunder is not so clear and evident as to be easily apparent.

The explanation for this remarkable quality of the Diary, and doubtless the chief reason why its real character escaped early detection, is probably due to the fact that the core of the Diary is an actual diary written in 1860–1861. By skillful use of that genuine diary the concocter or concocters of the Diary succeeded in escaping the pitfalls into which the fabricators of spurious diaries usually fall. Mention of persons in the entry for a particular day could be confined to those mentioned in a genuine diary. In the same manner, all treatment of news that would have come to a diarist of 1860–1861 by way of the newspapers could be confined to matters actually mentioned in the genuine diary. The vagueness of the Diary at certain points, apparently a studied vagueness, appears to have been in large degree due to caution lest explicit statements might lead to detection. These and other precautions appear to have been so carefully observed that no suspicion as to the real character of the Diary was aroused at the time of its publication or for many years thereafter. In a word, the work of the fabricator or fabricators was supremely well done.

Why did Allen Thorndike Rice and Sam Ward see fit to keep the authorship of the Diary a profound secret? The answer is to be found, I think, mainly in four considerations.

1. Disclosure of it would certainly have surprised and disappointed many of the readers of the *North American Review*. The editorial introduction gave no real clue to the identity of the Diarist, but readers of the *Review* were invited by implication to believe that he was a public man of prominence at the period covered by the Diary. Announce-

ment or admission that the Diarist was Sam Ward would have come as a great surprise and something of a shock in 1879. At that time Ward was known to the general public only as the King of the Lobby. In their eyes he was distinguished from other lobbyists only by the greater success with which he played that none too respectable game. The remarkable qualities of the man which differentiated him from other lobbyists were little known to the general public. An admission that Ward was the Diarist would have seriously discounted the value and importance of the publication.

2. Such an admission might well have led to exposure of the real character of the Diary as not altogether what it purported to be. Some of the men mentioned in the Diary as talking at length with the Diarist on certain occasions, and for that reason likely to remember any such conversation, might have put in emphatic denials that they had ever played the roles attributed to them by the Diarist. Such denials by Lord Lyons, Judah P. Benjamin, or Hiram Barney would have been seriously embarrassing. Concealment of the identity of the Diarist diminished the danger of such denials.

3. Both by temperament and the exigencies of their callings Rice and Ward were men accustomed to the practice of secrecy in regard to many things they did. Persistent secrecy in regard to everything connected with the Diary was for them altogether in character.

4. For Ward there was a special personal reason for making him desire to keep his connection with the Diary a complete secret. In it he had given rather free rein to his propensity to pour ridicule upon persons of whom he disapproved and especially upon any action savoring of pretense, pomposity, or hypocrisy.

Among those whom the Diary depicted in an unfavorable light was Charles Sumner. In several passages he was held up to ridicule. That feature of the Diary, if Ward's authorship had become known, would have been a grief to his sister, Julia Ward Howe, and to his intimate friend Longfellow, both of whom had been among Sumner's most intimate friends and admirers. For that reason, if for no other, Ward naturally desired that his connection with the Diary should remain a profound secret.

Can the various parts of the Diary—genuine core, recollections, inventions—be distinguished one from the others? I do not believe it can be done completely. The blending of the parts has been accomplished with such literary skill that a complete attempt to distinguish them would almost certainly fail to achieve its purpose. The rewriting of the genuine core has probably made such an undertaking practically impossible. Something, however, can be done. It does seem possible to distinguish certain portions as almost certainly sheer inventions.

The Lincoln portion, I believe, belongs in that category. The indications are overwhelmingly strong that none of the three interviews that the Diarist claims to have had with Lincoln actually occurred. Two of the three striking Lincoln incidents, those about Lincoln at the opera in New York City and the story about how Lincoln handled the delegation of Seward men who opposed the appointment of Chase to the Cabinet, appear to be inventions. The story that Douglas held Lincoln's hat while Lincoln delivered his inaugural address differs from the others only in that the alleged incident was not invented *in toto,* but was an elaboration based upon a highly dubious newspaper item. It too was virtually though not technically an invention.

Other features of the Diary that can with almost equal certainty be regarded as belonging in the same category include: the account of the Diarist's interview with James L. Orr, the commissioner from South Carolina, on December 28, 1860; the scheme attributed to Wigfall for the abduction of Buchanan; Thurlow Weed's remark about Harris, the newly elected senator from New York, "Do I know him personally? I should rather think I do. I invented him."; the interview of the Diarist with Lord Lyons on March 1, 1861; and the story about the telegram sent to Jefferson Davis at Montgomery at the behest of Seward.

A considerable portion of the Diary undoubtedly consists of recollections of conversations which the Diarist actually had with the persons in question, notably Seward and perhaps Douglas, and of stories he had heard at the time and later recalled. In such places recollection doubtless "improved" the actual conversation and stories the Diarist had heard in 1860–1861. Examples of this sort are afforded by the story about Cameron which the Diarist puts into the mouth of Charles Sumner; the story about Seward and the dinner in his honor at Richmond; the account of the dinner party on February 26, 1861. It seems probable that all or nearly all of the conversations which the Diarist reported that he had with Seward and Douglas belong in this category. While the Diarist may have had conversations with Seward and Douglas on most—but not all—of the occasions indicated in the Diary, his reports as to what they said appear to have been put down from recollection at a much later date and are not to be relied upon as reports of what they actually said.

At this point the reader will probably feel disposed to remark that if the foregoing analysis is to be accepted, it leaves very little of the Diary as material for the historian and the biographer. Such a remark, in my opinion, would be well warranted. "The Diary of a Public Man" ought not to be regarded as a reliable source in any of its details. It does present a striking picture of the Secession Winter at Washington. The general impression it conveys as to the confusion and uncertainty which prevailed in the national capital during that troubled time may well be accepted as substantially accurate, though the details taken separately ought not to be regarded as historical facts. As a semi-fictional production, deserving the critical attention of the lover of history, the Diary may well be held in high esteem. But it ought not to be regarded as history.

# Postscript

Suitable documentation for this book has presented a problem of considerable difficulty. Ideally, it may be asserted, there should be a citation in support of every statement of fact and expression of opinion. Such an array of citations, however, would probably amount to a thousand and would require fifty pages or more. Much of it, moreover, would be superfluous, being a repetition of data already set forth in the text, or dealing with matters of well-known and undisputed fact, or having to do with men or details of no particular consequence for the main purpose of the book. I have, therefore, tried to find a satisfactory solution for the difficulty by attempting to provide suitable citations in support of all matters of fact and expressions of opinion apart from these categories just mentioned. This will meet, I believe, all reasonable demands.

Allusions to the text of the Diary have been accompanied in nearly all instances by the date of the entry, thereby enabling ready reference to the Diary as reprinted from the *North American Review* of August to November, 1879. The editions of the books cited are indicated in the bibliography by the dates of their publication.

Grateful acknowledgment is due to friends who have aided me. Dr. Guy Stanton Ford first called my attention to the Diary. S. L. M. Barlow, Mrs. Arthur Chester, Calver Collins, H. W. L. Dana, J. R. Garfield, Ferris Greenslet, Allen Nevins, W. H. Seward, and the late Mrs. Maud Howe Elliott enabled me to have access to manuscript collections under their control or directed my attention to material that might have escaped my notice. F. Lauriston Bullard, Bernard De Voto, and J. G. Randall made suggestions by which I have greatly profited. None of them, however, is in any way responsible for the opinions to which I have given expression.

FRANK MALOY ANDERSON

*Hanover, New Hampshire*
*October, 1948*

180

# Bibliography

## Manuscript Collections

All collections are in the Manuscript Division of the Library of Congress unless otherwise indicated.

S. L. M. Barlow (New York); James A. Bayard; S. W. Crawford; Stephen A. Douglas (University of Chicago); William M. Evarts; James A. Garfield; Abraham Lincoln; Henry Wadsworth Longfellow (Cambridge); Manton Marble; S. F. L. Morse; E. L. Pierce (Harvard); Henry S. Sanford (Connecticut Historical Society); William H. Seward (Auburn); United States Army (Office of the Adjutant General); Martin Van Buren; Samuel Ward (Newport, New York Public Library, Harvard); Gideon Welles.

## Newspapers

Baltimore: *American, Exchange, Patriot, Sun.*
Boston: *Advertiser, Atlas and Bee, Courier, Globe, Herald, Journal, Post, Transcript.*
Charleston: *News and Courier.*
Chicago: *Interocean, Times, Tribune.*
Cincinnati: *Commercial, Enquirer, Gazette, Times.*
Detroit: *Free Press.*
Kalamazoo: *Gazette.*
London: *Times, Truth.*
Louisville: *Courier-Journal.*
Nashua: *New Hampshire Telegraph, Gazette.*
New York: *Commercial Advertiser, Daily News, Daily Transcript, Evening Post, Herald, Journal of Commerce, Sun, Times, Tribune, World.*
Philadelphia: *North American, Press, Public Ledger.*
Providence: *Journal.*
Richmond: *Enquirer.*
Sacramento: *Union.*
St. Louis: *Republican.*
San Francisco: *Examiner.*
Springfield (Illinois): *State Journal.*
Springfield (Massachusetts): *Republican.*
Washington: *Evening Star, National Intelligencer, National Republican, Post, States and Union.*

Files can be located through *The American Newspapers, 1821–1936*, a Union List of files available in the United States and Canada, edited by Winifred Gregory (1937).

## Periodicals

*Annals of Iowa, Atlantic Monthly, California Historical Quarterly, Critic, Frank Leslie's Weekly, Galaxy, Harper's Magazine, Harper's Weekly, Nation, North American Review, Overland Monthly.*

# Books

ADAMS, HENRY. *The Education of Henry Adams.* 1918.

*Appleton's Railway and Steam Navigation Guide.* 1861.

ARNOLD, ISAAC N. *The History of Abraham Lincoln and the Overthrow of Slavery.* 1866.

ATKINS, JOHN B. *The Life of William Howard Russell.* 2 vols. 1911.

BANCROFT, FREDERIC. *The Life of William H. Seward.* 2 vols. 1900.

*Biographical Directory of Congress, 1776–1927.* (1928.)

BULLARD, F. LAURISTON (editor). *The Diary of a Public Man.* Limited edition, 1945. Popular edition, 1946.

CARR, CLARK E. *Stephen A. Douglas.* 1909.

Columbia Historical Society. *Records.* 43 vols. 1898–1942.

CRAWFORD, FRANCIS MARION. *Dr. Claudius, a True Story.* 1883.

CRAWFORD, SAMUEL W. *The Genesis of the Civil War.* 1887.

CREWE, ROBERT O. A. *Lord Rosebery.* 2 vols. 1931.

CURTIS, GEORGE TICKNOR. *Life of James Buchanan.* 2 vols. 1883.

DAVIS, ELMER H. *History of the New York Times.* 1921.

DERBY, JAMES C. *Fifty Years among Authors and Publishers.* 1884.

*Dictionary of American Biography.* 21 vols. 1928–44.

DYER, BRAINERD. *Zachary Taylor.* 1946.

ELLIOTT, MAUD HOWE. *Uncle Sam Ward and his Circle.* 1938.

FORNEY, JOHN W. *Anecdotes of Public Men.* 2 vols. 1873–81.

GOBRIGHT, LAWRENCE A. *Recollections of Men and Things at Washington during the Third of a Century.* 1869.

GREELEY, HORACE. *The American Conflict: a History of the Great Rebellion in the United States of America, 1860–1864.* 2 vols. 1864–66.

HENDRICK, BURTON J. *Lincoln's War Cabinet.* 1946.

HOLLAND, JOSIAH G. *Life of Abraham Lincoln.* 1866.

HURLBERT, WILLIAM H. *France and the Republic* (1890); *Gan-Eden: or Pictures of Cuba* (1854); *General McClellan and the Conduct of the War* (1864); *Ireland under Coercion* (1888).

JOHNSON, ALLEN. *The Historian and Historical Evidence.* 1926.

KENDALL, AMOS. *Autobiography of Amos Kendall* (1870); *Letters on Secession* (1861).

KING, HORATIO. *Turning on the Light.* 1895.

KOERNER, GUSTAV P. *Memoirs of Gustav Koerner, 1809–1896.* 1909.

LAMON, WARD H. *Recollections of Abraham Lincoln.* 1895.

LOSSING, BENSON J. *Pictorial History of the Civil War in the United States of America.* 3 vols. 1866–68.

Massachusetts Historical Society. *Proceedings.* 67 vols. 1879–1945.

NICOLAY, JOHN G. AND HAY, JOHN. *Abraham Lincoln; a History.* 10 vols. 1890.

POLLARD, EDWARD A. *Southern History of the War. The First Year.* 1863.

POORE, BEN PERLEY. *Perley's Reminiscences of Sixty Years in the National Metropolis.* 2 vols. 1886.

RANDALL, J. G. *Lincoln, the President.* 2 vols. 1945.

REID, JAMES D. *The Telegraph in America. Its Founders, Promoters, and Men.* 1879.

RUSSELL, WILLIAM H. *My Diary, North and South.* 1863.

SCHURZ, CARL. *The Reminiscences of Carl Schurz.* 3 vols. 1907-8.

WALPOLE, HORACE. *The Letters of Horace Walpole.* Edited by Mrs. Paget Toynbee. 16 vols. 1903-5.

*War of the Rebellion. Official Records of the Union and Confederate Armies.*

WARD, SAMUEL. *Exploits of the Attorney General* (1860); *Lyrical Recreations.* 1865, 1871, 1883.

WATTERSON, HENRY. *"Marse Henry": an Autobiography.* 2 vols. 1919.

WIKOFF, HENRY. *The Adventures of a Roving Diplomist* (1857); *A Letter to Viscount Palmerston* (1861); *My Courtship and its Consequences* (1855); *The Reminiscences of an Idler* (1880).

WILSON, HENRY. *History of the Rise and Fall of the Slave Power in America.* 3 vols. 1874–77.

# Notes

[1] Hendrick, 115–121; Randall, I, 295.

[2] Among Lincoln biographers who have accepted the Diary as authentic are Carl Sandburg, W. E. Barton, Ida Tarbell, and N. W. Stephenson. Allen Johnson in his *The Historian and Historical Evidence,* 59–61 and in his life of Douglas, 461–474, did likewise. Frederic Bancroft in his life of Seward, II, 43, note, pronounced it "trustworthy evidence." George Ticknor Curtis in his life of Buchanan, II, 391–395, questioned its accuracy but accepted it as authentic.

[3] Curtis, *Buchanan,* II, 391, note.

[4] Massachusetts Historical Society, *Proceedings,* 2nd series, X, 489.

[5] *New York World,* Aug. 10, 1879.

[6] An assertion that Stuart was the Diarist also appeared in the *Boston Herald,* Nov. 10, 1879.

[7] *Chicago Tribune,* Aug. 26, 1879.

[8] *Ibid.*

[9] W. R. Leonard in the *Dictionary of American Biography,* X, 425.

[10] *Chicago Tribune,* Aug. 26, 1879.

[11] *Appleton's Railway and Steam Navigation Guide* for January, 1861, pp. 159, 161. See also the time tables as advertised in the *New York Evening Post,* Feb. 21, 1861.

[12] The Senate *Journal* for February 21, 1861, shows a vote which manifestly must have occurred about noon. Collamer was among those voting. *Journal,* 279.

[13] *Congressional Globe,* 1st Sess. 30th Cong., 571–572, 1027.

[14] See the biographical sketches in the *Biographical Directory of the American Congress,* 1434–5, 1495, 1614.

[15] *Springfield Republican,* March 21, 1861.

[16] M. A. Griffin in *Dictionary of American Biography,* XVI, 348–49.

[17] Welles Papers.

[18] Shortly after I made this discovery the Sanford Papers were impounded by a court order and are not now open to examination.

[19] Lincoln Papers, no. 4376.

[20] *Ibid.,* no. 4514.

[21] Pp. 217–223.

[22] The sketch about Kendall that follows is based in the main upon his *Autobiography.* I used also the correspondence between Kendall and Morse in the Morse Papers; Forney's *Anecdotes of Public Men,* II, 147–153; and numerous obituary notices in the newspapers for November, 1869.

[23] Pp. 311–317.

[24] Mrs. Arthur Chester of Rye, New York.

[25] *New York Times,* Sept. 20, 1860.

[26] *Washington Star,* Nov. 16, 19, 21, 25, 30; Dec. 5, 8, 11, 15, 20, 26, 28, 1860; Kendall's *Autobiography,* 589–619.

[27] J. D. Reid, *The Telegraph in America,* 142. Clearly shown also in Kendall's correspondence with Morse in the Morse Papers.

[28] Sumner's notes to R. C. Waterman, Nov. 23, 1860 and to David Chambers, Dec. 31, 1860 (Library of Congress) are good examples.

[29] Kendall to T. R. Howlett, Aug. 25, 1866, *Autobiography*, 671.

[30] Morse wrote to Kendall, Feb. 11, 1861, "How does my petition in *extension* progress?" Morse Papers, Letter Book E, 270–271.

[31] Senate *Journal*, 2nd Sess. 36th Cong., 98, 139.

[32] *New York Herald, Constitution* (Washington), *Evening Star*, Dec. 4, 1860.

[33] Copies of bitter letters exchanged in 1842 between Kendall and F. P. Blair, Sr. are in the Van Buren Papers, XLIV, nos. 10415–68, passim.

[34] His dealings with New Yorkers led him in 1854 to write Morse, "Do not be sanguine. New York is a curious place." Morse Papers, XXXIII, no. 102709–10.

[35] Morse Papers, Letter Book E, 297.

[36] Morse to William Stickney, Feb. 28, 1861. "All arrived safely, I on Tuesday & Mr. & Mrs. Kendall last night." Morse Papers, Letter Book E.

[37] See the items about Lincoln's callers and length of their calls as found in the Washington newspapers (*Star, States and Union, National Republican*) and in the Washington dispatches of the principal New York newspapers. His evening was fully occupied by the Spaulding dinner and the serenade in his honor at the Willard.

[38] *Philadelphia Press*, Dec. 31, 1860.

[39] *New York Commercial Advertiser*, March 1, 1861.

[40] *Harper's Magazine*, CIC, 500–503, May, 1945.

[41] Massachusetts Historical Society, *Proceedings*, 2nd series, X, 487–490.

[42] *Ibid.*, 489.

[43] Barney's name was not included among the guests listed in any of the New York newspaper accounts published on Feb. 21, 1861.

[44] Among the papers studied were the *Herald, Times, Tribune, Evening Post, World*, and *Daily News*.

[45] Brainerd Dyer, *Zachary Taylor*, 253.

[46] *Congressional Globe*, 1st Sess. 29th Cong., 791–795.

[47] Among the papers studied were the *Herald, Times, Tribune*, and *Evening Post*, of New York; the *Baltimore American;* the *Springfield Republican;* the *Cincinnati Commercial;* and all of the Washington papers.

[48] Among the many newspapers which in early 1861 gave highly favorable reports as to her appearance and manner were the *Evangelist* (reproduced by the *Sacramento Union*, Jan. 1); the *Home Journal* (reproduced by the *Richmond Inquirer*, March 19); the *Baltimore Exchange*, March 1; and the *Daily News*, March 5, the *Times*, Feb. 26, and the *World*, Feb. 28, of New York.

[49] Massachusetts Historical Society, *Proceedings*, 2nd series, X, 488.

[50] *New York Commercial Advertiser*, March 7, 1861.

[51] Contemporaneous newspaper accounts indicate clearly that the reception did not last more than about an hour.

[52] His name was listed in the *Evening Star* and the *States and Union* (Washington) on March 8, 1861, as among the arrivals at the National Hotel.

[53] *New Hampshire Telegraph*, March 16 and Nashua *Gazette*, March 21, 1861.

[54] The Crawford diary recorded on March 1, 1861, "Mr. Anderson of Tredegar Iron works of Va. came down today to visit the Major."

[55] Old Records Division, Adjutant General's Office (Washington).

[56] Among the longer and more detailed accounts appearing in the New York newspapers of Feb. 21, 1861, are those of the *Herald, World, Evening Post, Daily News*, and the *Day Book* (reprinted in the *States and Union*, Feb. 28). See also those of *Frank Leslie's Weekly*, March 2 and the *Atlas and Bee* (Boston), Feb. 22.

[57] The Washington dispatches of the New York newspapers seem to show Lincoln so occupied that a protracted conference such as that described in the Diary could not have occurred.

[58] B. P. Poore, *Perley's Reminiscences*, II, 65–67; Ward Lamon, *Recollections of Lincoln*, 35–38. While these accounts cannot be trusted as to details about the incident, there seems to be no good reason for doubt as the main point, i.e., that Robert Lincoln lost a valise containing the inaugural address, which had been written and privately printed in a few copies before Lincoln left Springfield.

[59] Koerner, *Memoirs*, II, 117–119.

[60] Without attempting to ascertain the full extent of its reproduction by other newspapers, I noted over twenty instances. There were doubtless many more.

[61] *Philadelphia Press*, March 7, 1861.

[62] The full text was in the *Philadelphia Press*, July 16, 1861.

[63] *Congressional Globe*, 1st Sess. 37th Cong., 27–40.

[64] *Ibid.*, 37.

[65] The article was unsigned, but a list of contributors kept for its own use by the *Atlantic Monthly* shows that Howard wrote it.

[66] Arnold, *Lincoln and the Overthrow of Slavery* (1866); L. O. Gobright, *Recollections*, XXX (1869); Greeley, *American Conflict* (1864–66); Wilson, *Rise and Fall of the Slave Power* (1874–77).

[67] Arnold, *Lincoln and the Overthrow of Slavery*, 174.

[68] Pollard, *First Year of the War*, 46; Holland, *Lincoln*, 278; Lossing, *Pictorial History of the Civil War*, I, 289.

[69] *Springfield Republican*, March 6, 1861; *Cincinnati Commercial*, March 6, 1861.

[70] *Ibid.*

[71] Aldrich, *Annals of Iowa*, VIII, 43–50 (1907); Arnold, *Lincoln and the Overthrow of Slavery*, 174 (1866); Carr, *Douglas*, 123 (1909); Poore, *Reminiscences*, II, 69–70 (1886); Schurz, *Reminiscences*, II, 219–220 (1907); Smith, *Records of the Columbia Historical Society*, XXI, 88 (1918); Watterson, "*Marse Henry*," I, 78 (1919).

[72] Smith.

[73] Carr.

[74] Carr, Poore, Schurz, Smith.

[75] F. W. Seward, *Seward at Washington*, 518.

[76] Alexander Rives to Seward, March 9, 1861. Seward Papers.

[77] Lincoln Papers, no. 7950.

[78] Seward's illness, reported in many newspapers, seems to have lasted from Thursday evening, March 7, to Sunday morning, March 10. During that period his only recorded absence from his own home appears to have been the hour he spent at the White House on March 8.

[79] Nicolay and Hay, *Lincoln*, III, 349.

[80] Seward's letter to Lincoln, Feb. 24, 1861 (Nicolay and Hay, III, 319–320) shows that Seward had examined the inaugural that day. Erroneous statements similar to that in the Diary were made by many newspapers at the time.

[81] The South Carolina commissioners appear to have left for Charleston via Richmond. If, however, they went by the alternative route, via Baltimore and Norfolk, they could not have gone from Washington "on the four o'clock morning train," for the earliest train left at 6:20 A.M. The schedules are in the Washington newspapers of January, 1861.

[82] The recently opened Lincoln Papers at the Library of Congress contain several copies of that draft showing the alterations made after Lincoln reached Washington.

[83] *Proceedings*, X, 487–490.

[84] Wikoff's books; Forney's *Anecdotes of Public Men*, I, 366–371; Derby's *Fifty Years among Authors*, 366–376; and numerous obituary notices in the newspapers of May, 1884, especially those of *Harper's Weekly*, May 17, the *Critic*, May 10, the *Nation*, May 8, and *Truth*, May 8.

[85] J. W. Forney, *Anecdotes of Public Men*, I, 366–371.

[86] Horace White to E. L. Pierce, May 30, 1896. Pierce Papers.

[87] A. F. Harlow in the *Dictionary of American Biography*, IX, 424; Mrs. Elliott's *Uncle Sam Ward and his Circle;* letters by and allusions to Hurlbert in the papers of Barlow, Douglas, Manton Marble, and Sam Ward; *Official Records of the Rebellion;* and many newspaper items, especially in 1862, 1891, and 1895.

[88] Elmer Davis, *History of the New York Times*, 44–46.

[89] The Ward, Barlow, and Evarts papers contain numerous specimens of his handwriting.

[90] F. Lauriston Bullard in the *Dictionary of American Biography*, XV, 535–536 and his edition of the Diary, 7–18; the *North American Review*, Volumes 124–142 passim; Frank L. Mott's *History of American Magazines, 1865–1880;* and numerous obituary notices in the newspapers of May, 1889.

[91] *Letters* (edited by Mrs. Paget Toynbee), III, 204.

[92] The Ward Papers; Ward's letters as found in the Longfellow, Seward, Garfield, Evarts, Bayard, and Barlow papers; Mrs. Maud Howe Elliott's *Uncle Sam Ward and his Circle;* the reminiscent books of Mrs. Julia Ward Howe and her daughters; Calver Collins' *Sam Ward in the Gold Rush;* Marion Crawford's *Doctor Claudius;* obituary notices in the newspapers of May, 1884.

[93] The Longfellow Papers at Cambridge contain 365 letters from Ward to Longfellow. Many of them are of great length.

[94] All are mentioned, often with interesting details, in Ward's unfinished Memoirs in the Ward Papers.

[95] *The Exploits of the Attorney General*. The copy that Ward presented to Ticknor is in the Boston Public Library.

[96] W. H. Russell, "Recollections of the American Civil War" in the *North American Review*, CLXVI, 237, Feb., 1898.

[97] Longfellow Papers and Mrs. Elliott's *Uncle Sam Ward and his Circle*, 526.

[98] In a letter to his friend, E. A. Stedman, Jan. 17, 1875, Ward acknowledged that the profession was "not commendable," but asserted that it was a necessity and that he had "endeavored to make it respectable." Ward Papers.

[99] Evarts to Ward, June 5, 1880. Ward Papers.

[100] See his undated letter in Mrs. Elliott's *Uncle Sam Ward and his Circle*, 489–490.

[101] *Ibid.*, 524–26.

[102] Crewe's *Lord Rosebery*, I, 67–68, 72, 81–82.

[103] Newspaper clipping in the Ward Papers.

[104] The delineation of Bellingham at pp. 180–187, 226–228, 235–242, 247–248, 304–319 is an exact description of Ward.

[105] P. 251 in the Houghton Mifflin edition, 1918.

[106] Garfield Papers.

[107] Quoted by J. B. Atkins in his life of William Howard Russell, II, 100.

[108] Seward Papers; Barlow Papers.

[109] Mrs. Elliott permitted me to examine two such diaries. There is a third in the Ward Papers at the New York Public Library.

[110] In his unfinished Memoirs he said he was so regarded. Ward Papers.

[111] For Ward and Sumner see the letters and comments cited under Sumner's name in the index to Mrs. Elliott's *Uncle Sam Ward and his Circle*, 697.

[112] Seward Papers. Frederic Bancroft has printed two of these notes in his life of Seward, II, Appendix K.

[113] Sam Ward to Douglas, April 1, 1861. Douglas Papers; *Cincinnati Commercial*, April 9, 1861.

[114] W. H. Russell, "Recollections of the Civil War" in the *North American Review*, CLXVI, 237, Feb., 1898; *My Diary, North and South*, 10; *New York Tribune*, March 18, 1861.

[115] *My Diary, North and South*, 113, 137, 154, 157, 204, 269, 361.

[116] Seward Papers. Printed in Bancroft's *Seward*, II, 542–43.

[117] Letters of early 1861 from Benjamin and Ward to Barlow are in the Barlow Papers. For the relations between Barlow and Aspinwall see the obituary notices for Barlow in the New York *Times, Herald,* and *Sun*, July 11, 1889. The Barlow Papers contain several letters from Ward to Barlow in 1860–61. One of these shows that Ward in Washington was then living in a house he had taken over from Barlow.

[118] Information from the late Mrs. Maud Howe Elliott.

[119] *California Historical Quarterly*, XI, 12, 14.

[120] John D. Wade in the *Dictionary of American Biography*, VIII, 64–65; Gwin's Memoirs in the *California Historical Quarterly*, XIX, passim.

[121] Some of Gwin's account in his Memoirs about the role he played as intermediary may be open to question, but there can be no doubt that he was warranted in saying, "The attachment of Mr. Seward to Mr. Gwin was well known throughout the Senate to all parties." Further proof of the intimacy is afforded in a note of Sam Ward to Seward, Feb. 16, 1861. "Dr. Gwin dines alone with me today . . . if not otherwise engaged you might find it a relief . . . to join us . . ." Seward Papers.

[122] Coleman, "Seward and Gwin" in the *Overland Monthly*, 2nd series, XVIII, 465–471.

[123] *California Historical Quarterly*, XL, 17.

[124] For Ward and Hurlbert see the letters and comments cited under Hurlbert's name in the index to Mrs. Elliott's *Uncle Sam Ward and his Circle*, 694.

[125] *New York World*, Aug. 16, 1879.

*The Diary of a Public Man*

# The Diary of a Public Man

## UNPUBLISHED PASSAGES OF THE SECRET HISTORY OF THE AMERICAN CIVIL WAR*

(As a contribution to what may be called the interior history of the American Civil War, the editor of the "North American Review" takes great pleasure in laying before his readers a series of extracts from the diary of a public man intimately connected with the political movement of those dark and troubled times. He is not permitted to make public the whole of this diary, and he has confined his own editorial supervision of it to formulating under proper and expressive headings the incidents and events referred to in the extracts which have been put at his service. When men still living, but not now in the arena of politics, are referred to, it has been thought best to omit their names, save in two or three cases which will explain themselves; and, in regard to all that is set down in the diary, the editor has a firm conviction that the author of it was actuated by a single desire to state things as they were, or at least as he had reason at the time to believe that they were. Those who are most familiar with the true and intimate history of the exciting times covered by this diary will be the most competent judges of the general fidelity and accuracy of this picture of them; nor can it be without profit for the young men of the present generation to be thus brought face to face, as it were, with the doubts, the fears, the hopes, the passions, and the intrigues through which the great crisis of 1861 was reached. It is always a matter of extreme delicacy to decide upon the proper moment at which private memorials of great political epochs should see the light. If there is danger by a premature publicity of wounding feelings which should be sacred, there is danger also in delaying such publications until all those who

---

* The Diary is reprinted in the following pages exactly as it originally appeared in the *North American Review*. The first installment was printed in the August issue, 1879 (Vol. 129, pp. 125–40).

figured on the stage of political affairs have passed away, and no voice can be lifted to correct or to complete the tales told in their pages. In this instance it is hoped that both of these perils have been avoided. While many of the leading personages whose individual tendencies, ideas, or interest, gravely and decisively affected the cause of American history just before and throughout the Civil War are now no more, many others survive to criticise with intelligence and to elucidate with authority the views and the judgments recorded in this diary from day to day under the stress of each day's crowding story.—EDITOR.)

## PRESIDENT BUCHANAN AND SOUTH CAROLINA

*Washington, December 28, 1860.*—A long conversation this evening with Mr. Orr, who called on me, which leaves me more than anxious about the situation. He assures me that he and his colleagues received the most positive assurances to-day from President Buchanan that he would receive them and confer with them, and that these assurances were given them by Mr. B——, who certainly holds the most confidential relations with the President, not only as an editor of the official paper but personally. He declared to Mr. Orr that Anderson's movement from Moultrie to Sumter was entirely without orders from Washington, and offered to bring him into communication with Mr. Floyd on that point, which offer Mr. Orr very properly declined, on the ground that he represented a "foreign state," and could not assume to get at the actions and purposes of the United States Government through any public officer in a private way, but must be first regularly recognized by the head of the United States Government. He said this so seriously that I repressed the inclination to smile which involuntarily rose in me. I have known Mr. Orr so long and like him so much that I am almost equally loath to think him capable of playing a comedy part in such a matter as this, and of really believing in the possibility of the wild scheme upon which the secession of South Carolina seems to have been projected and carried out. He absolutely insists that he sees no constitutional reason why the Federal Government should refuse to recognize the withdrawal of South Carolina from the Union, since the recognition of the Federal Government by South Carolina is conceded to have been essential to the establishment of that Government. He brought up the old cases of

North Carolina and Rhode Island, and put at me, with an air of expected triumph, the question, "If Massachusetts had acted on the express language of Josiah Quincy at the time of the acquisition of Louisiana, declaring the Constitution abolished by that acquisition, what legal authority would there have been in the Executive of the United States to declare Massachusetts in rebellion and march troops to reduce her?" I tried to make him see that the cases were not analogous, but without effect, nor could I bring him to admit my point that the provision made in the Constitution for the regulation of Congressional elections in the several States by Congress itself, in case any State should refuse or neglect to ordain regulations for such elections, carried with it the concession to the Federal Government of an implied power to prevent any particular State from invalidating the general compact by a failure to fulfill its particular obligations. He intimated to me that for his own part he would be perfectly willing to let the claim of the United States over the Federal property in South Carolina be adjudicated by the Supreme Court, under a special convention to that effect between South Carolina and the United States, after the President had recognized the action by which South Carolina withdrew her "delegations of sovereignty" to the Federal Government. He was careful to impress on me, however, that this was simply his own personal disposition, and not his disposition as a Commissioner.

All this was but incidental to his main object in calling on me, which was to urge my coöperation with Mr. Seward to strengthen the hands of the President in ordering Major Anderson back at once to Fort Moultrie. He explained to me that, by this unauthorized transfer of his small force to Fort Sumter, Anderson had immensely strengthened the war secessionists, not only in South Carolina but in other States, who were loudly proclaiming it as unanswerable evidence of an intention on the part of the United States to coerce South Carolina, and to take the initiative in plunging the country into a horrible civil strife, which would be sure to divide the North, and in which the West would eventually find itself on the side of the South. He had seen Mr. Seward during the day, who had fully agreed with him that Anderson's movement was a most unfortunate one, and had suggested that the matter might be arranged if South Carolina would evacuate Fort Moultrie and allow Anderson to reoccupy that post, both parties agreeing that Fort Sumter should not be occupied at all by either. This would, in fact, Mr. Orr said, be conceding almost everything to the United States, as Sumter could not be held against a sea force, and Moultrie commands the town. His explanation of Anderson's movement is that he lost his head over the excitement of two or three of his younger officers, who were not very sensible, and who had got themselves into hot water on shore with some of the brawling and silly young Sea Island bloods of Charleston. As to the willingness of South Carolina to come into such an arrangement of course he could not speak, though he did not believe that Moultrie would have been occupied to-day excepting to afford a basis for it. I agreed with him that anything which could properly be done to avert an armed collision between the forces of the United States and those of any State, in the present troubled and alarmed condition of the public mind, ought to be done; but I frankly told him I did not believe Mr. Buchanan would take the responsibility of ordering Anderson to evacuate Fort Sumter and return to Fort Moultrie, and asked him what reason, if any, he had to think otherwise. He hesitated a little, and finally told me that Mr. Seward had given him reason to think the decision could be brought about through the influence of Senator ———, whose term expires in March, but who has great personal weight with the President, and, as a Southern man by birth and a pronounced Breckenridge Democrat, no inconsiderable hold upon the more extreme Southern men, particularly of the Gulf States. Mr. Seward, in fact, told him that the subject had been discussed by him with this gentleman last night pretty fully, and that he thought Mr. Buchanan could be led to see that the crisis was an imminent one, and must be dealt with decisively at once.

### SOUTH CAROLINA NOT IN FAVOR OF A CONFEDERACY

For his own part, Mr. Orr admitted that he deprecated above all things any course of action which would strengthen the Confederate party in South Carolina. He did not wish to see a Confederate States government formed, because he regarded it—and there I agreed with him—as sure to put new obstacles in the way of the final adjustment so imperatively necessary to the well-being of all sections of the country. He thought that if the United States Government would at once adjust the Fort Sumter difficulty, and recognize the secession of South Carolina as an accomplished fact within the purview of the Constitution, the Independent party, as he called it, in South Carolina would at once come forward and check the now growing drift toward a new Confederacy. The most earnest and best heads in South Carolina, he said, had no wish to see the State linked too closely with the great cotton-growing Gulf States, which had already "sucked so much of her blood." They looked to the central West and the upper Mississippi and Ohio region as the railway history of the State indicated, and would not be displeased if the State could be let entirely alone, as Rhode Island tried to be at the time when the Constitution was formed. In short, he pretty plainly admitted that South Carolina was more annoyed than gratified by the eagerness of Georgia and the Gulf States to follow her lead, and that nothing but the threatening attitude given to the United States by such acts as the occupation of Fort Sumter could determine the victory in that State of the Confederate over the Independent movement.

I could not listen to Mr. Orr without a feeling of sympathy, for it was plain to me that he was honestly trying to make the best of what he felt to be a wretched business, and that at heart he was as good a Union man as anybody in Connecticut or New York. But when I asked him whether South Carolina, in case her absolute independence could be established, would not at once proceed to make herself a free State, and whether, wedged into the Gulf and the middle West as she is, she would not make any protective system adopted by the rest of the country a failure, he could not answer in the negative. He got away from the point pretty smartly though, by asking me whether a free-trade policy adopted from South Carolina to the Mexican border would not be a harder blow at our Whig system than a free-trade policy confined to South Carolina. I asked him whether Governor Pickens, who seems, from what Mr. Orr told me—there is absolutely nothing trustworthy in the papers about it—to have ordered the occupation of Moultrie and Fort Pinckney, is really in sympathy with the secession movement. He smiled, and asked me if I knew Mrs. Pickens. "Mrs. Pickens, you may be sure," he said, "would not be well pleased to represent a petty republic abroad. But I suppose you know," he went on, "that Pickens is the man who was born insensible to fear. I don't think he is likely to oppose any reasonable settlement, but he will never originate one." One of Mr. Orr's colleagues, whom I did not think it necessary or desirable to see, came for him and took him away in a carriage. Almost his last words were, "You may be perfectly sure that we shall be received and treated with."

## SENATOR DOUGLAS ON BUCHANAN AND LINCOLN

He had hardly gone before Mr. Douglas called, in a state of some excitement. He had a story, the origin of which he would not give me, but which, he said, he believed: that Anderson's movement was preconcerted through one Doubleday, an officer, as I understood him, of the garrison, with "Ben Wade," and was intended to make a pacific settlement of the questions at issue impossible. I tried to reason him out of this idea, but he clung to and dwelt on it till he suddenly and unconsciously gave me the cue to his object in bringing it to me by saying: "Mind, I don't for a moment suspect Lincoln of any part in this. Nobody knows Abe Lincoln better than I do, and he is not capable of such an act. Besides, it is quite incompatible with what I have heard from him"—he had said, when he checked himself with a little embarrassment, I thought, and went on—"what I have heard of his programme. A collision and civil war will be fatal to his Administration and to him, and he knows it—he knows it," Mr. Douglas repeated with much emphasis. "But Wade and that gang are infuriated at Seward's coming into the Cabinet, and their object is to make it impossible for Lincoln to bring him into it. I think, as a friend of Seward's, you ought to understand this."

I thanked him, but put the matter off with some slight remark, and, without giving him my authority, asked him if he thought it likely Mr. Buchanan would receive the South Carolina Commissioners. "Never, sir! never," he exclaimed, his eyes flashing as he spoke. "He will never dare to do that, sir!" "What, not if he has given them to understand that he will?" I replied. "Most certainly not, if he has given them to understand that he will. That would make it perfectly certain, sir, perfectly certain!" He then launched out into a kind of tirade on Mr. Buchanan's duplicity and cowardice. I tried to check the torrent by dropping a remark that I had merely heard a rumor of the President's intentions, but that was only pouring oil on the flames. "If there is such a rumor afoot," he said, "it was put afoot by him, sir; by

196

his own express proceeding, you may be sure. He likes to have people deceived in him—he enjoys treachery, sir, enjoys it as other men do a good cigar—he likes to sniff it up, sir, to relish it!" He finally cooled off with a story of his having got a political secret out about the Kansas-Nebraska business, which he wished propagated without caring to propagate it himself, or have his friends do so, by the simple expedient of sending a person to tell it to the President, after first getting his word on no account to mention it to any one. "Within six hours, sir, within six hours," he exclaimed, "it was all over Washington, as I knew it would be!"

### SECRETARY FLOYD AND THE PLOT TO ABDUCT BUCHANAN

*Washington, December 29th.*—This resignation of Floyd is of ill-omen for the speedy pacification of matters, as he would hardly have deprived Virginia of a seat in the Cabinet at this moment if he thought the corner could be turned. He is not a man of much account personally, and is, I believe, of desperate fortunes, at least such is the current rumor here; but it was of considerable importance that the post he held should be held by a Southern man at this juncture, if only to satisfy the country that South Carolina does not at all represent the South as a body in her movement, and his withdrawal at this moment, taken in conjunction with the lawless proceedings at Pittsburg the other day, will be sure to be interpreted by the mischief-makers as signifying exactly the contrary. The effects of all this upon our trade at this season of the year are already more disastrous than I can bear to think of. My letters from home grow worse and worse every week. No sort of progress is making in Congress meanwhile. B—— has just left me after half an hour of interesting talk. He shares my views as to the effect of Floyd's withdrawal; but a little to my surprise, I own, has no doubt that Floyd is a strong secessionist, though not of the wilder sort, and founds this opinion of him on a most extraordinary story, for the truth of which he vouches. Certainly Wigfall has the eye of a man capable of anything—"The eye of an old sea-rover," as Mary G—— describes it, but it staggers me to think of his contriving such a scheme as B—— sets forth to me. On Mr. Cushing's return from Columbia the other day, *re infecta*, Wigfall (who, by the way, as I had forgotten till B—— reminded me of

197

it, is a South Carolinian by birth) called together a few "choice spirits," and proposed that President Buchanan should be kidnapped at once, and carried off to a secure place, which had been indicated to him by some persons in his confidence. This would call Mr. Breckenridge at once into the Executive chair, and, under the acting-Presidency of Mr. Breckenridge, Wigfall's theory was, the whole South would feel secure against being "trapped into a war." He was entirely in earnest, according to B——'s informant —whose name B—— did not give me, though he did tell me that he could not have put more faith in the story had it come to him from Wigfall himself—and had fully prepared his plans. All that he needed was to be sure of certain details as to the opportunity of getting safely out of Washington with his prisoner, and so on, and for these he needed the coöperation of Floyd.

He went to Floyd's house—on Christmas night, I think B—— said—with one companion to make this strange proposal, which takes one back to the "good old days" of the Scottish Stuarts, and there, in the basement room, Floyd's usual cozy corner, set it forth and contended for it earnestly, quite losing his temper at last when Floyd positively refused to connive in any way at the performance. "Upon my word," said B——, when he had got through with the strange story, "I am not sure, do you know, that Wigfall's solution wouldn't have been a good one, for then we should have known where we are; and now where are we?" He agrees with Mr. Douglas in thinking that President Buchanan probably has given the South Carolina Commissioners to understand that he will receive them, and also that he as certainly will not receive them. That mission of Cushing's was a most mischievously foolish performance, and he was the last man in the whole world to whom such a piece of work ought to have been confided, if it was to have been undertaken at all. After sending Cushing to her Convention to treat and make terms, it will be difficult for the President to make South Carolina or anybody else understand why he should not at least receive her Commissioners. It is this perpetual putting of each side in a false light toward the other which has brought us where we are, and, I much fear, may carry us on to worse things. B—— has seen Cushing since he got back, and tells me he never saw a man who showed clearer traces of having been broken down by sheer fright. "He is the boldest man within four walls, and the greatest coward out of doors," said B——, "that I ever knew in my life!" His description, from Cushing's account, of the people of Charleston, and the state of mind they are in, was at once comical and alarming in the highest degree. Certainly, nothing approaching to it can exist anywhere else in the country, or, I suspect, out of pandemonium.

### WERE THE CAROLINIANS CHEATED?

*January 1st.*—I took the liberty of sending to-day to Mr. Orr, who brought me the story about President Buchanan's intentions toward the South Carolina Commissioners, to ask him what he thought now of his informant. To my surprise, he tells me that Mr. B——, whom I had supposed to be entirely devoted to the personal interests of the President, persists in his original story, and either is or affects to be excessively irritated at the position in which he has now been placed. Mr. Orr wishes the Commissioners to go home and make their report, but his colleagues insist upon sending in a letter to the President, which I fear will not mend matters at all; and which certainly must add to the difficulty about that wretched Fort Sumter, notwithstanding the singular confidence which Mr. Seward seems to feel in his own ability ultimately to secure a satisfactory arrangement of that affair by means quite outside of the operations of the present Government, whatever those means may be. The South Carolina Commissioners profess to have positive information from New York that the President has ordered reënforcements to be sent to Sumter, and they are convinced, accordingly, that he has been trifling with them simply to gain time for perfecting what they describe as a policy of aggression.

### WAS THE CONFEDERACY MEANT TO BE PERMANENT?

*January 13th.*—A very long and interesting conversation with Senator Benjamin on the right of Louisiana to seize Federal posts within her territory without even going through the formality of a secession. He is too able and clear-headed a man not to feel how monstrous and indefensible such action is, but he evidently feels the ground giving way under him, and is but a child in the grasp of his colleague, who, though not to be compared with him intellectually, has all that he lacks in the way of consistency of purpose and strength of will. Virginia, he is convinced, will not

199

join the secession movement on any terms, but will play the chief part in bringing about the final readjustment.

My own letters from Richmond are to the same tenor. After a while I told him what I had heard yesterday from Mr. Aspinwall, whom it seems he knows very well, and offered to read him the remarkable letter from Mr. Aspinwall's lawyer, a copy of which Mr. Aspinwall, at my request, was so good as to leave with me. It illustrates Benjamin's alertness and accuracy of mind that before he had heard six sentences of the letter read he interrupted me with a smile, saying: "You need not tell me who wrote that letter, Mr. ———. I recognize the style of my excellent friend Mr. B——, of New York, and I can tell you what he goes on to say." Which he accordingly proceeded to do, to my great surprise, with most extraordinary correctness and precision. In fact, I inferred necessarily that the views expressed by Mr. Aspinwall's counsel must have been largely drawn from Mr. Benjamin himself, so completely do they tally with his own diagnosis of the position, which is, curiously enough, that the leaders of the inchoate Confederacy are no more at one in their ultimate plans and purposes than, according to my best information, are the leaders in South Carolina. Mr. Benjamin thinks that the ablest of them really regard the experiment of a new Confederation as an effectual means of bringing the conservative masses of the Northern people to realize the necessity of revising radically the instrument of union. In his judgment, the Constitution of 1789 has outlived its usefulness. Not only must new and definite barriers be erected to check the play of the passions and opinions of one great section upon the interests and the rights of another great section, but the conditions under which the Presidency is created and held must be changed. The Presidential term must be longer, the President must cease to be reëligible, and a class of Government functionaries, to hold their places during good behavior, must be called into being. I could detect, I thought, in his views on these points, a distinctly French turn of thought, but much that he said struck me as eminently sound and sagacious. He thinks not otherwise nor any better of President Buchanan than Mr. Douglas, though his opinion of Mr. Douglas is anything but flattering.

He agrees with me that, by permitting the South Carolina forces to drive off by force the Star of the West, the Government have practically conceded to South Carolina all that she claims in the way of sovereignty, though he is not surprised, as I own I am, at the indifference, not to say apathy, with which this overt defiance to the Federal authority and this positive insult to the Federal flag have been received by the people of the North and West. Certainly, since we are not at this moment in the blaze of civil war, there would seem to be little reason to fear that we shall be overtaken by it at all. The chief peril seems to me now to lie in the long period of business prostration with which we are threatened, especially if Mr. Benjamin's views are correct. I do not believe that his Confederate Government will lose the opportunity of establishing its free-trade system wherever its authority can extend while conducting negotiations for a new organization of the Union, and irreparable damage may in this way be done our great manufacturing interests before any adjustment can be reached.

## SEWARD AND VIRGINIA

*February 8, 1861.*—I can anticipate nothing from the Peace Convention. The Virginians are driving things, as I told Mr. Seddon to-day, much too vehemently; and the whole affair already assumes the aspect rather of an attempt to keep Virginia from seceding than of a settled effort to form a bridge for the return of the already seceded States. Nor am I at all reassured by his singular confidence in Mr. Seward, and his mysterious allusions to the skillful plans which Mr. Seward is maturing for an adjustment of our difficulties. He obviously has no respect for Mr. Seward's character, and in fact admitted to me to-day as much, telling me a story of Mr. Seward's visit to Richmond, and of a dinner there given him by a gentleman of distinction whose name he mentioned, but it has escaped me. At this dinner, according to Mr. Seddon, a number of gentlemen were invited to meet Governor Seward expressly because of their greater or less known sympathy with what were regarded as his strong views on the subject of slavery. Among these was Mr. Benjamin Watkins Leigh, a man conspicuous for the courageous way in which he maintained the ground that gradual emancipation was the policy which Virginia ought to adopt. I noted this name particularly, because, in mentioning it, Mr. Seddon said: "Leigh couldn't come, and it was well he couldn't, for he was such an old Trojan that, if Governor Seward had made the avowal before him which he made before the rest of the company, I believe Leigh would have been hardly restrained from insulting him on the spot."

This avowal was in effect as follows: After dinner, in the general conversation, some one venturing to ask Governor Seward how he could utter officially what the Virginians regarded as such truculent language in regard to the way in which New York should treat Southern reclamations for runaway slaves, Governor Seward threw himself back in his chair, burst out laughing violently, and said: "Is it possible you gentlemen suppose I believe any such ——— nonsense as that? It's all very well, and in fact it's necessary, to be said officially up there in New York for the benefit of the voters, but surely we ought to be able to understand each other better over a dinner-table!" Now, it doesn't matter in the least whether Mr. Seward did or did not say just this in Richmond. Something he must have said which makes it possible for such a story to be told and believed of him by men like Mr. Seddon; and it is a serious public misfortune at such a time as this that such stories are told and believed by such men of the man who apparently is to control the first Republican Administration in the face of the greatest difficulties any American Administration has ever been called upon to encounter. From what Mr. Seward tells me, it is plain that he has more weight with Mr. Lincoln than any other public man, or than all other public men put together; and I confess I grow hourly more anxious as to the use that will be made of it.

### THE NEW YORK SENATORIAL CONTEST BETWEEN GREELEY AND EVARTS

I had a long conversation this evening with ———, of New York, on the issue of this senatorial election at Albany, which also puzzles me considerably, and is far from throwing any cheerful light on the outlook. He could tell me nothing of Judge Harris, the newly elected Senator, excepting that there is apparently nothing to tell of him beyond a good story of Mr. Thurlow Weed, who, being asked by some member of the Legislature, when Harris began to run up in the balloting, whether he knew Harris personally and thought him safe, replied: "Do I know him personally? I should rather think I do. I invented him!" Mr. ———

says there is more truth than poetry in this. He is a warm personal friend of Mr. Evarts, who was generally designated as the successor of Mr. Seward, and he does not hesitate to say that he believes Mr. Evarts was deliberately slaughtered by Mr. Weed at the instigation of Mr. Seward. They are the most incomprehensible people, these New York politicians; one seems never to get at the true inside of the really driving-wheel. In his indignation against Mr. Weed my friend ———— was almost fair to Mr. Greeley. He says that Mr. Weed did not hesitate to say in all companies during the contest at Albany that he believed Mr. Greeley wishes to see secession admitted as of the essence of the Constitution, not only because he sympathizes with the Massachusetts abolitionists who proclaim the Union to be a covenant with hell, but because he thinks he might himself be elected President of a strictly Northern Confederacy. In respect to Mr. Evarts he tells me that he has reason to believe Mr. Seward does not wish to be succeeded in the Senate by a man of such signal ability as a debater, who is at the same time so strong with the conservative classes. As the chief of Mr. Lincoln's Administration, Mr. Seward will have to deal with the reëstablishment of the Union by diplomatic concessions and compromises; and, while much of his work must necessarily be done in the dark and through agencies not appreciable by the public at all, he fears lest the whole credit of it should be monopolized with the public by such a skillful and eloquent champion as Mr. Evarts in the Senate. "In other words," said Mr. ————, "he would much prefer a voting Senator from New York to a talking Senator from New York while he is in the Cabinet." On this theory it is, my friend most positively asserts, that Mr. Evarts was "led to the slaughter." Unquestionably, as the ballots show, the Harris movement must have been preconcerted, and, if Harris is the kind of man my friend Mr. ———— makes him out to be, Mr. Seward will have nobody to interfere between him and the public recognition of whatever he may have it in his mind to do or to attempt. Whether a strong man in the Senate would not have been of more use to the country than a "voting Senator" under the present and prospective circumstances of the case, it is of little consequence now to inquire.

Hayne I am told is going home to-morrow, and this Sumter business gets no better. It is beginning to be clear to me that the

President means to leave it, if he can, as a stumbling-block at the threshold of the new Administration. And, in the atmosphere of duplicity and self-seeking which seems to be closing in upon us from every side, I do not feel at all sure that these South Carolinians are not playing into his hands. If they could drive away the Star of the West, there is nothing to prevent their driving out Major Anderson, I should suppose.

## MR. LINCOLN'S RELATIONS TO MR. SEWARD

*New York, February 20th.*—A most depressing day. Mr. Barney came to see me this morning at the hotel, from breakfasting with Mr. Lincoln at Mr. Grinnell's, to see if I could fix a time for meeting Mr. Lincoln during the day or evening. I explained to him why I had come to New York, and showed him what I thought best of Mr. Rives's letter from Washington of last Sunday. He was a little startled, but insisted that he had very different information which he relied upon, and, finding I could not be sure of any particular hour before dinner, he went pretty fully with me into the question about Mr. Welles, and gave me what struck me as his over-discouraging ideas about Mr. Seward. He assured me in the most positive terms that Mr. Lincoln has never written one line to Mr. Seward since his first letter from Springfield inviting Seward to take the Department of State. This is certainly quite inconsistent with what I have understood from Mr. Draper, and still more with the very explicit declarations made to me by Reverdy Johnson; nor can I at all comprehend Mr. Johnson's views in regard to the importance of Judge Robertson's mission to the South, if Mr. Barney's statement is correct. Of course, I did not intimate to him that I had any doubts on that head, still less my reasons and grounds for entertaining such doubts; but, after making due allowance for his intense personal dislike and distrust of Mr. Seward, about which I thought he was more than sufficiently explicit in his conversation with me, I can not feel satisfied that he is incorrect. If he is correct, matters are in no comfortable shape. He admitted, though I did not mention to him that I knew anything on that point, that Seward has written repeatedly and very fully to Mr. Lincoln since the election, but he is absolutely positive that Mr. Lincoln has not in any way replied to or even acknowledged these communications. I really do not see how he can possibly be mistaken about this, and, if he is not, I am not only at a loss to reconcile Mr. Seward's statements with what I should wish to think of him, but much more concerned as to the consequences of all this. . . .

Mr. Barney said that Mr. Lincoln asked after me particularly this morning, and was good enough to say that he recollected meeting me in 1848, which may have been the case; but I certainly recall none of the circumstances, and can not place him, even with the help of all the pictures I have seen of such an extraordinary-looking mortal, as I confess I ought to be ashamed of myself once to have seen face to face, and to have then forgotten. Mr. Barney says the breakfast was a failure, nobody at his ease, and Mr. Lincoln least of all, and Mr. Weed, in particular, very vexatious. Mr. Aspinwall, who came in just as Mr. Barney went out, confirms this. He says that Mr. Lincoln made a bad impression, and he seemed more provoked than I thought necessary or reasonable at a remark which Mr. Lincoln made to him on somebody's saying, not in very good taste, to Mr. Lincoln, that he would not meet so many millionaires together at any other table in New York. "Oh, indeed, is that so? Well, that's quite right. I'm a millionaire myself. I got a minority of a million in the votes last November." Perhaps this was rather a light and frivolous thing for the President-elect to say in such a company, or even to one of the number; but, after all, it shows that he appreciates the real difficulties of the position, and is thinking of the people more than of the "millionaires," and I hope more than of the politicians. I tried to make Mr. Aspinwall see this as I did, but he is too much depressed by the mercantile situation, and was too much annoyed by Mr. Lincoln's evident failure to show any adequate sense of the gravity of the position.

### THE BUSINESS ASPECT OF SECESSION

He had hardly gone, when in came S——, with a face as long as his legs, to show me a note from Senator Benjamin, to whom he had written inquiring as to the effect, if any, which the farce at Montgomery would be likely to have upon patent rights. Benjamin writes that of course he can only speak by inference, and under reserve, but that, in his present judgment, every patent right granted by the United States will need to be validated by the Government of the Confederate States before it can be held to be of binding force within the territory of the new republic. No wonder S—— is disquieted! If the thing only lasts six months or a year, as it easily may unless great and I must say at present not-to-be-looked-for political judgment is shown in dealing with it, what confusion and distress will thus be created throughout our manufacturing regions! I have no doubt myself, though I could not get Mr. Draper to see it as I do to-day, that these Confederate contrivers will at once set negotiations afoot in England and in France for free-trade agreements in some such form as will inevitably hamper us badly in readjusting matters for the national tariff, even after we effect a basis of political accommodation with them. . . .

### MR. LINCOLN ON NEW YORK, MAYOR WOOD, AND THE
### IMPORTANCE OF DEMOCRATIC SUPPORT

My conversation with Mr. Lincoln was brief and hurried, but not entirely unsatisfactory—indeed, on the main point quite the reverse. He is entirely clear and sensible on the vital importance of holding the Democrats close to the Administration on the naked Union issue. "They are," he said to me, "just where we Whigs were in '48 about the Mexican war. We had to take the Locofoco preamble when Taylor wanted help, or else vote against helping Taylor; and the Democrats must vote to hold the Union now, without bothering whether we or the Southern men got things where they are, and we must make it easy for them to do this, because we can't live through the case without them," which is certainly the simple truth. He reminded me of our meeting at Washington, but I really couldn't recall the circumstances with any degree of clearness. He is not a great man certainly, and, but for something almost woman-like in the look of his eyes, I should say the most ill-favored son of Adam I ever saw; but he is crafty and sensible, and owned to me that he was more troubled by the outlook than he thought it discreet to show. He asked me a number of questions about New York, from which I gathered for myself that he is not so much in the hands of Mr. Seward as I had been led to think, and I incline to believe that Mr. Barney is nearer the truth than I liked this morning to think. He was amusing about Mayor Wood and his speech, and seems to have a singularly correct notion of that worthy. He asked me what I had heard of the project said to be brewing here for detaching

New York City not only from the Union but from the State of
New York as well, and making it a kind of free city like Hamburg. I told him I had only heard of such visionary plans, and
that the only importance I attributed to them was, that they
illustrated the necessity of getting our commercial affairs back
into a healthy condition as early as possible. "That is true," he
replied; "and nobody feels it more than I do. And as to the free
city business—well, I reckon it will be some time before the
front door sets up housekeeping on its own account," which struck
me as a quaint and rather forcible way of putting the case.

I made an appointment for Washington, where he will be at
Willard's within a few days, and agreed to write to ———. My
cousin V—— came to me with a most amusing account of the
President-elect at the opera in Mr. C——'s box, wearing a pair
of huge *black* kid gloves, which attracted the attention of the
whole house, hanging as they did over the red velvet box-front.
V—— was in the box opposite, where some one, pointing out the
strange, dark-looking giant opposite as the new President, a lady
first told a story of Major Magruder of the army, a Southern
man, who took off his hat when a procession of Wide-awakes
passed his Broadway hotel last year and said, "I salute the pall-
bearers of the Constitution"; and then rather cleverly added, "I
think we ought to send some flowers over the way to the undertaker of the Union."

During one of the *entr'actes,* V—— went down into what they
call the "directors' room" of the Academy, where shortly after
appeared Mr. C—— with Mr. Lincoln, and a troop of gentlemen
all eager to be presented to the new President. V—— said Mr.
Lincoln looked terribly bored, and sat on the sofa at the end of
the room with his hat pushed back on his head, the most deplorable figure that can be imagined, putting his hand out to be
shaken in a queer, mechanical way. I am afraid V—— has a
streak of his sarcastic grandmamma's temper in him.

THE IGNOMINIOUS NIGHT-RIDE FROM HARRISBURG*

*Washington, February 24th.*—Since I sat and listened to the
silvery but truly satanic speech of Senator Benjamin, on his taking leave of the Senate three weeks ago, nothing has affected me

---

* The second installment, beginning here, appeared in the *North American
Review* in September, 1879 (Vol. 129, pp. 259–73).

so painfully as this most unfortunate night-trip of Mr. Lincoln's from Harrisburg here. It is in every imaginable way a most distressing and ill-advised thing, and I can scarcely trust myself to think of it, even here alone in my room. Mr. Seward feels about it as I do, though he affects, with his usual and rather exasperating assumption of levity, to laugh it off. But it has shaken my confidence, and it will shake the confidence of a good many more people in the reality of his influence over this strange new man from the West. It gives a weight and importance of the most dangerous sort, too, to the stories which the opponents of a peaceful and satisfactory adjustment have been so sedulously putting about in regard to the disposition of the border States, and particularly of Maryland; and it can not fail to excite a most mischievous feeling of contempt for the personal character of Mr. Lincoln himself throughout the country, especially at the South, where it is most important that people should at this moment have been made to understand that the new Administration comes into power in the ordinary legitimate way, and will be presided over by a man of law and order, who has confidence in himself, in the people of the country, and in the innate loyalty of Americans to the law. I do not believe one word of the cock-and-bull story of the Italian assassins, which Mr. Seward told me to-day had been communicated to Mr. Lincoln as coming from General Scott; and it was clear to me that Mr. Seward himself did not believe one word of it. Even with the brief glimpse I got in New York of Mr. Lincoln, I am slow to believe in his being so weak and vulgar a man as this performance indicates, and I am satisfied that some extraordinary pressure must have been exerted upon him to make him do a thing which, at any time, would have been deplorable and scandalous, and which appears to me, happening at this moment, to be nothing less than calamitous. I can think of nothing else. It really throws the whole machinery of our system off its center. Are we really drifting into the wake of Spanish America? This can not be; and yet, when we have reached a point at which an elected President of the United States consents to be smuggled through by night to the capital of the country, lest he should be murdered in one of the chief cities of the Union, who can blame the rest of the world for believing that we are a failure, or quarrel with desperadoes, like Wigfall, for taking it for granted? It is sickening.

*Washington, February 25th.*—A visit this morning from Senator Douglas, and who is as much concerned as I am at the turn affairs are taking. He feels exactly as I do over this wretched smuggling business; and both startles and shocks me by what he tells me of Mr. Seward's share in it, asserting positively, as of his own knowledge, that, at the urgent request of General Scott, Mr. Seward sent his son to Mr. Lincoln at Philadelphia, to impress upon him and his friends the imminent peril they would be in at Baltimore. I expressed my utter surprise, and asked him if he had spoken with Mr. Seward on the subject since Saturday. He had not. "But you must remember," he said, "that in all this business General Scott does with Seward as he pleases; and General Scott is an old woman in the hands of those born conspirators and makers of mischief—the Blairs." He went on from this to give me his reasons for believing that the Blairs were moving heaven and earth to get control of Mr. Lincoln's Administration; and that they have made more progress that way than is at all suspected, even by Mr. Seward. I do not like any of the Blairs, and indeed I know nobody who does. But of them all I like Montgomery least; and I can imagine nothing less to be desired than his entrance into the Cabinet, which Senator Douglas regards as inevitable. He goes further than I can in his views as to the policy which he thinks the Blairs are bent on cajoling or compelling Mr. Lincoln to adopt. They are coöperating now for the moment, he thinks, with the extreme anti-Seward men both here and in New York. "What they really want," said Senator Douglas, "is a civil war. They are determined, first, on seeing slavery abolished by force, and then on expelling the whole negro race from the continent. That was old Blair's doctrine, sir, long ago; and that is Montgomery's doctrine, sir," he said, with even more than his usual emphasis; "and, if they can get and keep their grip on Lincoln, this country will never see peace or prosperity again, in your time, or in mine, or in our children's children's time. They will be the evil genius, sir, of the republic. They, and nobody else, you may depend upon it, will be found at the bottom of this abominable smuggling scheme." I asked Senator Douglas how it could have been possible for anybody to persuade Mr. Lincoln into such a suicidal act, unless he is a lamentably weak and pliable character. "No, he is not that, sir," was

209

his reply; "but he is eminently a man of the atmosphere which surrounds him. He has not yet got out of Springfield, sir. He has Springfield people with him. He has his wife with him. He does not know that he is President-elect of the United States, sir. He does not see that the shadow he casts is any bigger now than it was last year. It will not take him long to find it out when he has got established in the White House. But he has not found it out yet. Besides, he knows that he is a minority President, and that breaks him down." Mr. Douglas then went on to give me some painful details as to Mr. Lincoln's domestic life and habitual associations in Illinois, which were very discouraging. He wound up by saying that he had made up his mind to see Mr. Lincoln at once and tell him the truth.

### MR. STANTON'S ESTIMATE OF LINCOLN

I called at Willard's Hotel, and left my card for Mr. Lincoln, who had gone out. But, as I was crossing Fourteenth Street, I met the Attorney-General, who stopped me to ask if I had seen the President-elect since he "crept into Washington." It is impossible to be more bitter or malignant than he is; every word was a suppressed and a very ill-suppressed sneer, and it cost me something to keep my temper in talking with him even for a few moments. When he found that I had only met Mr. Lincoln once, to my recollection, he launched out into a downright tirade about him, saying he "had met him at the bar, and found him a low, cunning clown." I could not resist telling him as we parted, that I hoped the President would take an *official* and not a *personal* view of his successor in any relations he might have with him. I think he felt the thrust, for he bowed more civilly than he is apt to do, when he left me. But Mr. Stanton's insolence shows how very mischievous the effect of this wretched blunder has already been; and, while it appalls me even to suppose that Mr. Seward can have had any hand in it, it is not much more satisfactory to believe that he really has so little influence with Mr. Lincoln as would be implied in his not having been consulted as to such a step at such a juncture.

### DID FLOYD ORDER ANDERSON TO FORT SUMTER?

*Washington, February 26th.*—At dinner to-day I sat next to Mr. ———, who told me positively, as of his own knowledge, that

Anderson's movement to Fort Sumter was made directly in pursuance of a discretion communicated to him as from the President himself, and he added an extraordinary assertion that he knew it to have been recommended by Floyd, and as he believed for the purpose, which of course Floyd was very careful not to betray to Mr. Buchanan, of creating a situation which should make an armed explosion inevitable, and should so force Virginia and the border States into secession. The withdrawal of Secretary Cass, he said to me (and his personal relations at the White House certainly ought to make him an authority, especially when speaking confidentially as he knew he was to-day), roused the President to a sense of the dangerous position in which he is placed by reason of his well-known political and personal good will toward the South and leading Southern men. "He has never been the same man that he was, since that day," said ———. He was positive about the instructions sent to Anderson; and reiterated his assertion two or three times with an emphasis which I thought well to moderate, though, as Mr. Flores, a lively little South American Minister, sat next him on the other hand, there is no great danger, I think, of his having been understood by anybody but myself.

### THE CONFUSION OVER MR. LINCOLN'S CABINET

Later on in the evening ——— came over and sat by me to urge me to go with him to-morrow to see Mr. Lincoln in regard to the Cabinet appointments. He was much agitated and concerned about them, having gotten into his head, for reasons which he gave me, that Mr. Lincoln, in his despair of harmonizing the Seward men with the Chase men, has concocted or had concocted for him a plan of putting Corwin into the State Department, sending Seward to England, and giving the Treasury to New York. I listened to him patiently, and I own I was startled by some of the facts he told me; but I have pointed out to him that, however close might be the ties between Mr. Corwin and Mr. Lincoln, Mr. Chase could not be counted out in this way unless with his own consent, which I did not believe could be got, and that I am beginning to think that Mr. Chase holds the new President a good deal more tightly in his hand than Mr. Seward does. I declined peremptorily to call upon Mr. Lincoln in the business; though I said I should certainly call upon him as a matter of respect, and that, if he gave me any reason or opportunity to speak of his Cabinet, I should tell him frankly what I thought. I found ———— quite as strongly impressed as Mr. Douglas by the machinations of the Blairs, and quite as fearful of their success. He showed me a letter he had received a fortnight ago from Mr. Draper, in New York, expressing great anxiety as to Mr. Seward's position in the Cabinet in case of the nomination of Mr. Chase, and intimating an intention of visiting Washington with several other gentlemen for the purpose of making Mr. Lincoln understand that he must absolutely drop the idea of putting Mr. Chase into the Treasury. I told him that Mr. Weed had to-day expressed the same ideas to me, and I asked him if he did not know that a counter-pressure was putting on Mr. Lincoln to exclude Mr. Seward. "Suppose," I said, "they should both be excluded?"

We were very late, and while the whist was going on I had a very interesting talk with ———— about Mr. Benjamin, in the course of which he told me a story so characteristic of all the persons so concerned in it that I must jot it down. We happened to speak of Soulé and the curious letter which he published the other day. "I dined with Benjamin," said ————, "in January, a day or two after that letter appeared, and calling his attention to what seemed to me the nut of it, being the passage in which Soulé eloquently calls upon Louisiana, if she must leave the Union, not to follow the leadership of men who, with the Federal power at their back, had not been able to protect her rights within the Union, I said to him, *'C'est de vous et de Slidell qu'il a voulu parler'?"* Benjamin laughed, as did St. Martin and Hocmelle of the French Legation, who were also of the company, and replied: "Of course" (he was speaking of us), "that is the ruin of poor Soulé, that he can not conceal his morbid hatred of both of us—that, and his congenital incapacity of telling the truth; he loves lying, loves it more than anything else; loves it *jusqu'à la folie!"* Then Benjamin went on to tell a story of an encounter between himself and Soulé, on the way to Mexico, whither Soulé was going to prevent, if possible, the carrying out of the Tehuantepec scheme. When he found Benjamin on board of the boat, which he had not expected, he volunteered the absurd statement to Benjamin that he was only going to Vera Cruz *en route pour Tampico!* Of course he did not go to Tampico, but to the capital;

and, when he got to the capital, he opened his batteries on Tehuantepec, by informing the Mexican President that he had been specially deputed by President Buchanan to advise with him on the international relations of the two countries; though he might have ascertained, with tact and a very little trouble, that Mr. Forsyth had already cautioned the Mexican Government, by direction of President Buchanan, against having any dealings with Soulé at all! I did not say to ———, though I was on the point of saying it, that I was not at all sure whether this curious story best illustrated the innate mendacity of Soulé, or the innate duplicity of a more exalted personage. ——— is very bitter now against Benjamin, though still under the glamour, as I must confess myself to be in a measure, of his charming personal ways, and his rare and lucid intelligence. At this very dinner to which he referred early in January, ——— tells me Benjamin spoke of the arrangements and projects of the Confederate organizers, with an apparent intimate knowledge of them all; saying that the Confederate Congress would assemble at Montgomery before February 15th, and choose a President, so that Lincoln should find himself confronted, when he took the oath in March, by a complete government, extending at least over eight States, and offering peace or war to his choice. ——— does not believe the story about Yancey from Montgomery to-day. He thinks Benjamin will be sent as Confederate Commissioner to Europe, to seek recognition; and certainly a more dangerous one could not be selected. He would hurt us abroad as much as Yancey would help us. On reaching home, I found a note from ———, full of hopes for to-morrow, which I can see no reason for sharing, and another from Mr. Weed to the same effect, telling me that Mr. Douglas would see Mr. Lincoln to-night. I do not see that the Peace Conferences have advanced us one step from the point where we were in January, when Mr. Ledyard came to see me, telling me that General Cass had been electrified into better spirits, ill as he then was, by the absolute certainty that Mr. Seward and Mr. Crittenden had so got their heads together as to insure a satisfactory settlement "the very next day." How many days have since gone by with no such result; and what is before us now but imbecility if not worse, in the government we have, and utter distraction in the councils of a government we are to have? Poor General Cass! I bade him good-by yesterday, and I suspect for ever. I should not be surprised if the journey brings him to the end, and I hope he has not been allowed to carry out his purpose of seeking an interview with Mr. Lincoln. He is not strong enough to bear the excitement, and it can do no good, I fear.

## WITH MR. LINCOLN IN WASHINGTON

*Washington, February 28th.*—Half an hour with Mr. Lincoln to-day, which confirms all my worst fears. I should say he is at his wits' ends, if he did not seem to me to be so thoroughly aware of the fact that some other people are in that condition. I told him frankly, on his own provocation to the subject, what I thought would be the advantages to his Administration, and to the country, of putting ——— into the Cabinet, and gave him to understand, as plainly as I thought becoming, that he must not look on me as acting in concert with any set of men to urge that nomination, or any other nomination, upon him. I think he saw that I was in earnest; and, at all events, he advised me to write to ——— in the terms in which I wished to write to him.

I was sorry to find him anxious about the safety of Washington, and he asked me some questions about Captain Stone, which surprised me a little, and annoyed me more. I told him what I knew of Stone personally, and what had been said to me about him, by the most competent men in the army, at the time when he first came here, by General Scott's wish, to reorganize the militia of the District. He seemed very glad to hear of this, and was very much taken with a story which I told him, and for the accuracy of which I could vouch, that when Captain Stone, upon an urgent recommendation of General Scott, was appointed to the command of the District militia, in January, Governor Floyd was excessively enraged, and tried to get his own nephew, "Charley Jones," who had been previously nominated for the post, and who is a desperate fellow, to insult Stone, pick a quarrel with him, and shoot him. Mr. Lincoln's melancholy countenance lighted up with a twinkle in his eye. "That was not such a bad idea of Floyd's," he said, in a slow, meditative sort of way. "Of course, I'm glad Stone wasn't shot, and that there wasn't any breach of the peace; but—if the custom could be generally introduced, it might lubricate matters in the way of making

214

political appointments!" After a little, he recurred to the dangerous condition of Washington. I then spoke very earnestly, for it
was clear to me that he must be still under the pressure of the
same evil counsels which had led him into that dreadful business
of the night-ride from Harrisburg; and I urged him to put absolute confidence in the assurances of Captain Stone. I told him,
what I believe to be perfectly true, that the worst stories about
the intended incursions into Washington, and the like, all originate with men like George Saunders, of New York, and Arnold
Harris, of Tennessee, once a particular follower of President
Buchanan, but now a loud and noisy secessionist—men who
came into my mind because I had passed them in the hall of the
very hotel in which we were talking, and in which they have
been telling wonderful stories of conspiracy and assassination,
from the hotel porches, to anybody who will listen to them for
weeks past. He listened to me very attentively, and, suddenly
stretching out his hand, picked up and handed me a note to look
at. I recognized Senator Sumner's handwriting as I took it, and
was not, therefore, particularly surprised to find it alarmish and
mysterious in tone, bidding Mr. Lincoln, for particular reasons,
to be very careful how he went out alone at night. I saw that
Mr. Lincoln watched me while I read the note, and I perhaps
may have expressed in my countenance an opinion of the communication which I did not think it civil to put into words,
merely reiterating, as I laid it back on the table, my own conviction that there was nothing to fear in Washington, and no
occasion for measures likely to influence the public mind unfavorably in other parts of the country. As I arose to go, Mr.
Lincoln pulled himself together up out of the rocking-chair, into
which he had packed himself, and, scanning me good-naturedly
for a moment, said, very abruptly, "You never put backs with
Sumner, did you?" I suppose I looked as much surprised as I
felt; but I laughed and said that I did not think I ever had done
so. "Well, I supposed not," he said; and then, hesitating a moment, went on: "When he was in here I asked him to measure
with me, and do you know he made a little speech about it." I
tried to look civilly curious, and Mr. Lincoln, with an indescribable glimmer all over his face, continued: "Yes," he said, "he
told me he thought 'this was a time for uniting our fronts and
not our backs before the enemies of the country,' or something

like that. It was very fine. But I reckon the truth was"—and at this point I was compelled against my will to laugh aloud—"I reckon the truth was, he was—afraid to measure!" And with this he looked down with some complacency on his own really indescribable length of limb. "He is a good piece of a man, though— Sumner," he added, half quizzically, half apologetically, "and a good man. I have never had much to do with bishops down where we live; but, do you know, Sumner is just my idea of a bishop." At that moment a door opened, and a lady came in, in not a very ceremonious way, I thought, dressed as if either just about to go into the street, or having just come in. Mr. Lincoln presented me to her as his wife, and I exchanged a few words with her. Perhaps I looked at her through the mist of what Senator Douglas had intimated to me; but certainly she made a disagreeable impression on me. She is not ill-looking, and, though her manners are not those of a well-bred woman of the world, there would be nothing particularly repulsive about them, were it not for the hard, almost coarse tone of her voice, and for something very like cunning in the expression of her face. With the recollection of Mr. Douglas's account of her relations with her husband, the thought involuntarily occurred to me of the contrast between his own beautiful and most graceful wife and this certainly dowdy and to me most unprepossessing little woman. I think if the wives had been voted for, even by the women, Mr. Douglas would be President-elect to-day.

The passages were thronged as I came out. On the stairs I met Mr. Bell, who stepped aside with me for a moment to tell me how much he was impressed with the conservative tone of Mr. Lincoln's mind, and to go over the story I had yesterday heard of the interview of Tuesday night. I did not think it worth while to dampen his feelings by hinting what judgments I had formed of it all from Senator Douglas's account of it, nor to ask him what hope there could be from these propositions of the Peace Congress after what took place yesterday in the New York delegation. But the truth is, I am losing all heart and hope; there has been more Cabinet-making than peace-making in the Peace Congress; and I am beginning to be afraid that the Virginia secessionists are trifling designedly with Mr. Seward and all our friends.

Mr. Douglas came to see me late this evening. He has been some time with Mr. Lincoln it seems—last night again, not of course at the jam and "reception," but in a private earnest talk about the Peace Congress and the efforts of the extreme men in Congress to make it abortive. He was more agitated and distressed than I have ever seen him; and it is impossible not to feel that he really and truly loves his country in a way not too common, I fear now, in Washington; but I really can not make out what he expected Mr. Lincoln to do. He told me he had urged Mr. Lincoln to recommend the instant calling of a national convention, upon which point Mr. Seward agrees with him, as his motion in the Senate shows to-day. But he admitted that he had no success in getting Mr. Lincoln to a point on the subject, and this led us to a question of what Mr. Lincoln really means to say in his inaugural. I found that Senator Douglas knew just as well as I knew that Mr. Lincoln has not confided this yet, even to Mr. Seward; but I could not get him to feel as I do how strangely compromising this is to all our hopes of a settlement through the influence of Mr. Seward. How is it possible that Mr. Lincoln can intend to put Mr. Seward at the head of his Administration, if he leaves him thus in the dark as to the purport of the first great act of his official life, now only four days off! I can not even reconcile Mr. Seward's acquiescence in such a course with the respect I would like to feel for him as a man; and it seems to me absolutely discouraging as to the outlook for the country.

## MR. LINCOLN HIS OWN PRIVY COUNCIL

Senator Douglas could not or would not see this, even though he admitted that he knew the inaugural address to have been prepared by Mr. Lincoln himself, without consulting anybody, so far as it appears, at Springfield; and though he could give me no good reason for believing that Mr. Lincoln has so much as shown it to Mr. Seward or anybody else since he reached Washington. Everything seems to me to be at sixes and sevens among the very men who ought to be consulting and acting together with united efforts to force the conservative will of the country on all the desperate intriguers of both sections. Senator Douglas tells me to-night that an effort is making now to get, not Corwin, but

Sumner, into the State Department, but that Mr. Adams has refused to have anything to do with it. It is only what was to have been expected of a man of Mr. Adams's good sense; it only illustrates the desperation of the rule or ruin faction in the Republican party; and that, I can not help but feeling, is a very formidable force to deal with, especially when brought to bear upon such a man as Mr. Lincoln, with his executive inexperience, and in the presence of the unprecedented difficulties with which he is to deal.

Still I can not think he will let go his hold on Mr. Seward and the great body of strong, sound opinion which Mr. Seward now undoubtedly represents. My chief fear, and as to this Senator Douglas agrees with me, is from Mr. Seward's own friends and representatives here. These New-Yorkers are the most singular combinations of arrogance and timidity in politics I have ever heard or read of. I do not wonder that the Western men dislike them; they are almost as much of a mystery to their nearest neighbors. Before going, Senator Douglas had a word to say about President Buchanan and the South Carolina Commissioners. He tells me that it has now been ascertained that the President nominated his Pennsylvania Collector at Charleston on the very day, almost at the very moment, when he was assuring Colonel Orr, through one of his retainers, that he was disposed to accede to the demands of South Carolina if they were courteously and with proper respect presented to him. They rewrote their letter accordingly, submitted it to the President's agents, who approved it and sent it to the White House. This, Senator Douglas says, was on January 3d, in the morning. The Commissioners spent the afternoon in various places, and dined out early. On coming in, they found their letter to the President awaiting them. It had been returned to them by a messenger from the White House, about three o'clock P.M.; and on the back was an endorsement, not signed by any one, and in a clerkly handwriting, to the effect that the President declined to receive the communication! They ordered their trunks packed at once, and left for home by way of Richmond on the four-o'clock morning train, feeling, not unreasonably, that they had been both duped and insulted.

### LORD LYONS ON THE SITUATION

*Washington, Friday, March 1st.*—I had a most interesting but gloomy conversation with Lord Lyons this morning, having to call on him in relation to ——'s business with those vexatious people in Barbadoes and Antigua. We fell into conversation after getting through with this; and, though he is the most discreet of men, he pretty plainly intimated to me that he was more concerned as to the outlook than most of our own people here seemed to be. He has old American blood in his veins, which does not perhaps count for much; but his family have had trouble enough with the emancipation business to make him grave, he says, when he contemplates the possible complications of the negro question to arise out of the conflict here, and he put the prospect as to that in quite a new light to me, I am ashamed to say, when he said that, to him, the question of peace or war did not appear to be in the least contingent upon anything that might or might not be said or enacted here in Washington. "How are you going to dispose of the actual occupation, unlawfully, or by force, of United States premises in these seceded States?" he said. "How can the new President acquiesce in that occupation? And, if he does not acquiesce in it, how will he put an end to it?" I really could make no answer to these questions, and they haunt me now as they have not before. How can any negotiations with Virginia affect the situation actually created for us in South Carolina, and Georgia, and Texas, and Florida? Can Mr. Lincoln pass over this difficulty in his inaugural? And yet how can he deal with it as things now stand without bringing the shadow of war over the land? Another thing that Lord Lyons said struck me, which was that, while England could not possibly have anything to gain by a real rupture of the Union, the case was clearly different with France, under her present policy and engagements on this side of the water.

I left the British Minister, feeling as if I had just landed at Washington, and come in contact with the seething peril of the day for the first time. I can not but think that his opinion of the situation is affected by his European training and ideas, and that he under-estimates the force here of that sober second thought of the people which has saved us so often, and I must hope will save us again now.

INCREASING BUSINESS TROUBLES AND COMPLICATIONS

*Washington, March 2d.*—The distress at home grows hourly

worse and worse. And this preposterous tariff which they have assumed to establish at Montgomery points to a still worse state of things. If there are many at Montgomery bent, like some of the worst men we have here, on really driving the two sections into war, they are taking the direct way to their horrible purpose. I can get no positive light as to the actual state of things in regard to Fort Sumter; though ———— writes to me from New York that he is positive Mr. Holt has taken measures to secure reënforcements for the fort, and that it will not be evacuated certainly before Mr. Buchanan retires. The news that the Confederates have made Mr. Toombs their Secretary of State is very ominous. There is no wilder or more unsafe man alive; and his last speech in the Senate was as detestable in point of spirit as the maiden speech, on the other side, of that noisy and vulgar cockney Orator Puff, Senator Baker, who came here heralded as such a wonder of eloquence, and who went to pieces so completely in his first effort under the close and withering fire of Benjamin. I met the man again to-day as I passed into the National, and I really could hardly speak to him civilly. It is such men as he who play into the hands of the worst enemies of the country and of common sense at the South.

### MR. LINCOLN MAKES HIS OWN CABINET

There can be no doubt about it any longer. This man from Illinois is not in the hands of Mr. Seward. Heaven grant that he may not be in other hands—not to be thought of with patience! These New York men have done just what they have been saying they would do, and with just the result which I have from the first expected; though I own there are points in the upshot which puzzle me. I can not feel even sure now that Mr. Seward will be nominated at all on Tuesday: and certainly he neither is nor after this can be the real head of the Administration, even if his name is on the list of the Cabinet. Such folly on the part of those who assume to be the especial friends of the one man in whose ability and moderation the conservative people at the North have most confidence; and such folly at this moment might almost indeed make one despair of the republic!

———— has just left me. He was one of the party who called on Mr. Lincoln to-day to bring matters to a head, and prevent the nomination of Chase at all hazards. A nice mess they have made of it! Mr. Lincoln received them civilly enough, and listened to all they had to say. Speaking one after another, they all urged the absolutely essential importance of the presence of Mr. Seward in the Cabinet, to secure for it either the support of the North or any hearing at the South; and they all set forth the downright danger to the cause of the Union of putting into the Cabinet a man like Mr. Chase, identified with and supported by men who did not desire to see the Union maintained on its existing and original basis at all, and who would rather take their chances with a Northern republic, extending itself to Canada, than see the Union of our fathers kept up on the principles of our fathers. After they had all said their say in this vein, Mr. Lincoln, who had sat watching them one after another, and just dropping in a word here and there, waited a moment, and then asked what they wanted him to do, or to forbear. They all replied that they wished him to forbear from nominating Mr. Chase as a member of his Cabinet, because it would not be possible for Mr. Seward to sit in the same Administration with Mr. Chase. He wouldn't wish it, and his friends and his State would not tolerate it—couldn't tolerate it—it must not be.

Then Mr. Lincoln sat looking very much distressed for a few moments, after which he began speaking in a low voice, like a man quite oppressed and worn down, saying, it was very hard to reconcile conflicting claims and interests; that he only desired to form an Administration that would command the confidence of the country and the party; that he had the deepest respect for Mr. Seward, his services, his genius, and all that sort of thing; that Mr. Chase has great claims also, which no one could contest—perhaps not so great as Mr. Seward; but what the party and country wanted was the hearty coöperation of all good men and of all sections, and so on, and so on, for some time. They all thought he was weakening, and they were sure of it, when after a pause he opened a table-drawer and took out a paper, saying: "I had written out my choice here of Secretaries in the Cabinet after a great deal of pains and trouble; and now you tell me I must break the slate and begin all over!"

He went on then to admit, which still more encouraged them, that he had sometimes feared that it would be as they said it was—that he might be forced to reconsider his matured and he thought judicious conclusions. In view of that possibility, he said he had constructed an alternative list of his Cabinet. He did not like it half as well as the one of his own deliberate preference, in which he would frankly say he had hoped to see Mr. Seward sitting as Secretary of State, and Mr. Chase sitting as Secretary of the Treasury—not half as well; but he could not expect to have things exactly as he liked them; and much more to the same effect, which set the listeners quite agog with suppressed expectations of carrying their great point.

"This being the case, gentlemen," he said, finally, after giving the company time to drink in all he had said—"this being the case, gentlemen, how would it do for us to agree upon a change like this?" Everybody, of course, was all attention. "How would it do to ask Mr. Chase to take the Treasury, and to offer the State Department to Mr. William F. Dayton, of New Jersey?"

―――― told me you could have knocked him or any man in the room down with a feather. Not one of them could speak. Mr. Lincoln went on in a moment, expatiating on his thoughtfulness about Mr. Seward. Mr. Dayton, he said, was an old Whig, like himself and like Mr. Seward. He was from New Jersey, which "is next door to New York." He had been the Vice-Presidential candidate with General Fremont, and was a most conservative, able, and sensible man. Mr. Seward could go as Minister to England, where his genius would find great scope in keeping Europe straight as to the troubles here, and so on, and so forth, for twenty minutes.

When he got through, one of the company spoke, and said he thought they had better thank him for his kindness in listening to them, and retire for consultation, which they did. But I fear from the tone and the language of ―――― that there is more cursing than consultation going on just now. I must own that I heard him with something like consternation. Whether this prefigures an exclusion of Mr. Seward from the Cabinet, who can tell? Nor does that possibility alone make it alarming. It does not prefigure—it proves that the new Administration will be pitched on a dangerous and not on a safe key. It makes what was dark enough before, midnight black. What is to come of it all?

### MR. SUMNER AND MR. CAMERON*

*Washington, March 3d.*—I received this morning a note from

*The third installment, beginning here, appeared in the *North American Review* in November, 1879 (Vol. 129, pp. 376–88).

———, asking me to come at once, if possible, to his house, and going there instantly, as I chanced to be free to do, I found to my surprise that he had sent for me to meet Senator Sumner, whom I found engaged in close conversation with him, and who greeted me with a warmth a little out of proportion, as I thought, to the relations between us, for I have never affected an admiration which I certainly have never felt for Mr. Sumner.

It was soon explained when I found that Senator Sumner had asked ——— to send for me in order that he might urge me to call at once upon Mr. Lincoln and represent to him "in the strongest language which you can command—for no language can be too strong"—the dreadful consequences to the influence and success of the new Administration which must follow his nomination of Mr. Simon Cameron to a seat in the Cabinet. Mr. Sumner's conviction was absolute that Mr. Lincoln had bound himself by a political bargain in this case, which would itself suffice to blast his reputation as an honest man were it made known, as it would surely be; but he treated this as a small evil in comparison with the mischief sure to be done by the presence in the Cabinet of such a person as Mr. Cameron, "reeking with the stench of a thousand political bargains worse than this."

When he had abated a little of the vehemence of his language, I took occasion to ask why I should have been requested to intervene in such a matter, and on what grounds Mr. Sumner and ——— had reached what seemed to me the extraordinary conclusion that I could be induced to meddle with it. Senator Sumner interrupted me by asking, somewhat more peremptorily than I quite liked, whether I needed to be informed of the true nature of this "political Judas from Pennsylvania, whom Providence had marked with the capillary sign of his character, and who might have sat to Leonardo da Vinci for the picture in the Milanese refectory." All this made me but the more indisposed to listen to him, but I finally succeeded in ascertaining that he had sent for me on the strength of ———'s assurances as to the way in which Mr. Lincoln had been kind enough to speak of me to himself. I hastened to assure them both that any good opinion which Mr. Lincoln might have of me must have been based upon my careful abstinence from precisely such interferences—"impertinent interferences," I quietly called them—with his affairs,

223

as the intervention to which they desired to urge me would certainly be. I told them how extremely slight my acquaintance was with the President-elect, to which ——— replied that Mr. Lincoln himself had cited my representations in favor of one gentleman whom he hoped to include among his advisers as having been "the most decisive endorsement" with him of that choice. I could only reiterate my surprise; and Mr. Sumner insisting upon his theme, began again with more fervor, if possible. He very soon gave me the true secret of his extreme anxiety on this point. He asked me what interest I or my friends could have in such a preponderance as the Middle States seemed destined to have in the Cabinet if Mr. Seward and Mr. Cameron were to enter it together, and in what way it could advance our wishes or purposes to allow the New England States, "the cradle and the spinal life of the Republican party," to be "humiliated and thrust below the salt at the board which, but for them, would never have been spread"—with much more to the same general effect, but all this with an intensity and bitterness quite indescribable.

——— was more temperate in his expressions, but almost equally urgent with me to do what I was compelled again and again in the clearest terms to let them understand that nothing under heaven could make me do, even if I had the fullest belief that my action could in any way affect the matter, which I certainly had not. It astonished me to see how hard it was apparently for Mr. Sumner to understand that my objections to coöperating with ——— and himself did not in some way arise out of some relations of my own with Senator Cameron—out of some doubt on my part as to the measure of mischief to be apprehended from Senator Cameron's political reputation, and from the nature of the appointments sure to be made and favored by him.

It was idle for me to assure him again and again that I knew perhaps as much of Pennsylvania politicians in general, and of Senator Cameron in particular, as other people, and should regret as much as he possibly could any "predominance" of Pennsylvania politicians in the new Administration. Nothing could stop him; and he insisted on telling me a succession of stories to illustrate the unscrupulousness of Mr. Cameron, one of which he declared had been told in his own presence and in a company of gentlemen by a chief agent in the transaction, who seemed to regard it, said Mr. Sumner, as a brilliant triumph of political skill, a thing to be proud of, and a decisive proof of the fitness of Senator Cameron for any office in the country.

A CURIOUS CHAPTER IN PENNSYLVANIA POLITICS

It was to the effect that, when Mr. Cameron found his election to the Senate in grave doubt, he turned the day in his own favor by taking a pecuniary risk which eventually resulted in his making a considerable sum of money. According to Mr. Sumner's version of the affair, the person who gave the history of it in his presence, and who is certainly a prominent man in the financial circles of Philadelphia, stated that a leading member of the Legislature (I think he said a State Senator) offered to vote for Mr. Cameron, and to induce two or more of his friends to do the same thing, if he could be relieved of some local indebtedness in the place where he resided and put in the way of a livelihood elsewhere, his constituents being so hostile to Mr. Cameron that it probably would not be agreeable for him to continue among them after Mr. Cameron's election through his help to the Senate. No bribe passed; but the local legislator was appointed to a remunerative position in the way of his calling (as a lawyer, I think) in one of the great Philadelphia corporations, and removed to that city, having previously paid off his local indebtedness with a loan from Mr. Cameron on the security of some stock which he happened to hold in a small railway, at that time of no appreciable value.

The loan was never called for, but through some subsequent legislation the small railway in question was brought into a more extensive railway system, and the collateral in Mr. Cameron's hands advanced to a value far exceeding the amount for which it had been ostensibly hypothecated. After listening to Mr. Sumner for a considerable time, I finally asked him why he did not go himself to Mr. Lincoln and depict the Senator from Pennsylvania in the dark colors in which he had represented him to us. He intimated that he had already done so, and after a little the conversation took a turn which confronted me with the painful conviction that all this indignation about Senator Cameron had its origin not so much in any real horror of the Pennsylvania element in politics as in the belief, which I hope is well grounded, that the presence of Mr. Cameron and Mr. Seward in the Cabinet will confirm Mr. Lincoln in his disposition to pursue a conservative conciliatory policy which may bring the seceded States back into the Union, rather than a policy aimed at a complete separation of the slaveholding from the non-slaveholding region.

### NO WAR FOR THE UNION, AND NO UNION

It did not surprise me, of course, to find Mr. Sumner aiming at such a result, but the acquiescence in his views of ———— does both surprise and pain me. I asked them if they did not think it better, from the point of view of the negroes, for whom they seem to be so deeply concerned, that slavery should be held for eventual execution within the Union—now that events had so clearly demonstrated the incompatibility of the institution as a permanent feature of Southern society with that general peace and order which must be as essential to the South as to the North —than that slavery should be excluded from the influences of freedom in a new confederacy, organized to uphold and develop it; but I could bring neither of them to reason on the subject. Mr. Sumner grew very warm again. He was as much horrified as I could be or any man at the idea of an armed conflict between the sections. "Nothing could possibly be so horrible or so wicked or so senseless as a war"; but between a war for the Union which was not to be thought of, and "a corrupt conspiracy to preserve the Union," he saw, he said, little choice, and he desired to see the new Administration formed "supremely in the interests of freedom." As for the slaveholding States, let them take their curse with them if they were judicially blinded so to do. He quoted some lines, I think of Whittier, about their right to make themselves the scandal and the shame of "God's fair universe," as embodying his conceptions of what we ought now to recognize as the policy of freedom, and then he recurred finally to the original theme, and once more in concert with ———— began about the visit they wished me to make to Mr. Lincoln. I was forced at last to tell them both explicitly that, while I fully agreed with them as to the supreme necessity of avoiding any collision or conflict between the States, and had no fear of any such catastrophe, my hope of averting it rested mainly upon my hope that Mr. Lincoln was of one mind with Mr. Seward on the subject, and would direct his efforts to a conciliatory preservation of the Union; and that neither Mr. Seward nor Mr. Cameron could possibly have less faith than myself in any "policy of freedom" which contemplated the possibility of a severed Union, or less disposition to favor such a policy. It was not at all a pleasant conversation, but it was a necessary conversation, as I am sorry to find, and it is painfully evident that the new Administration will have to contend with a Northern as well as with a Southern current of disaffection and disunion much stronger than I had allowed myself to suspect.

In the evening I saw Mr. Douglas, and, without telling him whom I had seen to bring me to such a conviction, I expressed to him my conviction that unless Mr. Seward entered the Cabinet, and entered it with some colleague upon whom he could rely for support in a conservative policy, Mr. Lincoln would be drifted out to sea, and the country with him.

I found that the incidents of Saturday had been communicated to him, and, as I inferred, though he did not say so, by Mr. Lincoln himself; and I was much relieved to find that he entertains no doubt of Mr. Seward's nomination, and of his confirmation. He told me that Mr. Seward yesterday received assurances to that effect from Senator Hunter, of Virginia, through ———, and he agreed with me that, whatever our private opinions of the political habits and ideas of Mr. Cameron might be, it was most important that no effort should be made to displace him at this hour from the Cabinet, at the risk of seeing a man, either of the type of the Blairs, put in who will press things to a bloody contest, or of the opinion which I fear Mr. Chase represents, that the South and slavery had better be gotten rid of once for all and together. Mr. Douglas used the strongest language as to his own determination to stand by Mr. Lincoln in a temperate, resolute Union policy, and I must own that I never saw him to such good advantage. He was perfectly frank in admitting that he would regard such a policy adopted by Mr. Lincoln as a virtual vindication of his own policy during and before the Presidential election, and that he believed it would eventually destroy, if successful, the organization of the Republican party as a political power; but a man who received a million and a half of votes in a Presidential contest has a right to feel, and Mr. Douglas evidently does feel, that he speaks for a great popular force in the country. But, as I have often felt before, so I felt again this evening, that Mr. Douglas really is a patriotic American in the strong, popular sense of that phrase. He had seen Mr. Lincoln to-day, and he intimated to me that he had heard that part of the message read which touches the assertion of the invalidity of the acts of secession, and that he was entirely satisfied with it. To use his own expression, it will do for all constitutional Democrats to "brace themselves against." I repeated to him what Lord Lyons had said to me the other day, and asked him what ground Mr. Lincoln has taken on the questions raised by the seizure of Southern forts, and by the fortifications put up in Charleston against Fort Sumter. He says that since Mr. Lincoln reached Washington he has inserted in the message a distinct declaration that, while he regards it as in his duty to "hold, occupy, and possess" the property and places belonging to the Government and to collect the duties, he will not attempt to enforce the strict rights of the Government where hostility to the United States is great and universal. I then told him that Mr. Seward, some days ago, had assured me that he believed he would be able to induce Mr. Lincoln to take such a position as this, and that it would suffice, he thought, as a basis of negotiation with the seceded States, and give the people breathing-time to recover their senses at the South; and we came to the conclusion, which I was very glad to reach, that Mr. Seward's counsels must have brought Mr. Lincoln to this stand, in which I have no sort of doubt, and Mr. Douglas has none, that the great majority of the Northern people of both parties will support him.

### TELEGRAPHING TO PRESIDENT DAVIS AT MONTGOMERY

It was late when I left Mr. Douglas, but when I reached home I found ―――― waiting for me with a most anxious face. He opened his business to me at once, which was to ask my advice as to what he should do with a message brought to him by ――――, one of Mr. Seward's New York men here, who desired him, in Mr. Seward's name, to have it sent to-night by telegraph to Mr. Davis at Montgomery, Alabama. ―――― had assured him that it was expected, arrangements having been made that such a message should be sent, and that he would do a public service by sending it. I asked if he had the message, which he produced. It bore a signature not known to me, and was a simple statement to the effect that the tone of Mr. Lincoln's inaugural message would be conciliatory. I asked ―――― what his objection was to sending such a message, which certainly could do no one any harm and which was probably enough true, when he called my attention to the fact that it was addressed to Mr. Davis as President of the Confederate States. I laughed, and told him that I saw no harm in that any more than in addressing Mr. Davis as Pope of Rome, and that I thought he might safely do as he preferred about it, especially as he had apparently agreed with Mr. Seward's friend to send it. I asked him then why this mysterious friend came to him with such a request, upon which he said that he had known the man very well in Wall Street, and had had occasion to avail himself of his services at various times. I finally advised him to send the message, rather than make any further confidences or communication about it, and to be a little more careful hereafter as to his associates and allies. He was in a curiously perturbed state of mind, and I am afraid has been going into stock speculations again.

As to ————, from whom he got his message, he told me a curious story, which helps to explain the sort of irritation which Mr. Seward's particular followers so often show about him, as well as to confirm my own not very high opinion of some of these New York men in whom he takes such an interest apparently. It appears that, before the message was handed to him, he had a long conversation with ———— on the subject of the President's message, and that, after trying in vain to get a definite statement about it from his New York friend, he had twitted the latter until he lost his temper so far as to admit that, when he had pressed Mr. Seward for light as to the President's message this very morning, Mr. Seward had finally put him off with the extraordinary statement that "all he had to do to insure a peaceful settlement of the whole business was to be sure and buy a lot of tickets to the inauguration ball and make it a grand success; that would satisfy the country, and lead to peace."

I really could not stand this, but burst into a fit of laughter, which seemed to annoy ———— more than it amused him. He grew quite hot as to Mr. Seward's levity and indifference to the interests of his "friends," protesting that it was nothing less than an outrage on the part of Mr. Seward to put off in this way a man of wealth and influence who was devoted to him, and who had a great material interest at stake in learning whether we were to have war with the seceded States or not, as he was a large owner of steamers which the Government would need to charter if there was to be a war or even a large warlike demonstration. I lost my patience a little with this, and told ———— promptly that, if these were the motives of his New York friend, Mr. Seward deserved credit for putting him off with a recommendation to buy ball-tickets, but he came back at me triumphantly with the dispatch to Montgomery which his New York friend had secured at the end of a second visit to Mr. Seward, as a decisive sign of the peaceful prospect before us, and which he finally took away, saying that he would send it.

### THE MILITARY INAUGURATION OF MR. LINCOLN

*Washington, March 4th.*—I am sure we must attribute to the mischievous influence of the Blairs the deplorable display of perfectly unnecessary, and worse than unnecessary, military force which marred the inauguration to-day, and jarred so scandalously upon the tone of the inaugural. Nothing could have been more ill-advised or more ostentatious than the way in which the troops were thrust everywhere upon the public attention, even to the roofs of the houses on Pennsylvania Avenue, on which little squads of sharpshooters were absurdly stationed. I never expected to experience such a sense of mortification and shame in my own country as I felt to-day, in entering the Capitol through hedges of marines armed to the teeth. ————, of Massachusetts, who felt as I did—indeed, I have yet to find a man who did not— recalled to me, as we sat in the Senate-chamber, the story of old Josiah Quincy, the President of Harvard College, who, having occasion to visit the Boston court-house during one of the fugitive-slave excitements in that city, found the way barred by an iron chain. The sentinels on duty recognized him, and stooped to raise the chain, that he might pass in, but the old man indignantly refused, and turned away, declaring that he would never pass into a Massachusetts court-house by the favor of armed men or under a chain. It is really amazing that General Scott should have consented to preside over such a pestilent and foolish parade of force at this time, and I can only attribute his doing so to the agitation in which he is kept by the constant pressure upon him from Virginia, of which I heard only too much to-day from ————, who returned yesterday from Richmond. Fortunately, all passed off well, but it is appalling to think of the mischief which might have been done by a single evil-disposed person to-day. A blank cartridge fired from a window on Pennsylvania Avenue might have disconcerted all our hopes, and thrown the whole country into inextricable confusion.

That nothing of the sort was done, or even so much as attempted, is the most conclusive evidence that could be asked of the groundlessness of the rumors and old women's tales on the strength of which General Scott has been led into this great mistake. Even without this the atmosphere of the day would have been depressing enough. It has been one of our disagreeable, clear, windy, Washington spring days. The arrangements within the Capitol were awkward, and very ill attended to. No one was at his ease. Neither Mr. Buchanan nor Mr. Lincoln appeared to advantage. Poor Chief-Justice Taney could hardly speak plainly, in his uncontrollable agitation.

### HOW MR. DOUGLAS STOOD BY THE NEW PRESIDENT

I must, however, except Senator Douglas, whose conduct can not be overpraised. I saw him for a moment in the morning, when he told me that he meant to put himself as prominently forward in the ceremonies as he properly could, and to leave no doubt on any one's mind of his determination to stand by the new Administration in the performance of its first great duty to maintain the Union. I watched him carefully. He made his way not without difficulty—for there was literally no sort of order in the arrangements—to the front of the throng directly beside Mr. Lincoln, when he prepared to read the address. A miserable little rickety table had been provided for the President, on which he could hardly find room for his hat, and Senator Douglas, reaching forward, took it with a smile and held it during the delivery of the address. It was a trifling act, but a symbolical one, and not to be forgotten, and it attracted much attention all around me.

### THE BEARING OF MR. LINCOLN HIMSELF

Mr. Lincoln was pale and very nervous, and did not read his address very well, which is not much to be wondered at under all the circumstances. His spectacles troubled him, his position was crowded and uncomfortable, and, in short, nothing had been done which ought to have been done to render the performance of this great duty either dignified in its effect or, physically speaking, easy for the President.

The great crowd in the grounds behaved very well, but manifested little or no enthusiasm, and at one point in the speech Mr. Lincoln was thrown completely off his balance for a moment by a crash not far in front of him among the people, followed by something which for an instant looked like a struggle. I was not undisturbed myself, nor were those who were immediately about me; but it appeared directly that nothing more serious had happened than the fall from a breaking bough of a spectator who had clambered up into one of the trees.

Mr. Lincoln's agitation was remarked, and I have no doubt must have been caused by the impressions which the alarmists have been trying so sedulously to make on his mind, and which the exaggerated preparations of General Scott to-day are but too likely to have deepened.

### THE INAUGURAL ADDRESS, AND THE EFFECT OF IT

The address has disappointed every one, I think. There was too much argumentative discussion of the question at issue, as was to have been expected from a man whose whole career has been that of an advocate in his private affairs, and of a candidate in public affairs, and who has had absolutely no experience of an executive kind, but this in the actual state of the country is perhaps an advantage. The more we reason and argue over the situation, the better chance there will be of our emerging from it without a collision.

I listened attentively for the passages about which Mr. Douglas had spoken to me, and I observed that, when he uttered what I suppose to be the language referred to by Mr. Douglas, Mr. Lincoln raised his voice and distinctly emphasized the declaration that he must take, hold, possess, and occupy the property and places belonging to the United States. This was unmistakable, and he paused for a moment after closing the sentence as if to allow it to be fully taken in and comprehended by his audience.

In spite of myself, my conversation with Lord Lyons and his remarks on this point would recur to my mind, and, notwithstanding the encouraging account given me by Mr. Douglas of the spirit and intent of Mr. Lincoln himself, this passage of his speech made an uncomfortable impression upon me, which I find it difficult even now to shake off. There is probably no good reason for this, as no one else with whom I have spoken to-day seems to have been affected by the passage of the speech as I myself was, and I am conscious to-night that I have been in a morbid and uneasy mood during the whole day. Mr. Lincoln was visibly affected at the close of his speech, and threw a tone of strange but genuine pathos into a quaint, queerly constructed but not unpoetical passage with which he concluded it, not calculated to reassure those who, like myself, rely more upon common sense and cool statesmanship than upon sentiment for the safe conduct of public affairs.

Upon the public here generally the speech seems to have produced little effect, but the general impression evidently is that it prefigures a conciliatory and patient policy; and, so far, the day has been a gain for the country. I anticipate little from it at the far South, but much in the border States, and especially in Virginia, which just now undoubtedly holds the key of the situation.

## AN INTERESTING MARYLAND VIEW OF THE SITUATION

On my way back from the Capitol, I met ———, of Maryland, who walked with me as far as Willard's. He spoke of the inaugural very contemptuously, and with evident irritation, I thought, and what he said strengthened my own feeling that it will be of use in allaying the excitement which his friends are trying so hard to foment, not only in Virginia, but in his own State. He makes no secret of his own desire to see Maryland and Virginia carry Washington out of the Union with them. When I suggested that other States had spent a good deal of money in Washington, and that there was a good deal of public property here which had been called into existence and value by the United States, and not by Maryland or Virginia, he advanced the singular doctrine that the soil belonged to these States, and that everything put upon it must go to them when they resumed their dominion over the soil. "The public buildings and the navy-yard here," he said, "belong to Virginia and Maryland just as much as the public buildings and the forts at Charleston belong to South Carolina." He did not relish my reply, I thought, which was to the effect that I agreed with him entirely as to the parity of the claims in both cases, and saw no more reason why the property of the United States at Washington should belong to Maryland and Virginia than why the property of the United States at Charleston should belong to South Carolina. He was very bitter about the presence of Senator Douglas at the side of Mr. Lincoln, and generally seemed to think that the day had not been a good one for the disruptionists. I hope he is right, and, in spite of my own forebodings, I think he is. The Blairs were alluded to in our conversation, and he thundered at them as traitors to their own people. He said they were execrated in Maryland, and that no man of them would dare to enter the doors of the Maryland Club, and assured me that, only a few weeks ago, the neighbors of old Mr. Blair had sent him word that "a tree had been picked out for him in the woods." Much as I dislike the Blairs, and dread their influence on the new Administration, I felt constrained to tell —— that, in my judgment, the amiable neighbors of Mr. Blair could do nothing more likely to make his son the next President of the United States than to execute the atrocious threat implied in such a message; and so we parted. This effervescence of local sympathy, in and about Washington, with the secessionist plans and leaders, is most unfortunate, for it gives color to the inflammatory representations of men like Mr. Montgomery Blair, and supplies them with excuses for persuading General Scott into a course of military displays and demonstrations, to which his own unparalleled vanity alone would sufficiently incline him without such help.

### THE CONFEDERATE COMMISSIONERS COMING

On reaching home I found a letter from Mr. Forsyth, telling me that he will be in Washington shortly, as a Commissioner from the Confederate States with others, and intimating his own earnest wish to secure an amicable adjustment of the separation, which he insists upon as irreparable at least for the present. I shall be very glad to see him, for he is a man of unusual sense, and I do not believe he can have persuaded himself into the practicability of the fantastic schemes represented in this wild confederacy. I hope his colleagues may be as able men as himself, for, though I do not see how they are to be in any way officially recognized, their presence here, if they will hear and talk reason, may be very beneficial just now.

Just after dinner I was called out by a card from Mr. Guthrie, introducing to me a man from his own State, who wished to see me on "business important, not to himself only." I found him a tall, quiet, intelligent-looking Kentuckian, who had an interest in a mail-route in the Southwest and in the Northern connections with it, and who was very anxious to get at some way of saving his interest, by inducing the "Confederate Government" at Montgomery to make terms with him such as the Government had made. The man seemed an honest, worthy fellow, very much in earnest. He had copied out, on a slip of paper, Mr. Lincoln's allusion to his intended purpose of maintaining the mails, and I found that what he wished me to do was, to tell him whether I thought Mr. Seward or Mr. Lincoln would give him a kind of authority to take a contract for carrying the mails for the Government at Montgomery, on the same terms on which he held a contract with the Government here, so that there might be no interruption in the mail service. I assured him that I could not give him any light as to what Mr. Seward or Mr. Lincoln would or would not do, but that I would with pleasure give him a note to Mr. Seward, stating who had sent him to me, and what he wanted. This I did, and he went away expressing much gratitude. The incident struck me as but a beginning and inkling of the infinite vexations, annoyances, and calamities which this senseless and insufferable explosion of political passions and follies is destined to inflict upon the industrious people of this country and of all sections. What is most to be feared is the exasperating effect on the people generally of these things, and my own letters from home bear witness daily to the working of this dangerous leaven among classes not commonly too attentive to political affairs.

### THE INAUGURATION BALL

I walked around for half an hour this evening to the inauguration ball, thinking as I went of poor ——'s amazement and wrath at Mr. Seward's extraordinary proposition that the success of this entertainment would settle the question in favor of peace. It was a rash assertion on Mr. Seward's part, for never was there a more pitiable failure. The military nonsense of the day has doubtless had something to do with it; for ——, whom I met just

after entering the great tawdry ballroom, assured me that the
town was full of stories about a company of Virginia horsemen
assembled beyond the Long Bridge with intent to dash into
Washington, surround the ballroom, and carry off the new
President a captive by the blaze of the burning edifice! The place
was not half full, and such an assemblage of strange costumes,
male and female, was never before seen, I am sure, in this city.
Very few people of any consideration were there. The President
looked exhausted and uncomfortable, and most ungainly in his
dress, and Mrs. Lincoln, all in blue, with a feather in her hair, and
a highly-flushed face, was anything but an ornamental figure in
the scene. Mr. Douglas was there, very civil and attentive to
Mrs. Lincoln, with whom, as a matter of politeness, I exchanged
a few observations of a commonplace sort. I had no opportunity
of more than half a dozen words with Mr. Douglas, but I was
glad to find that he was satisfied with the address and with the
general outlook, though he agreed with me that the military
part of the business had been shockingly and stupidly overdone.
He was concerned too, I was surprised to find, about the nomination of Mr. Seward to-morrow, and gave me to understand that
both the Blairs and Mr. Sumner have been at work to-day against
it still. I promised to see ———— in the morning, before the meeting of the Senate, on the subject. ————, of New York, who
walked out of the absurd place with me, and accompanied me
part of the way home, tells me that the real reason of Mr. Seward's anxiety for the success of this entertainment is, that the
whole affair is a speculation gotten up by some followers of his
in New York, and that he has been personally entreated by a
New York politician who is very faithful to him, a Mr. Wakeman, to interest himself in its success!

Certainly Mr. Seward is one of the most perplexing men alive.
I can not doubt his personal integrity or his patriotism, but he
does certainly contrive to surround himself with the most objectionable people, and to countenance the strangest and the
most questionable operations imaginable.

## MAJOR ANDERSON AND FORT SUMTER[*]

*Washington, March 6th.*—To-day ———— came to see me, having come directly through from Montgomery, stopping only a

[*] The last installment, beginning here, appeared in the *North American
Review* in November, 1879 (Vol. 129, pp. 483-96).

day in Charleston on the way, where he saw and had a long conversation with Major Anderson, who is a connection by marriage of his wife, and with whom he has long been on terms of particular good will. He astonishes me by his statements, which I can not doubt, as to the real status of things at Fort Sumter. That Major Anderson transferred his garrison to Fort Sumter from Fort Moultrie of his own motion, on discretionary instructions received last winter from the War Department, he has no sort of question; and indeed his very particular account given to me of the circumstances attending the act of transfer is most interesting—so interesting that I have asked him and he has promised to write it out for me, as it is too long for me to set down here. He tells me Major Anderson has no expectation whatever of the reëstablishment of the Government over the seceded States, and that he intends to be governed in his own future course (military considerations and the question of subsistence of course apart) by the course of his own State of Kentucky. He does not sympathize at all with the States which have now seceded, but he thinks the provocation given them in the action and attitude of the Northern abolitionists an adequate provocation; and ———— assures me that in his opinion Major Anderson would unhesitatingly obey the orders of a Confederate Secretary of War were Kentucky to withdraw from the Union and join this new and menacing organization. Fortunately, there seems no immediate likelihood of this, but it shows how much more perilous the situation is than I own I had allowed myself to think, and how mischievous in its effects has been the leaving open through all these years of the question of States rights, their exact limitations, and their relations to the Federal Government.

———— is convinced that Major Anderson would never have abandoned Fort Moultrie had he not thought wise to remove himself from a position in which he was liable to be commanded by the authorities of South Carolina, his determination being to retain the control of the position primarily in the interest of his own Commonwealth of Kentucky, so that Kentucky might in no way be committed by his action either for or against the retention of the forts in Charleston Harbor. I asked ———— to go with me and state these facts to Mr. Lincoln, pointing out to him their grave importance, and the decisive influence which an accurate knowledge of the feelings and disposition of Major Anderson might have upon the President's judgment of what may be expedient to be done in this most dangerous matter. His own conviction as to the quiet and positive character of Major Anderson, of whom he tells me that, though not a man of unusual abilities in any way, he is a very resolute and conscientious man, holding stubbornly to his own ideas of duty, I told him I was sure would weigh much more with the President than any representations on the subject coming through a third party possibly could. He was quite averse to doing this at first, but finally consented, on my urgent representations, to do so, and I have written a note this afternoon to the President, asking his permission to call on him about a public matter at some hour which may suit him to-morrow.

### THE SECESSIONISTS AT MONTGOMERY

Of the proceedings at Montgomery ———— gives me an account at once grotesque and saddening. He tells me that a sharp division is already showing itself in the councils of the secession leaders. Mr. Toombs has the wildest ideas of the immediate recognition by England and France of the new government, and insists that no concession shall be made to public opinion in those countries or in the North on the question of slavery. "Cotton is king" is in his mouth all the time. Mr. Memminger, the South Carolinian Secretary of the Treasury, ———— thinks much the ablest man they have there, and he takes a more business-like view of the situation, being of the opinion that, unless something is done to secure the seceded States under their new nationality a solid basis of credit abroad, they will not be able to carry on the ordinary operations of a government for any great length of time. None of them anticipate hostilities, and I am glad to learn from ———— that the number of persons of any weight and credit among them, who are disposed so to press matters in any direction as to make hostilities probable, is very small. Even in Charleston ———— assures me there is a perfect good temper shown in all intercourse between the United States authorities and those who have the present direction of affairs there. At Montgomery ———— found the women much more violent and disposed to mischief than the men, many ladies almost openly expressing their wish to see the "Confederate flag" planted at Washington. It appears too, that of this same Confederate flag a number of models have been furnished by ladies. Copies of some of these ───── had brought on, and he exhibited them to me. Nothing can be imagined more childish and grotesque than most of them were. The abler men at Montgomery he tells me are urgent that the seceded States should claim the flag of the United States as their own, a proposition which I should suppose would be quite agreeable to Mr. Sumner and others who have not yet got over their disposition to denounce the Union as a "covenant with death and an agreement with hell." I asked ───── what these people really mean to do or to attempt to do about patents, showing him some of my letters from home, which clearly indicate the trouble brewing in our part of the country on that very important subject. He could give me no reassuring views of the matter, but, on the contrary, led me to think that the seceded States will try to raise a revenue by exacting heavy sums of patentees for a recognition of their rights within the territory of those States. Such measures, like the adoption last week by their Congress of an act throwing open the coasting-trade of all the seceded States to the flags of all nations on equal terms, are too clearly aimed at the material interests and prosperity of the country not to arouse extreme and legitimate irritation. They are a sort of legislative war against the rest of the Union, which may lead, before we are well aware of it, into reprisals and warfare of a more sanguinary kind.

### MR. SEWARD'S NEGOTIATIONS WITH VIRGINIA

I asked ───── what information he brought as to the relations between the people at Montgomery and the border States, especially Virginia. He had no doubt, from what he heard there, that Virginia will secede, and was apparently very much surprised when I gave him my reasons for believing that nothing of the sort was to be expected. When I told him, as, in view of his position relatively to the well-disposed people of the South and of his intention to see the President to-morrow, I thought it right to tell him, that a messenger—and a messenger enjoying the direct personal confidence of Mr. Seward—left Washington this morning for Richmond with positive assurances as to the intention of the new Administration that no attempt should be made either to reënforce or to hold Fort Sumter, he was greatly surprised, but was forced to admit that such a communication might greatly alter the aspect of things and strengthen the hands of the Union men in Virginia. He thought it would, if made known, produce a great effect even at Montgomery.

AN INTERVIEW WITH MR. LINCOLN

*March 7th.*—Early this morning I received a message from the President, making an appointment for this afternoon. I called for ———— at his hotel and we drove to the White House. I could not help observing the disorderly appearance of the place, and the slovenly way in which the service was done. We were kept waiting but a few moments, however, and found Mr. Lincoln quite alone. He received us very kindly, but I was struck and pained by the haggard, worn look of his face, which scarcely left it during the whole time of our visit. I told the President, in a few words, why we had asked for this interview, and ———— then fully explained to him, as he had to me yesterday, the situation at Fort Sumter. It seemed to me that the information did not take the President entirely by surprise, though he asked ————— two or three times over whether he was quite sure about Major Anderson's ideas as to his duty, in case of any action by Kentucky; and, when ———— had repeated to him exactly what he had told me as to the language used to himself by Major Anderson, Mr. Lincoln sat quite silent for a little while in a sort of brooding way, and then, looking up, suddenly said: "Well, you say Major Anderson is a good man, and I have no doubt he is; but if he is right it will be a bad job for me if Kentucky secedes. When he goes out of Fort Sumter, I shall have to go out of the White House." We could not resist a laugh at this quaint way of putting the case, but the gloomy, care-worn look settled back very soon on the President's face, and he said little more except to ask ———— some questions about Montgomery, not I thought of a very relevant or important kind, and we soon took our leave. He walked into the corridor with us; and, as he bade us good-by, and thanked ———— for what he had told him, he again brightened up for a moment and asked him in an abrupt kind of way, laying his hand as he spoke with a queer but not uncivil familiarity on his shoulder, "You haven't such a thing as a postmaster in your pocket, have you?" ———— stared at him in astonishment, and I thought a little in alarm, as if he suspected a sudden attack of insanity, when Mr. Lincoln went on: "You see it seems to me kind of unnatural that you shouldn't have at least a post-

240

master in your pocket. Everybody I've seen for days past has had foreign ministers, and collectors, and all kinds, and I thought you couldn't have got in here without having at least a post-master get into your pocket!" We assured him he need have no concern on that point, and left the house, both of us, I think, feeling, as I certainly felt, more anxious and disturbed than when we entered it. Not one word had Mr. Lincoln said to throw any real light either on his own views of the situation or on the effect of ——'s communication upon those views. But it was plain that he is deeply disturbed and puzzled by the problem of this wretched fort, to which circumstances are giving an importance so entirely disproportionate to its real significance, either political or military.

### THE INVASION OF THE OFFICE-SEEKERS

We sent away the carriage and walked home. —— called my attention as we passed along to the strange and uncouth appearance of a great proportion of the people whom we encountered on our way or passed lounging about the steps of the Treasury Department and the lobbies of the hotels. I had not noticed it before, but certainly in all my long experience of Washington I have never seen such a swarm of uncouth beings. The clamor for offices is already quite extraordinary, and these poor people undoubtedly belong to the horde which has pressed in here to seek places under the new Administration, which neither has nor can hope to have places enough to satisfy one twentieth part of the number. After dinner I went in to see Mr. Seward, determined, if possible, to get some satisfactory statement as to the outlook of the immediate future from his point of view, and anxious also to ascertain what he knows, if he knows anything, either to confirm or to contradict the story of —— as to Major Anderson and Fort Sumter.

### MR. SEWARD'S EXPECTATIONS OF A SETTLEMENT

I found Mr. Seward in a lively, almost in a boisterous mood, but I soon induced him to take a more quiet and reasonable tone. I told him what —— had told me of Major Anderson, and that I had taken —— to see Mr. Lincoln. At this his countenance lighted up and he exclaimed, "I am so glad you did!" He then went on to assure me in the most positive and earnest terms that he had no doubt whatever that Fort Sumter would be evacuated at a very early day, that there were no military reasons whatever for keeping it, and no more or better reasons for holding it than there had been for holding Fort Brown, which certainly would not be and could not be held. He spoke very severely of what he called Major Anderson's folly in going into Fort Sumter at all—a folly the secret of which, as he said, I had now explained to him, but which was only the greater folly by reason of the motives which led to it, assuming the story of ———— to be true, as he added with a great deal of emphasis, "As I have no sort of doubt it is." I asked him how the surrender of Fort Sumter could be effected otherwise than by violence if ————'s story was true, since Major Anderson certainly would not give up the place on an express order from Washington if he cherished the notion of waiting for the action of his own State of Kentucky. That, he replied evasively, would be a matter for the negotiators, and he then gave me to understand that negotiations were, in fact, at this moment going on, which, in his judgment, would very soon relieve the Government of all anxiety on the score of Charleston Harbor and its forts. I then told him what account ———— had brought of the state of things at Montgomery, about which, however, he seemed to be himself very fully informed. He could give me no good reason for supposing it, but he seemed to be quite convinced that, as soon as the States of Virginia, Kentucky, and Missouri rejected the appeals of the secessionists, as he has positive information they will reject them, the disintegration of the new-born Confederacy will begin. I asked him how, admitting these expectations to be well founded, we were, in the interval during the process, to get on with our postal and business relations, mentioning to him what ———— had told me, that Mr. Toombs and others were strongly in favor of establishing a passport system by sea and land against all citizens of the United States. This apparently made little or no impression upon him, and I must say that I have come home quite discouraged and depressed. In the Senate no one of the Republicans seems to be just now thinking seriously of anything but the new appointments. I have been besieged for a week past with letters and applications asking me every day to see a score of persons whom I hardly know, in order to oblige a score of other persons whom, in many cases, I know only too well. It is a shameful and humiliating state of things, none the more tolerable that it was to have been expected. Mr. Seward was very anxious to get my views as to the proper treatment of Mr. Forsyth and the other commissioners. He seemed inclined to think that a mode might be found of receiving them and negotiating with them, without in any way committing the Government to a recognition of the Government which they assume to represent.

I found it difficult, indeed I may say impossible, to make him admit the hopelessness of looking for such a thing, but I told him frankly that I saw no earthly reason why he should not informally and in a private way obtain from these gentlemen—all of them, as we knew, honorable and very intelligent men—some practical light on the way out of all this gathering perplexity, if indeed they have any such practical light to give. He then gave me to understand that this was exactly what he had done and meant to do, and he repeated his conviction that the evacuation of Fort Sumter would clear the way for a practical understanding out of which an immediate tranquillization of the country must come, and in the not distant future a return of all the seceding States to their allegiance. I can only hope he is right.

### THE PROGRESS OF EVENTS AT RICHMOND

*Washington, March 9th.*— ——— came in to breakfast with me, having just returned from Richmond. He confirmed the story that an agent has been sent thither by Mr. Seward, with a most positive assurance that on no account shall Fort Sumter be reënforced, either with men or with supplies. He says this assurance reached Richmond the day after the confirmation by the Senate of the new Cabinet appointments, and he was told by ——— at Richmond, who certainly ought to know the facts in the case, that Senator Hunter agreed to press for the immediate confirmation of Mr. Seward in conformity with the precedents, on the express understanding that such a message should be forthwith dispatched to Richmond. Certainly, but for the attitude of Senator Hunter, and one or two other gentlemen of like views, the Chase and Sumner men in the Senate would have pretty surely, I think, given Mr. Seward some trouble before that body. As things are, ——— thinks the Union men will control the action of Virginia, and that we shall consequently have no war. Heaven grant it! But in all this I do not see what the Government of the Union is negotiating for, or what we are to get for the Union by all these concessions, beyond the boon—priceless, indeed, no doubt—of a peace which has not yet been seriously disturbed, and which the seceded States have at least as great an interest as we ourselves in seeing preserved. The whole thing seems to me much too onesided a piece of business, and I told ———— so plumply. Mr. Seward stopped to see me a moment, not long after breakfast, to say, with some appearance of fear, that the President's friends were "pestering" him about sending Mr. Corwin to England, and to intimate that he had put his foot down pretty forcibly in refusing to do anything of the kind. He showed me a note from a common friend of his and of Mr. Forsyth, asking him to receive and give audience to a certain Colonel ————, who had a matter to lay before him of great national importance, and asked me if I would object to seeing Colonel ———— myself, as he did not wish to do so, and yet was anxious to ascertain what Colonel ———— might have to say. I expressed some perplexity as to how such a thing could be arranged, but he laughed, and said that if I would name an hour there would be no trouble about it at all. I thought this odd, but named an hour for to-morrow morning.

## A GLIMPSE OF SENSE FROM THE SOUTH

A letter from ————, at Augusta. She writes in good spirits, but is evidently much impressed with the awkward situation, and with the feverish state of feeling all about her in Georgia. Certainly there is nothing bellicose or savage in her mood, but she tells me that her husband is disturbed and disquieted by what he thinks the imminent peril of great business disasters at the South, and especially in Georgia. He may well feel in this way, with the investments which he has made in factories sure to be ruined by the policy of his "Confederated" brethren at Montgomery.

## CERTAIN PLANS OF SOUTHERN LEADERS

*March 10th.*—While Mr. Douglas was talking with me this morning on some propositions which he means to offer in the Senate in a day or two, Mr. Seward's Colonel ———— sent his name in to me. I wished to excuse myself, but Mr. Douglas insisted I should not do so, and went away, promising to come back in the evening. I found Colonel ——— a very keen, bright, intelligent person, who was full of a great scheme in which he said that Mr. Davis and Mr. Forsyth both were very deeply interested, and in which he believed the eventual solution of the whole trouble in this country would be found. This was neither more nor less than a plan for the building of a great railway to the Pacific through the southwestern portions of the country, on the surveys made under the direction of Mr. Davis while he was Secretary of War. This, he said, the Confederate States Government would at once undertake. It would unite the Confederacy with California, and make it the interest of the whole North to seek a reunion on proper terms at the earliest possible moment with the Confederate States, which would then stretch from the Atlantic to the Pacific, "enveloping Mexico and the Gulf." I listened to the man in silent amazement for some time, for certainly I never heard such wild and fantastic propositions advanced with so much seriousness and apparent good faith, and, finally interrupting him, ventured to ask him what he wished or expected me to do in the premises, and why he should have been referred to me. He seemed not at all embarrassed, but said quietly that he had wished to see me as being a conservative man and a lover of peace, in order to show me that all we needed at the North was to have a little patience, and we should see the way opened out of all our difficulties by this notable project. Is it possible there can be truth in the old notion that, in times of great national trial and excitement, so many men do go mad, so to speak, in a quiet and private way, that madness becomes a sort of epidemic?

*Washington, March 11th.*—The debate on the expulsion of Wigfall has gone off to-day into abstractions, which vex and irritate one in the presence of the practical questions now pressing upon us. I could scarcely listen with patience to Mr. Foster's discussion of the point whether a Senator of the United States ought or ought not to consider his seat vacated upon the passage of an ordinance of secession by his State. Nothing will come of it all, and it only gives occasion to men like Mr. Mason to add fuel to the flame all over the country, by discussing and debating the circumstances in which it will be necessary for them to swell the list of seceders and for their States to go out of the Union.

As for Wigfall himself, his bearing for the last day or two has been rather better than it was on the day of his collision with Mr. Douglas, when he really looked like a tiger, and acted not unlike one. He and all the extreme men seem to be a great deal depressed, I am glad to say, by the intelligence which has crept out of the general agreement of the Cabinet to adopt the course recommended by General Scott on plain military grounds, and order Major Anderson to abandon Fort Sumter.

### THE ORDER TO EVACUATE FORT SUMTER

I had a long conversation on the subject with Senator Douglas to-day. He is entirely of my mind that the fort ought to have been abandoned already, and that much valuable prestige has been lost by the new Administration, which might have been secured had orders been sent at once to Major Anderson to that effect. The delay is attributable, no doubt, in part to the dilatoriness of Mr. Cameron in taking up the reins of the War Department; but I am sure Mr. Douglas is right when he lays a part of the responsibility on the influence of the Blairs, who keep pressing for a war policy. Even from their point of view, nothing can be more childish than to make an issue on the holding of Fort Sumter, which has already been abandoned in regard to Fort Brown, and to make that issue on the holding of an entirely untenable place. Mr. Douglas tells me, too, that a further difficulty has been raised by the friends of Major Anderson here from Kentucky, who insist that he shall not be ordered to leave Fort Sumter unless the order is accompanied by a promotion to one of the vacant brigadierships in the army, certainly under the circumstances a most scandalous and even foolish demand to make.

### THE PRESIDENT WISHES THE FORT EVACUATED

Mr. Lincoln has assured Mr. Douglas positively, he tells me, that he means the fort shall be evacuated as soon as possible, and that all his Cabinet whom he has consulted are of the same mind excepting Mr. Blair, which is precisely what I had expected. Mr. Douglas says that the President sent for him after his speech of Wednesday to assure him that he entirely agreed with all its views, and sympathized with its spirit. All he desired was to get the points of present irritation removed, so that the people might grow cool, and reflect on the general position all over the country, when he felt confident there would be a general demand for a National Convention at which all the existing differences could be radically treated. Meanwhile he did not see why the Executive should attempt to dispossess the seceded States of the forts occupied by them unless Congress insisted that he should, and gave him the means necessary for the work. "I am just as ready," he said to Mr. Douglas, "to reënforce the garrisons at Sumter and Pickens or to withdraw them as I am to see an amendment adopted protecting slavery in the Territories or prohibiting slavery in the Territories. What I want is to get done what the people desire to have done, and the question for me is how to find that out exactly."

Meanwhile, as I suggested to Mr. Douglas, no one is taking any steps that I can see to find out exactly or inexactly what the people desire to have done, and the secessionists are doing a good many things which for one I do not believe the people at all desire to have done.

### BREAKING UP THE UNION BY LEGISLATION

I called Mr. Douglas's attention to a letter received by me from Mobile yesterday, in which the opinion is expressed that, if the mission of Mr. Forsyth and his colleagues turns out a failure, the Confederate Congress will certainly adopt a sort of legal non-intercourse bill already in the hands of their Judiciary Committee, dismissing all cases from the courts to which citizens of other than the seceding States are parties. Mr. Douglas agreed with me, of course, that such legislation as this would be equivalent in some degree to a war, so far as its effects alike upon the country and upon individuals are concerned; and he was not less painfully struck by another bill, a copy of which I have just received from Montgomery, prohibiting absolutely the importation of slaves from the United States unless accompanied by their owners, and with an eye to settlement within the Confederate States. The object of this, of course, is to coerce Kentucky and Virginia, and particularly Virginia, into joining the new government. How long will it be possible for us to sit still and see all the conditions of our prosperity and importance thus nibbled at and taken away piecemeal?

It may be true, as Mr. Douglas suggests, that the introduction of such legislation at Montgomery indicates the obstinacy of the Union feeling in the border States, and may so far be taken as a sign rather of hope than of imminent danger. But the spirit and the intent of it all, so far as concerns the rest of the Union, are not the less hostile and mischievous. Certainly such steps can do little to promote the objects had in view by the Southern Commissioners.

## THE DIPLOMATIC PERPLEXITIES OF MR. SEWARD

*March 12th.*—Mr. Seward is much better to-day, and in unusually good spirits even for him; mainly, I think, because he has succeeded in getting Mr. Corwin to agree to take the mission to Mexico instead of the mission to England. He has news from Richmond, and I understood him from Mr. Summers, that the prospect of defeating the secessionists in the Convention brightens all the time, and that Virginia, after disposing finally of the importunities of the Southern States, will take the initiative for a great National Convention. Of this he feels as confident as of the complete overthrow of the schemes of the fire-eaters by the quiet evacuation of Fort Sumter, which can not now be long delayed. He is very much pleased with the tone and bearing of the Southern Commissioners, he says, "as reported to him," and certainly nothing can be more reasonable or pacific than the disposition shown by these gentlemen so far. But I do not see that they offer any practicable solution—and I told Mr. Seward so—of the situation; nor, indeed, do I see why it should be expected they could do so. The difficulties are not difficulties of sentiment, but of fact. Mr. Seward intimates to me pretty clearly that he already finds Mr. Sumner making trouble for him in the Senate, and pressing him disagreeably in his own department.

He is annoyed too, I thought, at having to send Mr. Cassius M. Clay to Spain, and said with a good deal of sagacity that if he must give a mission to Kentucky he thought it a pity to "waste it on a Kentuckian he was sure of already."

### MR. SEWARD AND THE CONFEDERATES

He is hopeful of the success of the Convention plan if we can but get the better of our own mischief-makers here, who are much more dangerous to us, he thinks—and I agree with him—than the people at Montgomery. Without precisely saying as much, he gave me very distinctly the impression that the intentions of the Administration to Fort Sumter have been made known at Montgomery, and have there produced a most beneficial effect. When I called his attention to the hostile and mischievous legislation going on there, he reminded me that the direction of the practical action of the seceded States just now rests with the Executive and not with the Legislature at Montgomery, and repeated several times his conviction that no one in the government there desired a collision more than he or I, which indeed I can readily believe.

I thought Mr. Seward seemed a little annoyed at the present attitude of Mr. Douglas; at all events, he showed an evident anxiety to lead me into expressing an opinion, which I positively declined to express, as to the efforts which Mr. Douglas has been persistently making to drive the Republican Senators into showing their hands, and which of course are not made in the interests of the Republican party. But he had nothing to say when I asked him why none of the Administration Senators were willing to speak for the Administration either one way or the other.

### THE SILENCE OF THE REPUBLICAN LEADERS

*March 15th.*—The declaration made yesterday in the Senate, that the seats of Davis, Mallory, Clay, Toombs, and Benjamin are vacant, has envenomed matters a good deal, and the debate of to-day will make them worse. It is a pity Mr. Douglas should have lost his temper, but certainly nothing could have been more irritating than Mr. Fessenden. It was perfectly obvious that the two Republicans who did most of the speaking after Mr. Fessenden—Hale and Wilson—knew Mr. Douglas to be really uttering the sentiments and sketching the policy of the President, and were pretty nearly half willing to admit as much and attack the White House, but they had discretion and self-command enough to forbear, so that Mr. Douglas really threw away his time for the moment. When the news of the evacuation of Fort Sumter comes, though, it will be his turn, and we shall then see collisions which will bring out the innermost truth as to the political chart of the new Administration, and which must pretty certainly lead to the complete reorganization of our political parties, if indeed it stops there.

# Index

# Index

Abrantes, Duchess of, 149
Adams, Charles Francis, 218
Adams, Henry, 137, 155
Adams, J. H., 58
Aldrich, Charles, 109
*American Quarterly Review,* 147
Anderson, Joseph R., 91–92, 185
Anderson, Robert, 7, 40, 58–59, 88, 90–92, 121, 166, 185, 192–93, 204, 211, 236–38, 240–42, 246
Appleton, D., and Co., 22
Arago, D. F. J., 147
Arnold, Isaac, 105, 107, 109
Aspinwall, William H., 40, 143, 163–64, 200, 205
Astor, Emily, 149
Astor, William B., 149
Astor House, 61, 62, 77, 94
*Atlanta Constitution,* 24
*Atlantic Monthly,* 105, 106, 186

"B——," Mr., 166, 192, 197–99
"B——," of New York, 163–64, 200
Baker, Edward D., 28, 40, 57–58, 143, 159, 220
Bancroft, Frederic, 69, 184
Bancroft, George, 42
Barlow, S. L. M., 155, 157, 164, 179, 187–88
Barney, Hiram, 21, 29, 37, 40, 45, 70, 72, 78, 125, 143, 185, 204–6
Barnwell, R. W., 58
Barton, W. E., 69, 184
Bates, Edward, 83, 97
Bates, Joshua, 128
Bayard, Thomas F., 132, 155
Bell, John, 216
Benjamin, Judah P., 14, 38, 70, 141, 163–64, 176, 187, 199–201, 205, 207, 212–13, 220, 249
Bennett, James Gordon, 127, 129
Benson, Eugene, 132
Black, Jeremiah S., 151

Blair, F. P., Sr., 234
Blair, Montgomery, 83, 121, 234, 246
Blairs, The, 40, 57, 84, 143, 159, 209, 212, 227, 230, 234, 236
Blanc, Louis, 127
Bonaparte, Joseph, 149
Bonaparte, Prince Louis-Napoleon, 127
Bonner, Robert, 153
*Boston Journal,* 46
Breckenridge, John C., 198
Browne, W. M., 166
Buchanan, James, 6, 9, 26–27, 40, 59, 74, 98, 119, 129, 166–67, 171, 177, 194, 196, 198, 200, 211, 213, 215, 218, 220, 231
Bull, Ole, 149
Bullard, F. Lauriston, 14, 66, 179

Cameron, Simon, 13, 34, 84, 144, 223–25, 227, 246
Carr, Clark E., 109
Cass, Lewis, 211, 213
*Charleston News and Courier,* 24
Chase, Salmon P., 10, 77, 84, 177, 211–12, 221–22, 227, 243
Chester, Mrs. Arthur, 179
*Chicago Tribune,* 25, 27
*Cincinnati Commercial,* 102–3, 107, 109, 111
Clay, Cassius M., 248
Clay, Clement C., 249
Clay, Henry, 48
*Cleveland Leader,* 24
Collamer, Jacob, 27–32
Collins, Carvel, 150, 179
*Constitution,* 166
Corwin, Thomas, 211, 218, 244, 248
"Cousin V——," 12–13, 93–94, 165, 207
Crawford, F. Marion, 155
Crawford, M. J., 14
Crawford, Samuel W., 90, 185
Crittenden, J. J., 213
Curtis, George Ticknor, 21, 69, 171, 184

St. *Louis Republican,* 108
St. Martin, Mr., 212
Sandburg, Carl, 184
Sanford, Henry S., 43–45, 161
*San Francisco Examiner,* 24
Saulsbury, Willard, 32
Saunders, George N., 6, 215
Schurz, Carl, 109
Scott, Winfield, 5, 116, 208–9, 214, 231–32, 234
Seddon, J. A., 14, 201–2
"Serendipity," 145
Seward, William H., 4, 9–10, 12–14, 36, 39–40, 44, 56–59, 75, 77, 83, 97, 116, 118–20, 123, 144–45, 157, 160–61, 164, 166–67, 171–72, 177–79, 186, 193, 196, 199, 201–6, 208–9, 211–13, 217–18, 220–22, 225–30, 235–36, 239–41, 243–44, 248–49
Sherman, John, 110
Sickles, Daniel, 127, 129
Smith, George Williamson, 109
Smith, Truman, 45
Soule, Pierre, 144, 160, 212–13
*Springfield Republican,* 24, 43
Stanton, Edward M., 127, 151, 159, 210
*States and Union,* 101
Stedman, E. A., 187
Stephenson, N. W., 184
Stickney, William, 49, 51, 185
Stone, Charles P., 5–6, 85–86, 214–15
Stroganoff, Baron Serge, 149
Strothers, D. H., 26
Stuart, Charles Edward, 25, 184
Sumner, Charles, 6, 7, 13, 33–34, 36–38, 46, 69, 78, 83, 86, 90, 124–25, 143–44, 160, 176, 178, 187, 215–16, 223–36, 239, 243

Taney, Roger B., 9, 98, 231
Tarbell, Ida, 69, 184

Taylor, Zachary, 4, 34, 80, 206
Thackeray, W. M., 127, 151, 155
Thayer, Sylvanus, 147
Thompson, James Westfall, 21–22
Thomson, John R., 32
Ticknors, The, 148
Tieck, Ludwig, 149
Tilden, Samuel J., 137
Tilton, Theodore, 132
*Times* (London), 129, 151, 162
Toombs, Robert, 143, 159, 220, 238, 242
*Transcript, Daily,* 63

Van Buren, John, 17
Van Buren, Martin, 17, 49
Vanderbilt, W. H., 164
Villard, Henry, 111
Vogelstein, Charles Chretien, 149

Wade, Benjamin, 117, 118, 160, 196
Wakeman, Abram, 236
Walpole, Horace, 145
Walsh, Robert, 147
Ward, Samuel, 146–70, 173–77, 187–88
Washburne, E. B., 110
*Washington Star,* 53, 101
Watterson, Henry, 109
Weed, Thurlow, 24–25, 65, 96, 177, 202–3, 212–13
Welles, Gideon, 44, 204
Wharton, Henry, 148
White, Horace, 130
White, J. W., 91
Wigfall, Louis T., 143, 159, 177, 197–98, 208, 245
Wikoff, Henry, 19, 126–30, 134–35
Willard Hotel, 4–5, 38, 82, 207, 210, 233
Wilson, Henry, 107, 249
Winthrop, Robert C., 42
Wood, Fernando, 4, 80, 142, 206

Yancey, W. L., 213